The management of everyday life

palgrave critical management studies

The management of everyday life

Edited by
Philip Hancock
Melissa Tyler

palgrave
macmillan

Selection, editorial matter and Introduction © Philip Hancock and Melissa
Tyler 2009

Chapter 6 © 2007 by Arlie Russell Hochschild. Reprinted by permission of
Georges Borchardt, Inc. on behalf of the author.
Individual chapters © individual contributors

First published 2009 by
PALGRAVE MACMILLAN

Palgrave Macmillan in the UK is an imprint of Macmillan Publishers Limited,
registered in England, company number 785998, of Houndmills, Basingstoke,
Hampshire RG21 6XS.

Palgrave Macmillan in the US is a division of St Martin's Press LLC,
175 Fifth Avenue, New York, NY 10010.

Palgrave Macmillan is the global academic imprint of the above companies
and has companies and representatives throughout the world.

Palgrave® and Macmillan® are registered trademarks in the United States,
the United Kingdom, Europe and other countries.

ISBN-13: 978–0–230–52479–8

This book is printed on paper suitable for recycling and made from fully
managed and sustained forest sources. Logging, pulping and manufacturing
processes are expected to conform to the environmental regulations of the
country of origin.

A catalogue record for this book is available from the British Library.

A catalog record for this book is available from the Library of Congress.

10   9   8   7   6   5   4   3   2   1
18   17   16   15   14   13   12   11   10   09

Printed and bound in Great Britain by
CPI Antony Rowe, Chippenham and Eastbourne

Contents

Acknowledgements

The editors and authors would like to thank numerous people who have commented on earlier drafts of the chapters presented here, or on the manuscript as a whole, or who have simply provided insight and inspiration in a number of different ways, including Gibson Burrell, Victoria Carruthers, Rick Delbridge, Chris Grey, Rolland Munro, Martin Parker and Hugh Willmott. We would also like to thank Ursula Gavin of Palgrave Macmillan for her commitment to the book, and also Mark Cooper and Cherline Daniel for seeing it through production. We are also very grateful to Germaine Koh and Phil Klygo for permission to reproduce an image from 'Sleeping Rough' (2003) in Chapter 5. Every effort has been made to trace right holders, but if any have been overlooked, the publishers would be pleased to make the necessary arrangements at the first opportunity.

Notes on contributors

Sharon Boden has worked at the Universities of Warwick and Keele, UK. Her research interests lie in the areas of gender and the body, consumerism, and the media. She has previously worked on projects examining the contemporary wedding experience, children's consumption of fashion, and representations of sleep in the media.

Mehdi Boussebaa is a postdoctoral research fellow at Saïd Business School, University of Oxford, UK. He received his PhD from the University of Warwick, UK. His main research interests centre on globalisation and its impact on organisations and their employees. He also has a peripheral interest in self-development technologies such as neuro-linguistic programming. His research has been published in *Human Relations and Critical Perspectives on International Business.*

Karen Dale is a lecturer in Organizational Analysis at the University of Lancaster, UK. Her work on organisational space, architecture and materiality, and on the body and organisation theory has been published in a range of international journals and edited collections. She is the author of *Anatomizing Embodiment and Organization Theory*, and co-author of *The Spaces of Organization and the Organization of Space: Power, Identity and Materiality at Work* (with Gibson Burrell).

Stephen Fineman is Professor of Organizational Behaviour in the School of Management, University of Bath, UK. He has had a long interest in emotion in organizations with publications such as *Emotion in Organizations, Understanding Emotion at Work* and *The Emotional Organization*. More recently, he has turned his attention to a critical examination of 'age' as embedded in a range of key organizational practices and prejudices.

Peter Fleming is Professor of Work and Organization at Queen Mary College, University of London, UK. He has previously held positions at Cambridge University and Melbourne University. He is the co-author of *Contesting the*

Corporation (with Andre Spicer), *Charting Corporate Corruption* and *Authenticity and the Cultural Politics of Work.*

Philip Hancock is an associate professor of Organization Studies at Warwick Business School, UK. He has published in a range of international journals and is co-author of *Work, Postmodernism and Organization* (with Melissa Tyler) and *The Body, Culture and Society* (with colleagues at Glasgow Caledonian University), and co-editor of *Art and Aesthetics at Work* (with Adrian Carr). His current research interests include organizational aesthetics, space and architecture, sleep, and the organizational aspects of Christmas.

Arlie Hochschild is a sociologist at the University of California, Berkeley, US. She is the author of *The Managed Heart, The Second Shift, The Time Bind, The Commercialization of Intimate Life* and co-editor of *Global Woman* (with Barbara Ehrenreich).

Bill Hughes is Professor of Sociology and Dean of the School of Law and Social Sciences at Glasgow Caledonian University, UK. His research interests include disability and impairment, social theory and the body. He is the co-author of *The Body, Culture and Society: An Introduction* (with several colleagues at Glasgow Caledonian University). He has published in *Sociology, Body and Society* and is a regular contributor to and a member of the Editorial Board of *Disability and Society.*

Craig Lair is a visiting assistant professor of Sociology at Gettysburg College, Pennsylvania, US. His interests include social theory, social processes of individualization, globalization and outsourcing. Craig's current work focuses on the sociology of outsourcing.

Alf Rehn is Chair of Management and Organization at Åbo Akademi University, Finland. His published research interests have ranged from anachronisms to zombies, with much in between, and try to explore the borders and limits of fields.

George Ritzer is Distinguished University Professor at the University of Maryland, US. Among his forthcoming books are *The Outsourcing of Everything* (with Craig Lair), *Globalization: A Basic Text, Globalization: Concepts, Debates, Extensions* (with Zeynep Atalay) and *Enchanting a Disenchanted World* (3rd edition). His current research deals with the 'prosumer'.

André Spicer is an associate professor of Organization Studies at Warwick Business School, University of Warwick, UK, and a visiting research fellow at Lund University, Sweden. He holds a PhD from the University of Melbourne, Australia. His work explores political dynamics in and around organizations. This work is brought together in *Contesting the Corporation* (with Peter Fleming).

Andrew Sturdy is a professor of Organisational Behaviour at Warwick Business School, University of Warwick, UK. His research focuses on issues of power, emotion and identity in different organizational domains, such as management consultancy.

Melissa Tyler is a senior lecturer in Organization Studies at Loughborough University, UK. Her work on gender, feminist theory and emotional and aesthetic forms of labour has been published in a range of international journals and edited collections. Her current research is on sales-service work in the children's culture industries, gender performativity and organizational space, and aesthetic labour in the retail sex industry.

Simon Williams is a professor of Sociology in the Department of Sociology, University of Warwick, UK. He has published widely in the fields of medical sociology, sociology of the body and the sociology of emotions, including ongoing research on sleep and society and new research on neuroscience, neuroculture and society. Current book projects include *The Politics of Sleep* and another co-authored book *NeuroFutures in the Making*.

Edward Wray-Bliss works as a senior lecturer in Management, at the University of Technology, Sydney, Australia. His research interests span the ethics and politics of organizational and academic life. More of his writings on the specific topic of drugs and intoxication can be found in the journals *New Technology, Work and Employment*, *Tamara* and *Culture and Organization*.

Introduction

The management of everyday life *Philip Hancock and Melissa Tyler*

> If reason is declared incapable of determining the ultimate aims of life and must content itself with reducing everything to a mere tool, its sole remaining goal is simply the perpetuation of its coordinating activity.
>
> *(Horkheimer, 2004: 1963)*

In this collection we present a series of chapters concerned with the ways in which managerial values and practices appear to be informing some of the most mundane and commonplace aspects of our everyday lives. They explore the extent to which management, as a historically specific logic of control and coordination, is extending beyond its established realm of competence, and offering ways in which the ever-intensifying pressures of contemporary life might be, if not controlled, then accommodated. It is not, however, a celebration of this process. As one might expect from a book that is part of a Critical Management Studies series each chapter demonstrates a deep unease regarding this process. They question the wisdom of allowing what is, in effect, a mode of rationality oriented towards the systematic regulation of complex systems to resource and mediate what, as we shall see, are some of the most intimate aspects of human life. In particular, each of the authors generally holds to the belief that management, as we broadly define it, fails to provide an adequate basis for human sociality due to its instrumentality, and its focus on individual achievement at the expense of social cooperation and conviviality. Not that this is to suggest that the views expressed in this collection are of a wholly negative character in terms of the extent to which such managerial influence is viewed as either totalising or uncontested. Many of the chapters are at pains to stress the ways in which such managerial incursions into everyday life are uncertain, contradictory, and sometimes even incoherent. Nonetheless, the general tenor of the writing you will find here is less than welcoming of such managerial values regardless of their sometimes contested, or limited, impact.

The origins of the collection stretch back to the summer of 1999, to a stream of papers on the management of everyday life, at the first of what was to become a biannual series of *International Critical Management Studies* conferences. The stream was inspired by what we felt was the rather disturbing comment made by our then head of management studies, in the face of a threat to his department's funding, that

> These are skills we all need! Management education is all about real transferable skills: leadership, problem solving, teamwork. Everyday we are faced with a problem we need to manage, that is why a degree programme like this is really valuable. They don't understand that!

Now, to be fair, one might be able to forgive the apparent hyperbole when considering that this was an outburst in the face of an impending institutional assault. Nonetheless, the idea that one should be able to directly equate the resources required to negotiate the trials and tribulations of everyday life with the formal language, techniques, and the largely taken for granted economic imperatives associated with the activity of professional management represented, we would suggest, a far stronger claim than it might at first have appeared. For in establishing such an equivalency it considered an education programme designed primarily to meet the needs of an occupation concerned with coordinating capitalist socio-economic relations to provide an appropriate template for the generalist acquisition of everyday life skills. Management as a formal, technocratic activity, it was being argued, represented both an epistemological and normative basis upon which everyday life could, and indeed should, be conducted, a proposition we found deeply disturbing and one which, we felt, required greater reflection.

As the time lag between the conference and the appearance of this edited collection might suggest, however, this was an idea whose time perhaps had not yet come. While the stream attracted a number of interesting papers (some of which appear here in an updated and modified form), overall there was not a sufficiently critical mass of contributions to justify developing the theme any further. Since then, however, both the temporal and spatial relationships that exist between the realms of what one might term work and non-work appear to have taken on a notable significance, not only in academic studies, but in both the popular media and the eyes of policy-makers and government officials. Terms such as 'work-life balance' have become national and international currency through debates over the average length of people's working hours, the role the state might legitimately play in the provision of say childcare facilities for working parents, or the legislating of flexible working rights for employees with dependants such as elderly relatives. Similarly, popular reading such as Madeline

Bunting's polemic on modern work, *Willing Slaves* (2004), has brought public attention to the realities of the UK's long-hours culture and the potential harm it is doing to individuals and families alike.

Not that this is a book about either of these topics per se. For while some of the authors do indeed draw on concerns about people's work-life balance and the apparent extension of their working hours, our aim here is to add a new dimension to these debates. It is not simply that people are finding it increasingly difficult, or indeed undesirable, to separate their everyday lives from their 'work lives', or that there is somehow a mutually constitutive relationship between them. Rather, by exploring the ways in which the principles and practices that manage life at work are being transferred into our non-working 'everyday' lives, we want to recognise what is perhaps an uncomfortable truth. Namely, that is, that it perhaps no longer matters whether or not we carry our working activities over into our private time either by extending our formal working hours, or by integrating work tasks into our leisure time; as increasingly our non-working lives are conceptualised, and indeed organised, in accordance with the same principles, regulations and expectations as our time at work.

There are, of course, many who would consider this something of a non-issue. Rather they might consider work, and all that goes with it, to be an inseparable element of their identity and something from which they derive an intense sense of pleasure and fulfilment. Well once again, this is not a personal worldview that we are seeking to directly challenge here. While one might wish to question the extent to which such an orientation to the values of waged labour is, ultimately both psychologically and, indeed, physiologically, healthy – considering, for instance, questions of personal burn-out amongst the most committed of employees – the value of work to certain occupational groups is a complex issue and one that has been explored elsewhere (cf. Warhurst et al., 2008). In short, while the interface between doing work and not doing work is a complex and, in itself, fascinating one, once again it is a critique of the possible erosion of that distinction and the elision of two, possibly antagonistic, ways of conceiving and being in the world that concerns us here.

Structure

In order to pursue this concern, the book is divided into three parts, topped and tailed, so to speak with stand-alone chapters that, in their own way, provide both opening and closing reflections on the theme of the collection as a whole. The opening chapter by Philip Hancock, entitled 'Management and colonization in everyday life', serves two functions. First, by way of an introduction it considers just what it is we might mean by both the terms management and everyday life in the context of this collection. Second, drawing in particular on the work and ideas of Jürgen Habermas (1984) it presents a particular analysis of the ways in which management values and ideas are increasingly permeating a range of popular, cultural resources. That is, Hancock argues, what we are currently witnessing is a process by which the capacity of certain cultural resources to provide a medium of everyday sensemaking is increasingly characterised by a largely technocratic and instrumental orientation to the negotiation of human relationships. By way of illustration, he draws on examples taken from both self-help books and lifestyle magazines, as well as reflecting briefly on the impact of modern communication technologies on the ways in which we negotiate the demands and expectations of everyday life as well as our relationships to others. While unable to offer any particular solutions to this situation, he concludes with an invitation for those interested in the issues raised by critical management studies to widen their perspective beyond that of the formal work organisation, and to consider the ways in which management, and the underlying rationality that characterises managerial ideas, has become an increasingly ubiquitous cultural presence in people's everyday lives.

Embodied living

Next we have the first of the three thematic parts of the book, which concerns itself with the impact of management on the lived experience of the body. Now, bringing the somatic to the fore in a study of the management of everyday life such as this should perhaps come as no surprise to those familiar with contemporary critical social theory. Since the mid-1980s, the body has become a significant site of research and reflection for those interested in the operation of control and authority within contemporary modern society evolving as a site upon which power and discipline have been increasingly exercised in order to fabricate subjects particularly suited to the demands of a technocratic, and essentially homogenising modernity.

Thus, the first chapter in this part explores some of these issues through what is perhaps the most intimate and personal aspect of one's embodied nature, namely sexuality. Here, Melissa Tyler considers the ways in which sexuality has become subject to a managerially orientated form of rationalisation. Drawing not only on Foucault, but also a range of other critical sources including the work of Axel Honneth and his consideration of recognition as an essential component of an intersubjective ethic, Tyler argues that the presentation of sexuality and sexual relations as favoured across a range of lifestyle magazines and associated media threatens to diminish the authentically erotic and intersubjectively ethical qualities of this particular dimension of everyday human being. Thus, as Tyler herself puts it, it is perhaps no longer sufficient that we should be doing or indeed even enjoying our sexuality. Rather the emphasis is increasingly on how we might manage it and improve it in order to ensure that, as both an integral element of our self-identity and public persona alike, disciplined sexual performance becomes a marker of our capacity to achieve in a competitive environment, as well as indicative of our final and full embrace of an all-pervasive work ethic.

From what we might consider to be one form of embodied leisure, or indeed recreational activity, to another, the following chapter by Edward Wray-Bliss concerns itself with the perhaps more controversial subject of drug and alcohol use. In a similar vein to Tyler, Wray-Bliss opens with the contention that in many respects, much like sexuality, the intoxication brought about by the use of drugs and alcohol might appear intuitively antithetical to the rational values of self-management. Nevertheless, he goes on to aptly illustrate many of the ways in which the consumption of such substances has become subject to a process of calculated control, if albeit in ways one might not have expected. So, for instance, while the consumption of alcohol has traditionally been subjected to highly disciplinary regimes of control and regulation, a whole series of other rationalities concerned with say the regeneration of city centres, and the proliferation of drinking establishments which often characterise this, have played an important part in configuring the ways in which such consumption is managed. Yet even in the face of various strategies to manage such activities, through health or legalistic discourses, control is never seen as total or complete. As such, Wray-Bliss offers a conclusion that is both wary, recognising as it does the continued influence of managerial rationality on the pursuit of pleasurable intoxication, but also optimistic recognising as he does the ultimately excessive nature of intoxication.

It might, of course, be that while managerial expert discourses relating to the consumption of drugs and alcohol present a particular example of an incursion into the realm of embodied health and well-being, we might want to extend our analysis more widely. In effect, such an extension is what Bill Hughes pursues in our next chapter, entitled 'Managing health in everyday life'. Here, Hughes explores the idea that what he terms 'post-medical' medicine serves primarily to perpetuate a culture of rational self-management – a preventorium – in which each of us is increasingly required to manage our health and the ways in which we live. As he puts it himself, we live in an age in which 'health and betterment have become everybody's business'. While on the one hand this can be viewed as an empowering process, whereby the individual patient has been elevated to the position of an active and engaged subject in terms of the informed provision of his or her own healthcare, on the other hand, a number of potential risks are also identified. Most notably, as Hughes observes, this culture of self-regulation is one that is continually permeated not only by expert discourses that are more than prepared to explain how such freedom should be exercised, but also by a moral injunction to self-reliance. One that, in its own way, marginalises any responsibility we also have for the other's welfare and health, as well as any claims we ourselves might also make for others' assistance.

In what is the final chapter of this first part, we shift back from the general question of health and its management to what one might consider to be a component, if not vital attribute, of healthy living, namely sleep. Based on joint research by Philip Hancock, Simon Williams and Sharon Boden, the focus here shifts from the everyday life of people to what we might term their everynight life. The authors observe how, over the last five years or so, a concern about the quantity and quality of our sleep has taken on the appearance of something approaching a moral panic. In response to this, a burgeoning industry in the management and regulation of sleep has emerged. Reflecting on the status of this 'sleep industry', the authors consider the ways in which sleep has become a site of a series of both commercial and managerialist interventions that positively valorise sleep as a medium of performative self-investment. Thus, from self-help books to drugs therapies, from space-age mattresses to alertness recovery programmes, the reconceptualisation of sleep as both an organisational resource and a form of individual capital is presented as an increasingly ubiquitous and, indeed, instrumentalised feature of modern life.

Everyday domesticity

In our second part we shift our attention away from an immediate concern with the management of the body towards the domestic and material environments such bodies frequently occupy during their everyday activities, focusing particularly on the home. The onus on us to manage our domestic environments is one that is, of course, enshrined in generations of popular magazines, in the activities of various women's guilds and organisations, and in the instruction young women have received for many decades, if not centuries, on how to be a good wife and mother. Increasingly, today, it is the object of a plethora of professional and expert interventions, ranging from the ever ubiquitous lifestyle magazines – beautifully described in an episode of the American animated comedy series *The Simpsons* as 'Homes Better Than Yours' – through home 'makeover' programmes on the television to domestic management companies and consultancies.

The first of our chapters, by Arlie Hochschild, explores the impact of a managerial orientation to the negotiation of domestic responsibilities particularly on the ways in which differing temporal priorities are handled. She focuses on the activities of 'Family 360' – the kind of management consultancy alluded to above – which was set up specifically to assist busy people in making improvements to their personal performance at home. In doing so, Hochschild identifies several personality or character types, ranging from what she terms 'endurers' to 'busy bees', each of which seeks to deal with the demands their increasingly hectic life schedules place upon them. While each of these character types reflects, in different ways, what she considers to be an actively engaged response to the pressures placed on the individuals to effectively manage their everyday domestic lives, the very existence of an organisation such as Family 360 remains intensely disturbing for Hochschild. For while such services might well meet a very real need in a culture within which success at work is closely entwined with domestic efficiency, what might the long-term consequences be when, as she puts it herself, a child's 'most vivid memory may be of those meetings around the dining room table with the expert who coached dad in how to get to the bottom line in love'?

Next we have Craig Lair and George Ritzer developing this theme with particular reference to the idea of outsourcing as something that is becoming increasingly common in middle-class families, particularly in the US. Referring to what they call metamanagement – a term taken from mainstream management literature referring to the inclusion of external sources of support, as well as internal – Lair and Ritzer chart the development of a burgeoning, domestic metamanagement industry. This industry encompasses services such as the personal concierge, nursery or daycare for children, as well as the periodic employment of personal chefs. And while, as both authors note, this may well seem to be a highly rational and empowering way of managing one's domestic life, the consequences may be far from rational, or indeed beneficial, for those involved. In particular, if what we are talking about here is the outsourcing of peripheral domestic affairs, such as gift buying, looking after children or even cooking a family meal, then it begs the question what, in the realm of everyday family life, remains too important or too precious to hand over to the 'experts' and, therefore, just what might still be beyond such rationalisation?

In the final chapter of this part, the relationship between management and domestic organisation is once again brought to the fore. Yet the focus here is somewhat different. Karen Dale, rather than considering domestic practices as such, explores rather the materiality of domestic life and how, in many ways, a largely managerial orientation to domestic space has promoted a particular view of what constitutes the 'ideal home'. Drawing on cultural resources ranging from the ever-expanding number of popular magazines that draw attention to the latest styles and domestic fashions to the aforementioned TV make-over shows, Dale unravels the aesthetic and architectural imperatives, and the language and priorities which are embedded within them, in such a way as to draw attention to the values of manageability that underpin their assertions of legitimacy and authority. Furthermore, she demonstrates that this is not as one might expect a neutral relationship. Rather it is one clearly embedded within, and informed by, the priorities of industrial capitalism and the production and control of particular relations of identity. Most notably, it must be said, in so far as they reproduce established relations of social stratification – such as class and gender – albeit perhaps in increasingly flexible and adaptable ways.

Lifestyle and the lifecourse

While, as in the chapter outlined directly above, the talk of lifestyle, and those cultural resources that increasingly mediate it, has informed much of what is written here, our final three chapters focus more exclusively on this particular issue. In particular each one explores what, following Titian's beautifully captured image, can be viewed as one of the three ages of man [sic], as life moves through childhood, into the world of the adult and, finally, into the realm of old age and retirement. Thus, management emerges as something that accompanies us, not only through space, but also through time; guiding us from one life stage into the next, ever watchful and ever ready to lend a helping [sic] hand.

Entitled 'From "My First Business Day" to "The Secret Millionaire's Club" – Learning to manage from early on', our opening chapter by Alf Rehn offers a critical evaluation of the extent to which managerial values and aspirations are increasingly embedded within a range of games and products aimed directly at the (very) young and aspiring business executive. From the entrepreneurial role model of Disney's Scrooge McDuck, to the managerial accoutrements of the 'My

First Business Day Playset' – which includes everything from an attaché case to a personal digital assistant – Rehn charts the ways in which such juvenile resources permeate the lifeworld of children's play, promoting cultural roles attuned not only to the practices but also to the values of kiddie-sized management. This is not to say that he believes that such resources are received or adopted in an unmodified form by those at whom they are targeted; children are, after all, far too creative and naturally iconoclastic for that. Equally, however, he acknowledges the ways in which the relationship between managerial discourse and childhood play is a complex and potentially precarious one, whereby the cues to subject formation such playtime resources offer cannot be simply disregarded. As such his is a call for further research, as well as continued critical vigilance, when asking both 'what does management do to children?' as well as 'what might children do to management?'.

Next, moving on from the realm of childhood innocence – if indeed such a thing exists – and into the struggles and conflicts of everyday adult life, André Spicer and Mehdi Boussebaa introduce what they term the curious case of neuro-linguistic programming (NLP), and reflect on its role in the management and rationalisation of everyday conflict. Both authors commence with an assumption that conflict is an inevitable, and in many respects productive, aspect of human relationships. Yet, as they observe, we are today offered, on a regular basis, if not always solutions and cures, then the belief that conflict can be confidently managed. As their title suggests, one particular prominent example of this promise is that to be found in what is termed neuro-linguistic programming. Commencing with a brief history of conflict, Spicer and Boussebaa then go on to explore the promises of NLP, particularly the proposition that it is possible to uncover rational motivations and, ultimately, deeply embedded mental maps or models, which if openly discussed and realised can mitigate many conflictual situations. Yet as the authors note, such a unitarist and ultimately individualist understanding of conflict ignores what are often the very real material conditions of lack and need that underpin conflict, and which cannot be addressed simply by delving into, and managing more effectively, our individual psyches.

In what is the final chapter of this part, and indeed the penultimate chapter of the collection as a whole, we shift our attentions to what many would regard as the final chapter of our everyday lives, namely retirement. Here, Stephen Fineman reflects on the extent to which the life of the retiree has itself become increasingly subject to a rationalisation process that underpins the offer of a better managed, and therefore better lived, retirement. While for many, the time it might be seen as offering the possibility of an escape from the calculative, and indeed performance, imperatives of working life, the expectation that retirement will be well thought out and well organised is one that is increasingly difficult to escape from. To consume, to invest, to maximise the capacity of one's ageing body, or to settle down in the purpose-built retirement community, all present themselves as exclusive, yet seemingly necessary, decisions to be taken as one maps out a successful, and indeed efficient, retirement portfolio. From the cradle, and now into the grave, we are adjured to plan, monitor, control and invest in our lifestyle and lifecourse in order to enjoy, and of course consume, to the best of our heightened abilities lest we should miss the opportunity to maximise our investment and fail to achieve the required standard of excellence.

Bringing the everyday back to work

The ultimate chapter of this collection, like the opening one, stands somewhat outside of the three parts described above. For, as the authors Peter Fleming and Andrew Sturdy observe, while the primary concern of the rest of the chapters has been the ways in which managerialism manifests within various aspects of life outside of the workplace, this is not the case here. Rather the question they choose to ask is, to what extent might managers also be increasingly drawing on the mundane values and practices of everyday life in order to further pursue the rational objectives of the organisation? In particular, and by way of concluding the collection as a whole, they evaluate the extent to which organisations are increasingly encouraging employees, at all levels, as they put it, to 'be themselves' at work. That is, to celebrate their differences, their passions and perhaps the most intimate aspects of themselves as integral to their work and organisational identities. Drawing on a case study, derived from their own research, the authors chart what they consider to be yet another process by which the distinctions between the values of organisational rationality, and the spontaneity, ambiguity, and playful uncertainties of everyday life are purposefully eroded in order to produce what are, in consequence, more effective, efficient and, ultimately, rationalised subject positions.

And on this note, we bring the collection to an end. As with all edited volumes, we do not claim either an exhaustive consideration of all the issues it has raised or indeed a comprehensive exploration of all the sites on which everyday life and management might be coming into evermore contact with one another. Nonetheless, what we hope to have provided is a constellation of ideas, perspectives and challenges all of which, while perhaps offering a temporary and contingent unity here, will provoke a diverse and, in their own way, critical series of engagements with not only the everyday life of management but, as we have pursued it here, the management of everyday life.

References

Bunting, M. (2004) *Willing Slaves: How the Overwork Culture is Ruling Our Lives.* London: Harper Collins.

Habermas, J. (1984 [1981]) *The Theory of Communicative Action. Vol. One: Reason and the Rationalization of Society* (trans. T. McCarthy). Cambridge: Polity Press.

Horkheimer (2004 [1963]) *Eclipse of Reason.* London: Continuum.

Warhurst, C., Eikhof, R. E. and Haunschild, A. (eds) (2008) *Work Less, Live More? A Critical Analysis of the Work-Life Boundary.* Basingstoke: Palgrave Macmillan.

Chapter 1

Management and colonization in everyday life

Philip Hancock

Introduction

Some 60 years ago Henri Lefebvre published the first volume of his critical evaluation of the condition of everyday life in advanced capitalist economies. In it (and the further volumes that were to follow), he offered a dialectical account of the struggle between what he considered to be the rationalizing and alienating values of capitalism, and the possibilities for liberation that exist within the activities and ambitions of everyday life. In this opening chapter, taking my inspiration from Lefebvre, I adopt the category of everyday life in order to critically explore what I consider to be the increasing presence of a particularly managerial rationality within the realm of the everyday, and those cultural resources that contribute to its reproduction.

The phrase 'the management of everyday life' is not, therefore, simply an empirical observation. Rather it intends a critical evaluation of the presence of management – and those modes of rationality and practice which underpin it – within a number of influential cultural resources that increasingly provide the foundations of personal sensemaking and the communicative practices that structure it. This chapter not only presents a discrete argument, therefore, but also establishes a framework within which the following chapters of this collection might be read. It considers just what might be meant by everyday life, a 'vague and vacuous term' (Highmore, 2002: 37), as well as asking what, for the purposes of this collection, might constitute management and how they might be seen to increasingly intersect.

Rationalization and the administered society

The proposition that everyday life is subject to a range of structuring forces aligned to the rational administration of the workplace organization is not without a history. Amongst other sources it can be traced back to early twentieth-century sociology and the discipline's approach to the socio-cultural consequences of industrial modernization. Perhaps the most influential source of this approach is to be found in the work of Max Weber. Weber's writings on what he considered to be the rationalization of modern life, resulting from the cultural dissemination of bureaucratic practices, are central to the argument I will present here. While Weber's attitude to bureaucratic forms of administration was more complex than is often assumed, what is clear was his unease with their impact on the more mundane aspects of people's lives. Weber (1968: 22) envisaged a situation whereby personal creativity, judgement and the human spirit would eventually be subsumed by a bureaucratized and increasingly disciplinary regime in which society is characterized by the production of a subject who is 'consistently rationalized, methodically trained and [oriented towards the] exact execution of the received order'. His obvious dismay at the potential consequences of such a process is aptly illustrated in one of his more often quoted reflections on what he considered to be the potential end point of this process:

> It is horrible to think that the world could one day be filled with nothing but those little cogs, little men clinging to little jobs and striving toward bigger ones – a state of affairs which is to be seen once more, as in the Egyptian records, playing an ever increasing part in the spirit of our present administrative systems, and especially of its offspring, the students. This passion for bureaucracy ... is enough to drive one to despair. (Weber, 1991: 78)

While central to Weber's fears regarding social bureaucratization was the prominence of modern rationality to its functioning and systems, it was not rationality per se that concerned him, however. Rather, Weber (1964) distinguished between what he termed 'formal rationality', a form of decision-making which orientates itself to the calculation of the most effective means to increase the chance of success in a particular endeavour, and 'substantive rationality', which concerns itself with the evaluation of values and ethical norms in relation to the outcomes of the formally rational. It was, as such, the predominance of the former in society that particularly concerned him, especially its apparent tendency to subsume questions of value under what increasingly appeared to be an uncritical logic of necessity.

It was this dimension of Weber's work that was subsequently taken up by a number of later twentieth-century academics, perhaps most notably a group of German intellectuals collectively referred to as the Frankfurt School. For the members of the Frankfurt School, Weber's understanding of the character of formal rationality – translated in their writings into *instrumental* rationality – was considered to be one of the greatest threats of the twentieth century. Theodor

Adorno, one of the School's most prominent members between the 1930s and the 1960s, referred to what he termed the emergence of an 'administered life' (Adorno and Horkheimer, 1979: 35) in which the values of equivalency and instrumentality associated with instrumental rationality and the calculative concerns of capitalism, expanded into every fold of human existence. This, he argued, reduced qualitative to quantitative experience and, as economic value and an adherence to policies and procedures became the measure of all things, produced an alienation of the modern subject from even the most intimate aspects of his or her everyday lives. As Max Horkheimer, another leading member of the School, expressed it,

> Just as all life today tends increasingly to be subjected to rationalization and planning, so the life of each individual, including his most hidden impulses, which formerly constituted his private domain, must now take the demands of rationalization and planning into account: the individual's self-preservation presupposes his adjustment to the requirements of the preservation of the system. (Horkheimer, 2004: 65)

Thus, drawing on Weber's own observation that rationalization is premised on 'the extension of formalistic quantifying reason to the phenomena of social life' (cited Cook, 2004: 5), the Frankfurt School sought to map out such incursions in areas such as popular culture, politics and even ethics, as part of a critical project oriented towards a radical re-evaluation of the proffered achievements of modernity.

While the work of the Frankfurt School continues to be influential, as we shall shortly see, by the close of the century its critical pre-eminence had been somewhat overshadowed by the rise of various poststructuralist and postmodern schools of thought. Yet despite a range of theoretical divergences, these shared with the School's work a number of similarities, most notably a congruent discomfort with the disciplinary and limiting effects of instrumental modes of thinking within society (cf. McCarthy, 1990). A notable instance of this can be found, for example, in Jean Francois Lyotard's (1984) interest in the increasingly performative character of contemporary knowledge which he viewed no longer as oriented towards the goal of truth but rather that of efficiency and, ultimately, power. Similarly, Michel Foucault (1979) was concerned with the ways in which the body – amongst other things – had become subject to a regime of similarly rational discipline, while Giles Deleuze (1995) analyzed how control pervades even the most mundane aspects of people's lives, serving not individual desires, but those of the corporations for whom they work and are ultimately accountable to.

More recently, academics associated with what is known as 'critical realism', a philosophical position that would generally locate itself in stark opposition to the poststructuralist worldview, have engaged in a similar critique of what is known as Rational Choice Theory (Archer and Tritter, 2000) and its largely instrumental orientation to the process of public policy-making. Nor has Weber's immediate legacy diminished in importance. Reiger (1985), for instance, has pointed to the ways in which the influx of expert technologies into the home during the twentieth century has led to an extension of instrumental reason into the everyday management of household and personal relationships. Similarly, George Ritzer's (1993) massively influential McDonaldization thesis has drawn our attention to the metaphorical parallel between what he considers to be an ongoing process of societal rationalization and the operations of the McDonald's fast food restaurant.

What follows in this chapter reflects, in many respects, therefore, a continuing dialogue with the diagnosis of modern life offered by Weber and those who have drawn inspiration from him. Or to put it another way, the theme of total administration sets the scene for what is, in effect, a reimagining of Weber's concerns regarding the rise of formal rationality within the context of the rise of modern management. Not that I consider these terms synonymous. There is much about what one might term the new managerial spirit that is clearly distinct from the characteristics of formalized reason described by Weber. This fact notwithstanding, however, the orientation to a critique of the process of societal rationalization that is to be found in Weber, his hermeneutic of suspicion to coin a phrase, is one that deeply influences the ideas and conclusions discussed here.

From administration to management

While the likes of Adorno employed the term 'administration' to characterize what was effectively the repression of human creativity, spontaneity and freedom, today, I would suggest, it has taken on a far more benign tone. In many respects the term administration is seen in a markedly positive light when compared with what one might consider to be its youthful usurper, namely management. In my own academic profession, for example, to describe oneself as involved in administration is to court, at worst, a slightly demeaning response, while to describe oneself as a manager is to invite, at best, derision if not outright hostility. This is because while the former tends to be associated with a relatively passive set of practices geared towards necessary systems maintenance, the latter is viewed frequently as a far more aggressive form of agenda setting and behavioural regulation.

Whatever one's view of the character of modern management, however, there would seem to be little reason to doubt, as Boltanski and Chiapello (2006) have recently recognized, its status as an important medium for the proliferation throughout society of formal rationality. Not only that, but as the likes of Protherough and Pick (2002: vii, *original emphasis*) have observed, we have, for some time now, lived in an age in which managerial ideas and principles appear almost overwhelmingly ubiquitous and whereby

Every aspect of life – hospitality, friendship, eating out or caring for one's family – ha[s] to be *managed*, with managerial 'targets' set for each part of its operation, and with league tables tabulating successes and failures.

Yet what exactly does the term management mean in such a context, and just how might it influence social relations above and beyond what one might consider to be its illegitimate sphere of not only interest, but indeed competence? Without entering into an extended discussion of the etymology of the term which can be found elsewhere (cf. Parker, 2002), the term management – along with the related terms managerial and managerialist – generally refers – one might argue – to a particular way of organizing, and deploying resources which, in principle, enable other activities to take place. To cite Parker (2002: 7), in this instance, management suggests

> a separation between the actual doing of whatever is being managed and the higher-level function of control of these processes.

With its origins in Taylor's (1911 much cited belief in the separation of managerial conception from employee execution, this is a generic version of management that views it as a largely neutral, but nonetheless highly directive, activity.

For most people, however, there is more to management than simply an abstract process of higher-level coordination. First and foremost, managerial activity tends to be concerned not with the control and coordination of just any process, but specifically with the production, distribution and exchange of economic resources or commodities. Managerial principles and the act of management are, therefore, closely associated with the coordination of specifically capitalist business practices and a set of specific institutional arrangements congruent with these.[1] These arrangements provide both the conditions of possibility within which management might exercise its perceived function – that is, a business community – while, at the same time, generate such conditions through an assemblage of historical and cultural expectations, economic necessities, and material artefacts and resources.

Second, managerial competency is no longer simply equated with administrative skills, even within, say, the not-for-profit sector of the economy. Rather it bears a host of additional expectations, the most notable being those of leadership, and perhaps even more prominently, entrepreneurialism. Western economies during the latter decades of the twentieth century, rocked as they were by the consequences of economic downturn, industrial unrest and the gradual unraveling of the postwar consensus, grew uneasy with the limitations of a managerial identity founded on the values of safe stewardship and technocratic competence. In response, management was reformulated in what were to become more pro-active and dynamic terms. Western industry, it was argued for example, needed fewer administrators and more leaders if it was to maintain its global pre-eminence (Zaleznik, 1977; Bass, 1985; Kotter, 1990). Influential texts such as those by Kotter (1990) redefined effective management, therefore, as leadership, with its ability to provide vision, direction and indeed motivation to an organization.

Also around this period, however, while management was increasingly coming to be redefined not only as an administrative and possibly visionary function, another discourse of managerial aspiration was exerting an increasing influence, that of the importance of entrepreneurship. While the image of the successful entrepreneur was seldom entirely disassociated from that of the great leader in the popular media, with figures such as Richard Branson and Anita Roddick both cases in point, the entrepreneurial spirit was something that was now seemingly available to all. Entrepreneurialism has even been touted as the new rock 'n' roll (Jones, 2005), suitable for the resurrection not only of the West's private industries but of its ailing public sector as well (Osborne and Gaebler, 1992).

This entrepreneurial spirit is one of daring initiative and self-organization; characteristics which, in many respects, diverge sharply from those traditionally associated with the administratively orientated manager. Nonetheless, in the public perception of such matters, great managers and great entrepreneurs have come to be seen as largely synonymous, an idea increasingly formalized in the notion of the intrepreneur. Perhaps of most interest in this context, however, are observations that have been made by some of the more critical voices in the debates surrounding enterprise. Most notable amongst these is Du Gay (1996), who recognizes that at the heart of the entrepreneurial project is a concomitant process of subjectification; that is, the production of enterprising subjects who have internalized these values, and ultimately, who become what can be termed entrepreneurs of the self. That is, they eventually come to see their physical and intellectual selves also as projects; projects oriented towards the maximization of personal opportunities, financial, as well as emotional, spiritual and cultural.

Before I go any further, however, I should perhaps make it clear that none of this is to suggest that the ways in which actual managers carry out their various administrative and associated functions can itself necessarily be formulated in such terms. While, as Grey (1997) has observed, there may be some aspiration towards such a formulaic model within the pages of the management textbook, the reality of managerial lives is often more complex. Managers tend, as Watson (1994: 35) has noted, to combine the application of formalized processes and practices with an ongoing process of sensemaking and adaptation or, to put it somewhat more crudely, making it up as they go along. As such, organizational management is often a more open-ended and indeterminate activity than one might suppose. It is contingent on environmental factors – both internal and external – and the meanings the individuals concerned ascribe to them and, as such, less amenable to the application of simple, universalistic, solutions.

Nevertheless, it is not the day-to-day activities of managers that so much concern me here, but rather how the values of managerialism – as a cultural ideology – permeate and resonate with a host of socio-cultural forms and lived practices that, to a lesser or greater extent, continue to lie outside the formal domain of the workplace. For, however, management is practised within the environment of the work organization, its validating logic is one that is clearly and very publicly articulated through a range of conceptual and symbolic resources that both structure and validate its claims to authority and, increasingly, universality. As I observed above with reference to Grey (1997), the managerial ethos as exemplified in its own literature and language[2] draws upon a host of performatively governed imperatives of action. That is, it invokes, more often than not, the language and values of effectiveness, efficiency, measurement, achievement, control and increasingly, as I have suggested above, entrepreneurialism, as representing an unproblematic and coherent orientation to the world. Add to this the hyperbole of heroic opportunity for those who submit to its particular worldview – including the possibility that one might unlock 'the mysteries of self-renewal' (Pascale, 1990: 15), identify 'the split/fix paradox' (ibid.: 36) and 'thrive on chaos' (Peters, 1988) while increasingly take control of our own destinies (Handy, 1997) – and what one is confronted with is a potentially very powerful cultural, and indeed ethical, technology. One that offers a means by which the indeterminacy and unpredictability so often characteristic of everyday life might be, if not rendered fully benign, then certainly 'manageable'.

To summarize then, what I am arguing for is an understanding of management that focuses not so much on the lived experiences of professional managers, but rather on a fundamentally ideological discourse that legitimates particular modes of engaging with, and being in the world, over others. One that directs individual decision-making and socially embedded practices towards an overriding prioritization of instrumentally orientated action, combined with an almost heroic valorization of individual entrepreneurialism, both of which are presented as a universalistic panacea in the face of the uncertainties of everyday life. Moreover, it is one that frequently evokes the language and symbolism of an idealized version of management practice – particularly the values of quantification, strategic planning and the marketing function – combined with a justificatory appeal to the efficiencies of the free market economy.

Considering everyday life

As the title of both this chapter and the book itself suggests, the question here is not one simply of management or managerialism, but of its influence on everyday life. Yet while social scientists have long been concerned with the category of the 'everyday', it has always been something of a contested concept. While interest in it appears to have experienced something of an upturn over the last decade or so, with books such as *The Body in Everyday Life* (Nettleton and Watson, 1998), *Music in Everyday Life* (DeNora, 2000) and *Governmentality, Biopower, and Everyday Life* (Nadesan, 2008) appealing to a broad spectrum of social scientific interests, the term nevertheless remains difficult to define and, in some instances, it is even considered symptomatic of the fallibilities of certain modes of social theorization (cf. Crook, 1998).

Despite this the category of the everyday has a well-established history, having been long associated with the phenomenological and ethnomethodological traditions within sociology,[3] and specifically with figures such as Schutz (1973, 1982), Goffman (1969) and Berger and Luckman (1967). Less concerned with developing a critical account of everyday life as we are here, however, writers in this tradition have primarily been interested in charting and making transparent the sensemaking accomplishments of people in and through their everyday interactions. As Dant (2003: 66) observes,

> To generalize, this sociological tradition rejects macro-social processes as determining the form of social life and regards social actors as collectively and collaboratively responsible for creating the social worlds they live in.

Nevertheless, while it is true that this tradition has, to a lesser or greater extent, tended to focus on the intersubjectivity of everyday life, many of the underlying propositions that characterize it do resonate with a more avowedly critical approach; in particular the unavoidable significance of shared resources and cultural frameworks within which agreements to the legitimacy of certain interpretations of meaning and claims to truth might be adjudicated. As such, some reference will be made to these ideas within the context of the critical approach to the everyday I consider here.

Leaving to one side the previously discussed work of the early Frankfurt School for one moment, perhaps the most prominent figure associated with a more critical relationship to the everyday is Henri Lefebvre (1992, 2000) whom I referred to at the opening of this chapter. For Lefebvre (1992: 97 *original emphasis*), a French Marxist intellectual, everyday life should be viewed as that

> Which is profoundly related to *all* activities, and encompasses them with all their differences and their conflicts; it is their meeting place, their bond, and their common ground ... In it are expressed and fulfilled those relations which bring into play the totality of the real, albeit in a certain manner which is always partial and incomplete: friendship, comradeship, love, the need to communicate, play etc.

Yet while a champion of the need to study the contours of the mundane and everyday he was, unlike the phenomenologists, by no means an uncritical bystander. For when he spoke of the partiality and incompleteness of the everyday, as he did above, it indicates what he considered to be its essentially contested nature. For while the everyday is, in Lefebvre's view at least, the realm of 'authentic' human value and agency, it nevertheless remains a mediated space; mediated, in particular, by what he termed the 'technocratic' (read formal or instrumental) rationality of market exchange. This is a rationality that he considered increasingly pervasive of the most intimate of our daily practices producing an alienation that is both integrating – in terms of a reified totality – and yet, at the same time, destructive of the fabric of meaningful human relationships. As he expressed it in one of his later works, *Everyday Life in the Modern World*, first published in 1971,

> [Everyday life] is no longer the place in where human suffering and heroism are enacted, the site of the human condition. [It] has become an object of consideration and the province of organization; the space-time of voluntary programmed self-regulation ...

where demands are foreseen because they are induced and desires are run to earth.
(Lefebvre, 2000: 72)

For Lefebvre, therefore, it was in the everyday that the contradictions and
paradoxes of an age in which human potential is both realized and retarded are
increasingly played out, where the 'dialectic of enlightenment', as Adorno and
Horkheimer (1979) termed it, is most starkly exposed.

Notwithstanding the force and insight of Lefebvre's account what it lacked,
however, was a systematic theorization of the nature of the interrelationship
between the qualities he associates with the everyday and the contrasting sphere
of technocratic rationality. One possible solution to this absence, however, is that
to be found in the work of a contemporary critical scholar, Jürgen Habermas.
While Habermas enjoys the status of one of the most prominent intellectual heirs
to the work and ideas of the Frankfurt School – having worked, for instance,
as research assistant to Adorno – his ideas diverge from many of those of his
mentors. Of notable significance is his rejection of what he considers to be
their unnecessarily totalizing vision of a society dominated by an instrumental
process of rationalization. Rather, through his theory of *communicative action*
(Habermas, 1984, 1987), Habermas offers instead a bifurcated conception of
society, comprising of what he terms the *lifeworld* and the *system*, each with its own
distinct, but ultimately interrelated, mode of organizing rationality.

While not entirely reducible to the idea of everyday life employed either by
the phenomenologists or by the likes of Lefebvre, Habermas's conception of the
lifeworld shares a number of important features with both of these perspectives.
As it did for Schutz and Garfinkel, the lifeworld represents for Habermas (1984:
335) the backdrop to human action which is 'the prereflective form of taken-
for-granted background assumptions and naively mastered skills'. It is where
consensus is pursued around values and aspirations, a process based on rational
dialogue and the presumed goal of achieving truth and mutual understanding.
It is this conception of the lifeworld that is subsequently contrasted with what
he terms the system which now, in a vein more akin to Lefebvre's bifurcation,
refers to the sphere of 'formal' or 'instrumental' rationality whereby the values
of differentiation and the rational calculation of means take precedence.
Embedded primarily within the state and economy, the rationality of the system
is said to orientate itself to the need for formal strategies directed at the efficient
coordination of complex socio-economic relations required for the reproduction
of 'the institutional cores that define society's "base"' (Habermas, 1987: 173).

Unlike his Frankfurt predecessors, therefore, Habermas is not entirely
antagonistic to the operation of a more formal mode of systems rationality, viewing
it, as he does, as necessary to the coordination of a complex society. Ideally, for
Habermas, however, such systemic activity should be governed by the values
and imperatives established in and through the communicative practices of the
lifeworld via what he terms *steering media* – most notably money and administrative
power – which translate such particular expectations derived from the normative,
everyday constitution of social relations into the general patterning of large-scale

economic and political transactions. Thus, formal, or instrumental, reason should ultimately be answerable to a more consensus-orientated, value-driven rationality; one that emerges from the communicative practices of the lifeworld. Yet where Habermas continues the critical tradition of his Frankfurt School predecessors is in his recognition that, under the conditions of modernity, there has been an ongoing reversal of this relationship, whereupon such aforementioned steering media act back upon the lifeworld, distorting those communicative practices through an imposition of the formal rationality which has come to characterize their functioning.

Habermas's concern, therefore, is with the tendency of aspects of the 'lifeworld' to fall increasingly under the direct dominance of instrumental reason (associated with the regulation and maintenance of capitalist exchange relations). This is characterized by the ways in which the symbolic resources we employ to legitimize the intersubjective rationality of our communicative interactions are increasingly displaced by a rationality orientated not towards critique or the establishment of truth or consensus, but rather the technical control and effective deployment of economic and socio-cultural resources. Hence, in his own words,

> Media such as money and power attach to empirical ties; they encode a purposive rational attitude toward calculable amounts of value and make it possible to exert a generalized, strategic influence on the decisions of other participants which *bypass* processes of consensus orientated communication. Inasmuch as they do not merely simplify linguistic communication, but *replace* it with a symbolic generalization of rewards and punishments, the lifeworld contexts in which processes of reaching and understanding are always embedded are devalued in favour of media-steered interactions. (Habermas, 1987: 183, *original emphasis*)

Now, it is with reference to such incursions into the communicative space of the lifeworld, incursions that distort and undermine the cultural and ethical foundations of everyday communicative practices and their critical (reflexive) potential, that Habermas attaches the term 'colonization'. Such colonizing incursions are not, however, 'all or nothing' processes. As Power et al. (2003) have argued, steering mechanisms can exert their influence on the lifeworld in two ways. When acting in a regulative sense, such mechanisms can provide valuable resources and information for the communicative reproduction of the lifeworld, acting as tools so to speak. When operating in what he terms a constitutive sense, however, such mechanisms reconstitute the very structure of the lifeworld, colonizing its consensual communicative practices with structures of thought, language and action regulated by the imperatives of instrumentality and utility.

As noted above, however, Habermas does not consider this a totalizing process. For while intense periods of assault on the communicative integrity of the lifeworld may result in an increase in certain social pathologies, like Lefebvre before him, Habermas is also at pains to acknowledge the dialectical and, therefore, resistive potential of everyday life in the face of these. As such, any such critical exploration of the everyday again shares in common with the phenomenological tradition a commitment to revealing and understanding how, in our everyday communicative practices, we may resist and challenge such colonizing processes and reassert what Habermas would consider to be apposite to lifeworld priorities.

Now, while I intend to return to this aspect of Habermas's argument, and its limitations, towards the end of the chapter, what I want to do now is articulate the main thrust of this chapter, namely that management can itself be understood not simply as a particular manifestation of such steering media, but particularly as one that possesses significant implications for the integrity of the contemporary lifeworld. In the aforementioned work by Power et al. (2003) it is claimed that accounting, for instance, can itself be understood and analyzed in terms of its relationship to the steering media of administrative power, money and law; steering media that increasingly function in a constitutive mode within the organizational sphere. Here I want to similarly explore the proposition that management, which can also be understood in such terms, increasingly demonstrates the potential to exert a similar constitutive influence on the realm of everyday life beyond such (albeit permeable) organizational boundaries. This means that management, or at least the constitutive rationality of management, increasingly has the potential to infuse the communicative and symbolic realm of the lifeworld and, in doing so, potentially distort both everyday processes of intersubjective sensemaking and the capacity to reason beyond the parameters such a limited mode of rationality favours.

Managerial colonization

The idea that interests related specifically to corporate performance present a significant force for the colonization of the everyday is not itself a new argument. In addition to the Weberian tradition I discussed earlier, Deetz (1992), for example, has developed an extensive analysis of the ways in which corporate values and demands have – through the media, the education system and so on – increasingly colonized the public democratic sphere including family and individual identities. Yet the argument I am presenting here differs in that it is not solely the direct pursuit of corporate interests that concerns me, but rather the integration of the values and principles of modern management itself, as a self-contained and reproductive ideology, into the cultural resources that contribute to the values and practices of everyday life.

Perhaps the most visible illustration of this has been the increasing prominence of what Habermas (1987: 397) refers to as 'expert cultures'. While the presence of a range of discourses of expertise is nothing intrinsically novel, either within organizations or society at large, what has been increasingly tangible over the last 20 years or so has been the almost direct transference of the imperatives, logics and values associated with managerial expertise, exemplified via the work of management consultants and various associated gurus, into cultural resources associated with the idea of 'everyday-managing'. Now, in using this hybrid term here what I acknowledge is that it is possible to think about managing in a way that is very different to the way in which we defined management earlier. Managing in the sense of 'everyday-managing' is about making sense of the world and getting by in such a way that is congruent with the idea of the lifeworld; that is, as a space within which learning, negotiation and adaptation take place as an intersubjective process, one grounded in shared resources and communicative engagements. After all, as Watson (1994: 12) notes,

> to survive in the world we have to manage our situation; to meet our material needs and to stay sane we struggle to exert some control. Notice the language used here: 'we have to manage'.

This exemplifies, I would argue, a dominance of lifeworld imperatives over systemic concerns whereby formal rationality serves the values of both survival and socially determined need. To stress the point once again, therefore, what I am concerned with here then is the reversal of this form of relationship, whereby the steering media manifest in management ideas increasingly configure the discursive and material resources and are increasingly presented as necessary for the successful maintenance of our everyday lives.

Now, in some cases this relationship between the system imperatives and techniques of management is, it has to be said, more obvious than others. Equally so, other system resources are often brought into play in order to further legitimate the universality or rigorous objectivity of its claims, such as medicalized discourses, or those of cognitive or behavioural psychology. Perhaps one particularly ubiquitous example of this inverted – in Habermasian terms – relationship is to be found on the shelves of pretty much every high street bookstore under the heading of 'self-help'.[4] I refer here, of course, to those books that offer us the promise of personal salvation from a host of personal ills and misfortunes through a combination of entrepreneurial, managerial and pop-psychological techniques. Take, for instance, McDermott and Shircore's (1999) *Manage Yourself, Manage Your Life*, within which the rationality of systems management is fused with the psychologism of neuro-linguistic programming (NLP), or perhaps Dryden's (2001) invocation to *Manage Your Emotions by Controlling Your Thoughts*, in which the principles of cognitive therapy provide a direct route to the restoration of the effectively and efficiently self-managed 'you'. Both of these titles and their contents illustrate a view of human subjectivity as something that must be closely regulated in order to ensure the individual is able to 'maximize life opportunities' while 'striving for personal excellence' and 'achieving sustainable peak performance'.

Similarly, in the increasingly popular field of professional life coaching, which appears geared towards the pursuit of competitive advantage in a world in which other people are either obstacles or resources rather than the source of meaning and self-understanding, individual self-improvement is offered as thoroughly amenable to such quantification. Yet the slippage from system to lifeworld is even starker than one might realize. It is not purely the rationality, language and values that, as exemplified in titles such as *The 10-minute Life Coach: Fast-Working Strategies for a Brand New You* (Harrold, 2002), demonstrate this, but the direct appropriation of management processes and procedures. Eileen Mulligan (1999), for example, a British 'coach' with a background in industry and business consultancy, offers a 7-day programme designed to improve everyday life achievements. It commences with the design and production of personal appraisal forms and questionnaires, and continues through a range of formalized tasks, including the production of a personalized mission statement. As Mulligan (1999: 30) herself 'pitches' it,

> For some individuals, their mission statement becomes the single and most significant aspect in their life. Mother Theresa dedicated her life to God and caring for the poor. Many religious leaders have spent a lifetime in prayer and meditation, their mission being enlightenment. There is one thing for sure: having a mission in life gives you a sense of purpose.

It is, of course, difficult to disagree with the underlying sentiment being expressed here, wrapped up, as it is, in an undeniable yet essentially meaningless tautology. Such managerial 'expert culture' does not, however, only find popular expression through the pages of relatively specialized, if apparently banal, self-help texts and professional services. If this were the case then perhaps it would all be far less interesting.

The imperative to have a 'mission' in life and to manage that mission also permeates, however, the much more visible and popular media of the contemporary, and highly popular, lifestyle magazine. It is here that readers are invited to become their own life coaches, 'inspired and motivated' to pursue 'instinct as the logical choice', eat 'mood food', take '6 steps to happiness'[5] and so become effective and efficient managers of the self. Indeed, this burgeoning publishing genre appears fixated with management language and imperatives. For example, readers across a range of publications are encouraged to ensure that their everyday lives are brought to order, reconceptualized and then reconstructed as 'well planned', 'controlled', 'efficient' and 'effective', regularly reviewing performance and ensuring any necessary modifications or interventions are undertaken accordingly.

Headings and sub-headings such as 'MOT Your Life: 25 point problem fixer' (Men's Health, April 2001: 6), '7 Steps to Happily Ever After' (SHE, November 2008: 71), 'Quality Time: 10 New Ways to Clock Off' (Woman and Home, November 2008: 54) where a 'top life coach' advises on ten ways to systematically improve quality of life, 'Calm the chaos, tame the tumult and nail down every second of your time as *FHM* brings order to your life in 18 easy steps' (FHM, November 2000: 5) and 'Finding and Keeping Friends You Need', which requires a detailed analysis of your friendships through the production of a written 'friendship audit' (Psychologies, November 2008: 151) all reflect, in equally soundbite fashion, the need to embrace the self as a marketable commodity, or as an entrepreneurial brand called 'you', as management writer Tom Peters (1997) put it. Within such texts, then, the self in relation to others is positioned as a managerial project to be subject to constant performance appraisal: 'spring clean your life – career wobbles? Love traumas? *Elle* shows you how to go for the big clean up' (*Elle*, April 2001: 7).

It is not simply to lifestyle texts that I would want to point to as illustrative of such a colonization process of contemporary cultural resources, however, despite their evident popularity. Take, in addition, the increasing importance of personal communication technologies in our everyday lives, technologies with the expressed purpose of ensuring that self-management is rendered evermore rapid, extensive and efficient. Leaving aside for one moment the almost – in this context anyhow – obsolete deskbound PC, the development and proliferation of a whole host of hi-tech devices including tablet PCs, PDAs, smartphones and even Internet-configured entertainment devices, such as Apple's ipod touch, have increasingly sought to blur not only previous distinctions between the temporal and spatial contexts of work and leisure (cf. Towers et al., 2006), but equally distinctions between relatively spontaneous action and pre-planned, coordinated and systematically pursued activities. Thus, rather than simply meeting a friend for a meal in a restaurant that you both know, by using say a device such as the Apple iphone, you are able to identify all the relevant restaurants in your area, look up their various reviews on the web, and then call up directions to the establishment of your (their?) choice based upon this information. Guess work, spontaneity and serendipity all appear largely obsolete as organizing an intimate social occasion is rendered calculable and potentially as efficient as generating a stock inventory.

The limits of everyday management

Before I proceed further with this line of argument, however, it should be acknowledged that such developments might well not be of concern to everybody. As one might expect in a book attached to a series in critical management studies, the resources I have drawn on here inevitably encourage one to view such developments in a somewhat jaundiced light; as symptomatic of the essentially homogenizing character of market capitalism which, while appearing to offer choice and opportunity, effectively curtails the possibility of thinking outside of the market and what it chooses to make available to us. Yet as Crook (1998: 538) insists, for instance, 'human experience is always mediated' and, as such, it might be equally argued that such colonizations could be more fruitfully considered as the networking of resources, and judged not so much against some metaphysical yardstick of human potentiality, or the devaluing of formal rationality, but rather against the usefulness people ascribe to them (as in the case of a smartphone which enables one to book a table in a recommended restaurant).

Perhaps one important source of inspiration for such a mode of critique is the work of Michel de Certeau who, while equally concerned with the experience of the everyday in contemporary society, certainly favours a less pessimistic reading of the conditions within which the modern subject finds himself or herself. For de Certeau, despite a shared concern with the negative impact on contemporary cultural forms of contemporary capitalism, he does not consider such an impact to be totalizing in its reach or impact. Rather, it always leaves room for what he terms 'tactics' (de Certeau, 1984: xii); that is, the ways in which people negotiate everyday life and, in doing so, inscribe their own meanings on place and time, and resist – sometimes through reappropriation – the kinds of colonizing rationalities of concern here.

What I would want to emphasize in response to this, however, is that it is neither my contention to deny the joy and personal advantages that might be obtained from such resources nor the existence of individual or cultural resistances by those who oppose them. Indeed, such views would be inimical to a perspective that takes seriously Lefebvre's account of the potentialities of the everyday to offer alternatives spaces and practices of life in the face of what he considers to be the systematic production of alienation. Nor, from a Habermasian conception of the lifeworld, can it simply be reduced to a condition of homogeneous stasis if it is to be truly understood as a communicative space of intersubjectivity which, by its very nature, remains as such only if it is constantly engaged with, through a process of re-evaluation, reorientation and reconstitution. As Habermas (1987: 185, *original emphasis*) himself observes in this respect,

> We cannot directly infer from the mere fact that system and social integration have been largely uncoupled to linear dependency in one direction or the other. Both are conceivable, the institutions that anchor steering mechanisms such as power and money in the lifeworld could serve as a channel *either* for the influence of the lifeworld on formally organized domains of action, *or*, conversely, for the influence of the system on communicatively structured contexts of action.

Indeed, the idea that human subjectivity can ever be wholly colonized or constituted as a singular and determined entity is one that has rightly been challenged from a number of perspectives within management and organization studies and beyond. As Jones and Spicer (2005) have argued with reference to the work of Lacan, for instance, if one accepts that each subject remains in a permanent state of becoming in terms of their individual identity, that it is never finally fixed or static, then no cultural ideology – be it managerial or not – can wholly create a state of closure in terms of the dynamics of human identity and agency.[6] Indeed, even if such theoretical claims are set aside, empirical illustrations of such ongoing everyday tactics abound. Spoof self-management books (cf. Woodhouse, 2001) and the critical reception that the directive contents of the lifestyle magazine often receives, even from those who read them (cf. Hancock and Tyler, 2004), all suggest the possibility of a critically engaged consciousness.

Practically, then, it might appear difficult in the light of what I have written above, to sustain an argument that focuses primarily on colonization by management at the expense of a consideration of possible sites of reappropriation and resistance. Well in part this may represent a fair criticism. Yet what is important, for me at least, is the need to promote recognition of the need to at least commence questioning management's role in how we evaluate and position ourselves in relation to the practices of our everyday lives; something that has been largely absent within the established parameters of critical management studies. Furthermore, in part my aim in this chapter has been to set the scene for the contents of this collection as a whole. I have, therefore, offered a particular theoretical orientation towards thinking about the relationship between management and everyday life; one that seeks to draw attention to the asymmetries such a relationship engenders when manifest as it is through the pages and associated cultural resources of the mass media. This is not, I stress once again, to either exaggerate the power of management or downplay the possibilities of play and resistance, but rather to identify its cultural presence as a first step towards rethinking the scope and objectives of studying management critically in the light of this.

Conclusion

In this chapter, I have attempted to establish something of a backdrop to the collection as a whole. In doing so, I have drawn primarily on the critical conception of a bifurcated social totality offered by Habermas and his concern with the nature of the relationship between the instrumental logic of commodity capitalism and the everyday space of intersubjective communication and sensemaking. This has led me to argue that management represents an increasingly pervasive and, indeed, colonizing rationality; one that is having a ubiquitous influence on the content of a range of socio-cultural resources which themselves can be said to play a not insignificant role in the structuring of the landscape of everyday life. It is, therefore, an influence that transcends the confines of the work organization and the formal labour relationship, and increasingly manifests within the resources and fabrics of everyday life, oriented as it is towards the apparent amelioration of some of our most pressing personal concerns and tribulations.

It is, of course, a somewhat particular version of management that I have presented here. It combines the rationality and principles of mass administration – instrumentality, quantification, systematization and so on – with the entrepreneurial language of innovation, (self) creativity, and even courage. In doing so, it offers not only a particular view of the world, but a means by which the vagaries and challenges of modern life might be negotiated, and perhaps, ultimately, overcome. In an age defined by the aforementioned new spirit of capitalism (Boltanski and Chiapello, 2006), or fast subjectivities (Thrift, 2005), in which novelty, excitement and indeterminacy are the order of the day, it offers what might be seen as a highly rational settlement whereby the irrationalities produced by a system which constantly accelerates and complicates the quality of everyday life are offered – somewhat dialectically – as their own solution.

Nonetheless, however one ultimately views both the legitimacy and utility of such a viewpoint, my overriding concern in writing this chapter is not that you uncritically accept what I say. Rather it is that you take some time to reflect on these issues in your critical studies of management, and perhaps ask yourself just where does management end today and, therefore, where might a critical study of management also end? Is it at the gates of the office or the factory, or perhaps at the home of the remote worker? Or, as part of a larger critical endeavour, should it perhaps venture even further, bringing its critical gaze to bear on the flotsam and jetsam of everyday life in order to fully grasp and render transparent this apparently ubiquitous of cultural ideologies? Hopefully this, and the chapters that follow, will provide you with a starting point when it comes to asking such questions as well as encourage you to think of new ones that are still to be asked.

Notes

1. By 'arrangement', I am not simply referring to a particular hierarchical configuration of offices or a division of labour within the context of an organizational structure, but rather a complex patterning of discursive and practical logics underpinned by a series of both tacit and explicit agreements as to their utility and socio-cultural legitimacy.
2. See, for example, Handy (1989, 1997), Drucker (1989), Peters (1988, 1992, 1997), Senge, (1990) as well as a host of management education textbooks.
3. The philosophical foundations of these interpretive approaches are to be found largely in the phenomenological philosophy of Hegel (1977) and Husserl (1970) and their conceptions of the intersubjective constitution of reality and the *lebenswelt* or 'life-world', respectively.
4. In the US, where many of these books are first published, sales continue to be more than healthy. In 2007, for instance, the US market in self-help books was estimated to be worth around $600 million (Loomis, 2008).
5. Echoing the one best way of Taylor, here the crude quantification and pseudo-scientific rhetoric (the discipline of 'positive psychology') is accompanied by an imperialistic universalism that allows the authors to claim that 'This new discipline demonstrates that the same basic principles about happiness apply to virtually everyone, across all age groups, nationalities and cultures' (Stauth, 2004: 37).
6. See also Hancock and Tyler's (2001) argument in relation to Hegel's philosophy of recognition.

References

Adorno, T. and Horkheimer, M. (1979) *Dialectic of Enlightenment*. London: Verso.
Archer, M. and Tritter, J. Q. (2000) 'Introduction', in M. Archer and J. Q. Tritter (eds) *Rational Choice Theory: Resisting Colonization*. London: Routledge, pp. 1–16.

Bass, B. M. (1985) 'Leadership, Good, Better, Best', *Organizational Dynamics*, 13: 26–40.

Berger, P. and Luckmann, T. (1967) *The Social Construction of Reality*. Harmondsworth: Penguin.

Boltanski, L. and Chiapello, E. (2006) *The New Spirit of Capitalism*. London: Verso.

Cook, D. (2004) *Adorno, Habermas and the Search for a Rational Society*. London: Routledge.

Crook, S. (1998) 'Minotaurs and Other Monsters: "Everyday Life" in Recent Social Theory', *Sociology*, 32: 523–540.

Dant, T. (2003) *Critical Social Theory: Culture, Society and Critique*. London: Sage.

de Certeau, M. (1984) *The Practice of Everyday Life*. Berkeley: University of California Press.

Deetz, S. (1992) *Democracy in an Age of Corporate Colonization*. Albany, NY: University of New York Press.

Deleuze, G. (1995) *Negotiations: 1972–1990*. New York, NY: Columbia University Press.

DeNora, T. (2000) *Music in Everyday Life*. Cambridge: Cambridge University Press.

Drucker, P. (1989) *The Practice of Management*. London: Heinemann.

Dryden, W. (2001) *How to Make Yourself Miserable: Manage Your Emotions by Controlling Your Thoughts*. London: Sheldon Press.

Du Gay, P. (1996) *Consumption and Identity at Work*. London: Sage.

Foucault, M. (1979 [1975]) *Discipline and Punish: The Birth of the Prison* (trans. A. Sheridan). London: Penguin.

Goffman, I. (1969) *The Presentation of Self in Everyday Life*. Harmondsworth: Penguin.

Grey, C. (1997) 'Management as Technical Practice: Professionalization or Responsibilization?', *Systems Practice*, 10: 703–726.

Habermas, J. (1984) *The Theory of Communicative Action, Vol. 1: Reason and Rationalization of Society*. Cambridge: Polity.

Habermas, J. (1987) *The Theory of Communicative Action, Vol. 2: The Critique of Functionalist Reason* (trans. T. McCarthy). Cambridge: Polity.

Hancock, P. and Tyler, M. (2001) 'Managing Subjectivity and the Dialectic of Self-Consciousness: Hegel and Organization Theory', *Organization*, 8: 565–585.

Hancock, P. and Tyler, M. (2004) 'MOT Your Life': Critical Management Studies and the Management of Everyday Life', *Human Relations*, 57: 619–645.

Handy, C. (1989) *The Age of Unreason*. London: Business Books.

Handy, C. (1997) *The Hungry Spirit: Beyond Capitalism – A Quest for Purpose in the Modern World*. London: Random House.

Harrold, F. (2002) *The 10-minute Life Coach: Fast-Working Strategies for a Brand New You*. London: Hodder & Stoughton General.

Hegel, G. W. F. (1977 [1807]) *Phenomenology of Spirit*. Oxford: Clarendon.

Highmore, B. (2002) 'Introduction To Part One', in Ben Highmore (ed.) *The Everyday Life Reader*, London: Routledge, pp. 37–38.

Horkheimer, M. (2004 [1947]) *Eclipse of Reason*. London: Continuum.

Husserl, E. (1970 [1954]) *The Crisis of European Sciences and Transcendental Phenomenology: An Introduction to Phenomenological Philosophy*. Evanston, IL: Northwestern University Press.

Jones, C. and Spicer, A. (2005) 'The Sublime Object of Entrepreneurship', *Organization*, 12: 223–246.

Jones, P. (2005) 'Entrepreneurialism; the new rock 'n' roll', *BBC News*. http://news.bbc.co.uk/1/hi/business/4542280.stm

Kotter, J. (1990) *A Force for Change: How Leadership Differs from Management*. New York, NY: Free Press.

Lefebvre, H. (1992 [1947]) *Critique of Everyday Life: Volume I*. London: Verso.

Lefebvre, H. (2000 [1971]) *Everyday Life in the Modern World*. London: Athlone.

Loomis, N. (2008) 'American Authors See Their Self-Help Books Flying Off The Shelf in Brazil', *Los Angeles Times*, 26 July.

Lyotard, J-F. (1984 [1979]) *The Postmodern Condition: A Report on Knowledge* (trans. G. Bennington and B. Massumi). Manchester: Manchester University Press.

McCarthy, T. (1990) 'The Critique of Impure Reason: Foucault and the Frankfurt School', *Political Theory*, 18(4): 437–469.

McDermott, I. and Shircore, I. (1999) *Manage Yourself, Manage Your Life: Simple NLP Techniques for Success and Happiness*. London: Piatkus Books.

Mulligan, E. (1999) *Life Coaching: Change Your Life in Seven Days*. London: Judy Piatkus.

Nadesan, M. (2008) *Governmentality, Biopower, and Everyday Life*. London: Routledge.

Nettleton, S. and Watson, J. (eds) (1998) *The Body in Everyday Life*. London: Routledge.

Osborne, D. and Gaebler, T. (1992) *Re-inventing Government*. Reading, MA: Addison-Wesley.

Parker, M. (2002) *Against Management*. Cambridge: Polity.

Pascale, R. (1990) *Managing on the Edge: How Successful Companies Use Conflict to Stay Ahead*. London: Penguin.

Peters, T. (1988) *Thriving on Chaos*. London: Macmillan.

Peters, T. (1997) *The Circle of Innovation*. London: Macmillan.

Peters, T. (1992) *Liberation Management*. London: Macmillan.

Power, M., Laughlin, R. and Cooper, D. (2003) 'Accounting and Critical Theory', in M. Alvesson, and H. Willmott (eds), *Studying Management Critically*. London: Sage, pp. 132–156.

Protherough, R. and Pick, J. (2002) *Managing Britannia: Culture and Management in Modern Britain*. Exeter: Imprint Academic.

Reiger, K. M. (1985) *The Disenchantment of the Home: Modernising the Australian Family 1880–1940*. Melbourne: Oxford University Press.

Ritzer, G. (1993) *The McDonaldization of Society: An Investigation into the Changing Character of Contemporary Social Life*. Newbury Park, CA: Pine Forge Press.

Schutz, A. (1973) *The Problem of Social Reality*. The Hague: M. Nijhoff.

Schutz, A. (1982) *Life-Forms and Meaning Structures*. London: Routledge & Kegan Paul.

Senge, P. (1990) *The Fifth Discipline*. London: Random House.

Stauth, C. (2004) ' 6 Steps to Happiness', *Be Unlimited*, 2: 37–41.

Taylor, F.W. (1911) *The Principles of Scientific Management*. New York: Norton.

Thrift, N. (2005) *Knowing Capitalism*. London: Sage.

Towers, I., Duxbury, L. Higgins, C. and Thomas,J. (2006) 'Time Thieves and Space Invaders: Technology, Work and the Organization', *Journal of Organizational Change Management*, 19: 593–618.

Watson, T. (1994) *In Search of Management: Culture, Chaos & Control in Managerial Work*. London: Routledge.

Weber, M. (1964 [1925]) *The Theory of Social and Economic Organization* (ed. T. Parsons). New York: NY: Free Press.

Weber, M. (1968 [1925]) *Economy and Society: Vol. 1* (ed. and trans. G. Roth and C. Wittich). New York, NY: Bedminster Press.

Weber, M. (1991 [1948]) *From Max Weber: Essays in Sociology* (ed. H. H. Gerth and C. Wright Mills). London: Routledge.

Woodhouse, M. (2001) *The 9 Life Habits of Highly Effective Cats: The Ultimate Guide to Feline Success.* London: Harper Collins.

Zaleznik, A. (1977) 'Managers and Leaders: Are They Different?', *Harvard Business Review*, 47 (May–June): 67–78.

Part **1**

Management and embodied living

Chapter 2

Managing under the covers

Lifestyle media and the management of sexuality in everyday life *Melissa Tyler*

Introduction

> Managerial work is about life itself, in a sense, managerial work is the essence of human activity. (Mintzberg, 2004: 207)

In many ways our sexuality has never been so unmanageable. The ubiquitous porn industry is arguably circumvented by frequenters of *You Porn*, and by subscribers and contributors to websites such as *Voyeur Web*, which claims to be the world's most visited amateur erotic photo and video site where (so they suggest) 'fantasies are played out' in what amounts, to all intents and purposes, to something of a (virtual) erotic community. Places such as the London-based club *Amora*, the 'academy of sex and relationships', promise us an erotic escape route from the pressures of work and everyday life, a sexual experience unmarred by intolerance or inhibition, one that is 'sexy, fun and inspiring'. Even in the workplace, as Fleming and Spicer (2004) have outlined (see also Chapter 12, this volume), many contemporary employers often welcome an (albeit relatively bounded) sexual pluralism according to which we are encouraged to 'be ourselves' as opposed to conforming to some narrowly defined sense of sexual normality. And yet, commercial pornography continues to account for by far the majority of internet traffic and, while we may be inspired or encouraged to simply be our (sexual) selves in a variety of settings, including the workplace, it seems fair to say that we experience and evaluate our sexualities and those of others against a cultural backdrop that is largely performance orientated. What this suggests is that while in contemporary capitalist societies we may be accorded considerable erotic freedom, compared to say, previous generations or to those living in more conservative cultures, we also seem to be increasingly subject to the performance pressures that often accompany such freedom.

And it is to this conditional freedom that this chapter turns it attention, considering some of the various ways in which the discourses and techniques associated with the management of work organizations, and with a societal preoccupation with management as the 'essence' of human activity, as Mintzberg puts it, have come to be incorporated into the management of sexuality in everyday life. After all, sexuality is perhaps one of the most personal and intimate aspects of everyday life outside of the confines of formal work organizations; more traditionally (romantically?) thought of as an essential human activity. Considering the intersection between management, sexuality and contemporary cultural resources such as lifestyle magazines, my focus here is on the extent to which the discourses and techniques associated with managerialism have become a significant part of the cultural landscape guiding the (self-) management of sexual identities and relationships. The basic premise of the chapter is that the contemporary management of sexuality constitutes a notable example of a managerial colonization of everyday life, signifying not only an intensification of what Gramsci (1988) called 'Fordist sexuality', but more substantially a corresponding threat to our erotic imagination and capacity for 'spiritual ingenuity' (Rose, 1995: 63). Drawing on critical social theory, as well as a range of examples taken from management texts and lifestyle magazines, the chapter argues that contemporary cultural discourses on sexuality, those involved in what Bauman (1998) describes as the 'cultural processing of sex', permeated as they are by references to managerial imperatives such as efficiency and effectiveness, reduce intimate relations to yet another aspect of a narrowly conceived performative project of the self.

Of course, the degree to which people internalize and live by the 'rules' of conduct they encounter in these particular media forms, or even attribute any meaning or significance to them beyond a 'quick flick' is not something that can simply be read off from an analysis of their content (Tyler, 2004). It does seem fair to say though that the ubiquity of lifestyle media suggests that they provide an important backdrop, a social landscape as it were, shaping the cultural imaginaries according to which people live their lives and against which sexual identities are forged and relationships are enacted, made meaningful and potentially evaluated. Such media provide, we might say, a degree of certitude in response to ontological anxieties; they provide a kind of cultural 'comfort zone' or reference point replete with discursive and commercial resources (especially given that a large proportion of their content consists of advertising) with which to handle changing and challenging circumstances and experiences, or simply a proliferation of choice and possibility. These are not simply cultural forms that reflect or represent social processes and relations, then, but in part constitute them; they are effectively 'guides to living' (Giddens, 1992: 2). The intention here is to reflect on the role they play in re-imagining the erotic in largely managerial terms. As Elliott and Lemert (2006) have noted, a marked series of changes have affected sex, intimacy and eroticism in market societies in recent decades. These changes relate broadly to a rapid rise in what, following Foucault, we might call discursive sexuality; that is, sexuality framed and regulated through advertising, mass media and information. As part of this process, sexuality has arguably become a central aspect of the entrepreneurial project of the self.

My discussion of the character and consequences of this process begins by considering the rational organization of everyday life and, particularly, the evolution of the self as an entrepreneurial project, one driven by the pursuit of a largely aesthetic form of reflexivity. It then considers critical perspectives on the modernist repression and administration of sexuality, focusing particularly on the characteristics of 'Fordist sexuality' and a so-called 'Taylorization of sex' (Jackson and Scott, 1997), before reflecting on the extent to which these characteristics have given way to a more pluralistic ethic of sexual tolerance. The following part of the discussion examines the prevalence of managerial discourse, techniques and imperatives in contemporary cultural resources such as lifestyle magazines and argues that, while much of what we might call discursive sexuality focuses on the promotion of sexual health, in mainstream media the emphasis is largely on sexual performance, efficiency and effectiveness. The final part of the chapter turns to the work of contemporary critical theorist Axel Honneth, to reflect on some of the consequences of this underlying performance imperative for intersubjective social relations, and for the lived experience of sexuality in everyday life.

The rational organization of everyday life

Focusing on the rationalizing impact of the so-called 'enterprise culture' on the management of everyday life, Du Gay and Salaman (1992) have argued that everyday life has fallen prey to the totalizing and individualizing effects of the imperatives of economic rationality upon which the concept of the enterprising self is based. This means that social relations come to be perceived largely as exchange relations in which social subjects are re-imagined as customers. Hence, through the discourse of enterprise the distinctions between production and consumption, between the inside and outside of organizations and, crucially, between work- and non-work-based identities are progressively blurred such that we all engage in a process of self-management. They illustrate this argument with reference to the ways in which the language of enterprise has traversed its traditional limits and has 'colonized our interiors' (Du Gay and Salaman, 1992: 629). Hence, by living one's life as an entrepreneur of the self, modes of existence that might otherwise appear to be politically or philosophically opposed can be brought into alignment.

Grey (1994: 481) notes similarly, in his account of career as a project of the self, how the pursuit of a career 'offers a vehicle for the self to become', one that effectively embraces the individual's whole life, including relations with friends, family and sexual partners. Hence, the conflation of self and career becomes 'an instrumental project which is to be managed and achieved' to the extent that self-management, both in and of everyday life, constitutes 'a more productive and economical form of managerial control than disciplinary power, with its costs and unintended consequences, could ever be' (Grey, 1994: 495).

In terms of the lived experience of sexuality and sexual relationships, this evolution of the self into an entrepreneurial, instrumental project is illustrated, we might say, in the increasingly common practice of drawing up pre-nuptial contracts and cohabitation agreements setting out joint financial arrangements and even how often couples can reasonably expect to have sex. Another interesting example of the rational pursuit of the self as an entrepreneurial project in this respect can be seen in the increasingly widespread use of dating advertisements and also dating agencies, or in the practice of 'speed dating', for the purposes of meeting a partner. Janice Coupland (1996) has suggested that the use of such resources is an efficient and 'rational' response to the contemporary organization of work and everyday life which imposes an irrational configuration of life circumstances – time-pressured, work-centred, mass-mediated and so on. As she puts it, 'in dating advertisements, the identities of the advertiser and her/ his would-be partner *are managed*' (Coupland, 1996: 188, emphasis added).

Providing the philosophical backdrop to many of the recent critical approaches to understanding the rationalization of everyday life in circumstances such as these, Habermas's account of the colonization of the lifeworld stresses that the latter has become increasingly subject to bureaucratic administration (see Chapter 1, this volume). Rather than a particular region of social space, the concept of the lifeworld designates, for Habermas, a series of presuppositions given form, repeatedly, in our 'everyday acts of mutual understanding' (Habermas, 1987: 124). His analysis emphasizes that the lifeworld has become increasingly colonized by imperatives of money and power, and that the pathologies of contemporary society largely flow from this colonization and a corresponding fragmentation of 'everyday consciousness' (Habermas, 1987: 355). The emancipatory task of critical theory, then, is to facilitate the lifeworld in regaining confidence in its own consensus-generating capacity in the face of this colonization by systems such as the state and other bureaucratic organizations. In this sense, Habermas's defence of modernity assigns particular significance to the role of 'communicative action', an aspect of his writing that he grounds in an (early) Hegelian philosophy of intersubjectivity and in which he argues that subjectivity evolves socially in an environment (the lifeworld) in which individuals must recognize themselves. The lifeworld, in this respect, is the condition of a self formed dialogically, through engaging and coming to terms with others. Hence, central to Habermas's critique of colonization is the presumption that becoming a subject is founded on 'the intuition that a telos of mutual understanding is built into linguistic communication' (Habermas, 1987: 99).

Although the teleological assumptions on which this 'intuition' is based are not everyone's cup of tea, and his concept of the everyday is clearly open to the charge of 'romantic nostalgia' (see Crook, 1998), Habermas's intersubjective philosophy seems particularly appropriate for developing a critical appreciation of sexuality and sexual relations. For, we might argue, it is precisely the colonization of this intersubjective process of becoming that underpins the management of sexuality in the contemporary era. Before considering the ways in which this process is culturally embedded in lifestyle media, however, it is important to acknowledge its historical evolution and, in particular, its early analysis in what Gramsci called 'Fordist sexuality'.

Fordist sexuality and the Taylorization of sex

Given what has been described as the ascetic spirit of modernity, it is perhaps not surprising that sexuality became a prime candidate for managerial attention and repression (Burrell, 1984; Hawkes, 1996). As Marcuse (1955) argued in *Eros and Civilization*, 'the scientific management of instinctual needs has long since become a vital factor in the reproduction of the system'. As Foucault (1979) in particular emphasized in his critique of the repressive thesis, this reproduction of the system came to be reflected not simply in the outright prohibition of sex, but rather through the reordering of ways of knowing, thinking and speaking about sexuality. As he put it, sexuality came to be regarded

> not merely as a thing to be condemned or tolerated but *managed*, inserted into systems of utility, regulated for the greater good of all, made to function according to an optimum. (Foucault, 1979: 24, emphasis added)

The progressive administration of sexuality that we see subject to critique in his work was underpinned, he argued, both by what is prioritized and by what is marginalized. While the former was characterized by a scientific association of sexuality with 'nature'; an enduring convergence of behaviour and identity, and the privileging of (re)productive (heter)sexuality in the construction of healthy, moral and rational sexual subjects, the latter involved a marginalization if not outright pathologization of women's sexual autonomy; same-sex desire; expressions of youthful sexuality, and of auto-eroticism. In the process of 'modernization', sexuality became, therefore, increasingly subject both to systematic organization and to scientific analysis. Indeed, sexology emerged, during the late nineteenth and early twentieth centuries, in a period in which scientific approaches to the investigation and management of human behaviour were dominant. Many of the central tenets of sexology, of course, sat quite comfortably with earlier, pre-modern religious ideas about sex being for procreation rather than pleasure. Yet sexology (founded as it was on a claim to the enlightening power of reason) also espoused a replacement of prejudice and fear with a series of truth claims to knowledge of what is 'natural' and 'normal' sexually. Despite a strong shift away from the positivist influence of biology, medicine and sexology, towards a much greater emphasis on the social construction of sexuality from the 1960s onwards, the essentialist ontology of sexology has continued to bequeath us with a legacy of sex as unavoidable – as a given, uncontrollable urge needing to be managed.

Sociologist Gail Hawkes (1996) maps out the history of this process, arguing that through the subjection of sexuality to scientific discourse, modernity came to be characterized by a specific mode of sexual production, according to which issues of efficiency and effectiveness came to the fore. Modernist regimes of sexual efficiency came to replace pre-modernist discourses of physical and moral danger, as the 'science' of sex offered a blueprint for the rationalization of the erotic. With this in mind, Jackson and Scott (1997) have argued that erotic pleasure has gradually been rationalized in line with Taylorist principles of scientific management. For Jackson and Scott (1997: 558–559), 'trends towards rational constructions of the sexual, coupled with a pedagogic approach to the management of everyday life' have contributed to a Taylorization of sex involving 'the production of rationalized means of producing pleasure'. This Taylorization process, one underpinned by a rationalization of intimacy, assumes 'a series of stages to be gone through before the final output' driven primarily by a performance imperative.

Both Hawkes's (1996) account of modernist sexuality and Jackson and Scott's (1997) analysis of the Taylorization of sex reflect Gramsci's (1988) earlier work, (written in the 1920s) on the relationship between sexuality and Fordism, in which he argued that modern sexuality and its management should be understood in relation to Fordist accumulation imperatives. In particular, he emphasized the extent to which Fordism demanded a mode of regulation that extended well beyond the immediate site of production so that sexuality became sublimated to the interests of calculative rationality. Himself echoing earlier writing by Weber on the containment of pleasure (see Burrell, 1984), Gramsci maintained that Fordism required that sexuality be mechanized and excluded from the sphere of the work organization. Just as the activities of workers in the labour process must be shaped carefully towards a given end, so their appetites outside of work must reflect the prevailing ideology of ordered rational action:

> The truth is that a new type of man demanded by the rationalization of production and work cannot be developed until the sexual instinct has been suitably regulated and until it too has been rationalized. (Gramsci, 1988: 282)

Gramsci emphasized, therefore, that a distinctly Fordist sexuality was a necessary correlate of mass production, one characterized by 'a new sexual ethic' (Gramsci, 1988: 282) of regulation and rationalization, of sexual asceticism, 'assimilated ... in the form of more of less permanent habits' (Gramsci, 1988: 288). An important question to ask ourselves then, given some of the changes outlined above, is to what extent has this Fordist sexual ethic given way to a post-Fordist sexuality, one characterized by a more postmodern proliferation of sexual possibilities, and the pursuit of a more sexually entrepreneurial project of the self?

It seems fair to say that the critical tradition outlined above has been largely underpinned by the conviction that, ultimately, 'eroticism represents a form of escape from the iron cage of rationality' (Burrell, 1987: 95–96). Erotic reality, within this tradition, occupies a distinct social space (the 'other dimension' of alienated reality, in Marcuse's terms), one that has a logic of its own, and a regime of laws and rules which, if violated, are liable to return us abruptly to the everyday realities of our damaged lives. Ideally, these laws and rules incorporate various elements and expectations pertaining largely to the embodied pursuit of pleasure underpinned by an ethic of mutuality. For some, recent changes in sexuality and sexual relations indicate that we have already begun to shift away from the repressed, administered sexuality outlined above, towards a more pluralistic, democratic sexuality underpinned by an ethic of tolerance and experimentation, signifying a move towards this erotic ideal becoming a lived reality, a perspective that represents an important counter argument to the 'colonization' thesis.

Sexual postmodernization and the enterprising self

Recent sociological approaches to sexuality tend to emphasize the extent to which modernist or Fordist sexuality has given way to a process of sexual postmodernization. Postmodern sexualities are understood largely in terms of a progressive disengagement of the enduring modernist association of sexuality with nature discussed above. The essentialist ontology on which modernist sexuality rested is replaced largely by a conception of sexuality as a lifestyle choice, a shift that feminists and queer theorists especially have argued releases sexuality from the strictures of heteronormativity. 'Sexual postmodernization' is therefore understood largely in terms of a rejection of the science of sex, and its pre-social conception of sexuality as an innate drive, in favour of a more performative ontology, emphasizing process, paradox and play. Hence, a postmodern sexual ontology is seen to be 'far more rooted in the poetic than the physical or biological' (Simon, 1996: 148), characterized by erotic multiplicity, experimentation, and an ethic of tolerance underpinned primarily by the pursuit of pleasure. For Simon, sexuality is an aspect of social life that is increasingly multiple, fragmented, diffuse and contested, forged out of the contingent circumstances of choice, pluralism and complexity that ultimately link together in the creation of a sexual self.

Where those of a postmodern persuasion differ from more critical perspectives on this dissolution into sexual pluralism is that where the former focus on the political potential of a proliferation of lifestyle choices, the latter see increasing scope for commercialization, commodification and colonization – a point I return to below. For the former, in the separation of sexuality from religion, from traditional familial structures, from communities and other repressive aspects of everyday life such as restricted forms of communication and representation, a socially and politically significant space is seen to open up for new kinds of sexualities to emerge. Such sexualities are understood to be characterized, as noted above, by a 'de-naturalization of sex' (Simon, 1996: 30) and a blurring of sexual boundaries (Gergen, 1991). In line with a proliferation of lifestyle choices offering a multiplicity of sexualities with which to experiment, the perception is that, as Plummer (1996: xv) has put it, 'a supermarket of sexual possibilities pervades'.

Emphasizing this sexual proliferation as a defining feature of late modernity, Giddens (1992) in particular has argued that the gradual social and economic liberation of women, the demise of ideologies of romantic love and the separation of sexuality from procreation have all been fundamental in promoting a new form of intimacy: the 'pure relationship'. Pure relationships presume 'equality in emotional give and take' (Giddens, 1992: 58) and an opening up of the self as a precondition of confluent love. This democratic form of intimacy involves what Giddens calls 'plastic sexuality': the pursuit of sexual pleasure severed from its ties to reproduction and obligation. Giddens maintains that the intimate equality on which plastic sexuality and the pure relationship depend is characteristic of late modernity, an era in which the biological justification for heteronormativity has lost its foothold, and in which sexuality has been released from the confines of a heterosexual, monogamous, procreative hegemony and replaced, instead, with a sexual pluralism driven by the hedonistic pursuit of pleasure and lifestyle choice.

Seidman (1989: 295), who also champions the emergence of a postmodern sexual ethic 'as a domain of pleasure and self-expression . . . erotic choice, experimentation and diversity', argues that critics of the liberating potential of sexuality have not fully grasped the shift in sexual ethics that has occurred in parallel with the move towards a reflexive, postmodern sexual ontology. This shift, he argues, is signified by a change from a morality centred on the sex act to one concerned more with the communicative, interactive context of sexuality; in other words, with the nature of the erotic exchange. In a similar vein to Giddens, Seidman argues that the humanizing, anti-instrumental character of contemporary sex manuals and other lifestyle resources such as magazines signifies a discursive shift towards a sexual ethic underpinned by a postromantic ideology of erotic pluralism, and an emphasis on the pursuit of sexual pleasure through non-procreative sexualities.

In contrast to the likes of Giddens and Seidman, who see a proliferation of sexual possibilities in these developments, my concern is more with the potential for a commercialization and colonization of intimate relations as a consequence of recent developments in the way in which we think about and experience our sexualities. Gramsci (1971), Foucault (1977) and Bourdieu (1984) have all emphasized the hegemonic significance of 'experts' and 'cultural agents' – intermediaries who intervene in the relationship between culture and subjectivity shaping this relationship in a particular way. The key site of hegemony, for Gramsci, is the myriad of everyday activities and experiences that culminate in common-sense assumptions that become cemented in some semblance of normality, thus concealing or mystifying the interests of dominant groups whose definitions of reality and whose norms and standards appear as natural, rather than as political and therefore contestable. Foucault (1977), of course, recalls this aspect of Gramsci's work in his account of the ways in which 'experts' operate as the architects of power/knowledge. Bourdieu (1984) also emphasizes the role played by cultural agents in shaping the investments we make in cultural capital in his account of the petit bourgeoisie as a symbolic elite. His emphasis on an investment orientation towards the self, in this case towards the self as an investor in 'sexual capital', encourages us to reflect critically, for instance, on the process through which 'disappointment in the bedroom, once considered part of life's normal ups and downs, has become the next frontier ... another enemy to be conquered' (Grady, 1999: 1). Here, journalist Denise Grady, writing in the *New York Times*, reflects on the overwhelming commercial success of new drug technologies such as Viagra as a means of investing in our sexual selves. Since its commercial launch in March 1998, Viagra has reportedly become the fastest selling prescription drug in history. Combined with the rise of the sex therapy industry as the provider of 'quick fix' solutions, such drug technologies arguably constitute examples of what Bauman (1994: 38) describes as our understanding of life-processes and collective living as 'a succession of "problems" to be resolved', and of our deeply ingrained dependence on 'ever-more expert and technique-intensive solutions' to such problems.

As Hochschild (1994) has emphasized in this respect, like other commercially based advice-givers, the editorial collectives of lifestyle magazines and the authors of self-help books act as 'investment counsellors', recommending to readers of various types how much and in whom to 'invest'. Hochschild cites the role played by such advice-givers as indicative of a more general trend towards what, drawing on Weber, she refers to as a 'commercial spirit of intimate life'. Lifestyle magazines appear to contribute to the spread of this commercial spirit, at least in part, by linking their advice on investment strategies to inspirational images, products and ideas appropriated largely from feminism, but also more generally to the management of everyday life, and to living one's life as an entrepreneur of the self, a theme to which I now turn.

Sexuality and managerialism in lifestyle media

In the second half of the twentieth century, the demands of reflexive modernity opened up a vast market for advice and guidance books, magazines, counselling services and therapy focusing on how to build, develop and rebuild relationships, bodies, selves and sex lives. As suggested above, representing the enlightening power of reason, sexology and the sex manuals it produced intended to replace prejudice and fear with scientific knowledge in order to 'liberate' our repressed sexuality. The authors of *The Joy of Sex*, for instance, emphasized how one of the chief rationales for their focus on sex as pleasure and play is its genuinely humanizing, anti-instrumental character: 'sex is the one place where we today can learn to treat people as people' as author Alex Comfort put it (1970: 9). At one level, sexology and the sex manual culture it spawned represented a significant challenge to residual Victorian mythologies, particularly those relating to women's endurance rather than enjoyment of sex.

Yet, sexologists also helped to affirm the idea that sex is principally a matter of technical skill, laying the foundation for a discourse that was widely disseminated in successive decades through a steady supply of best-selling sex manuals and sex education films, set against a broader cultural backdrop of liberation by the 'permissive' attitudes of the 1960s and by newly available methods of contraception such as the pill. Contemporary lifestyle magazines seem to have taken their discursive cue from the work of the sexologists in this respect, combining a clear preoccupation with sexual technique with, as Hochschild notes, emancipatory language and imagery culled largely from feminism. Hence, while a significant element of contemporary sexual discourse is concerned with strategies for managing risk and safety in relation to sexual health and well-being, much of that to be found in mainstream media culture, particularly in what we might broadly term the lifestyle media, is concerned largely with an intensified performance principle, underpinned by an instrumental pursuit of pleasure and a corresponding preoccupation with technical efficiency and effectiveness.

Indeed, such magazines are replete with language more usually associated with management texts, concerned as they seem to be primarily with an instrumental investment in ourselves (and others) as entrepreneurial projects. Readers are invited to ensure that their sex lives are well planned and controlled, efficient and effective, and to appraise their own (and their partner's) performances accordingly. For instance, while *New Woman* magazine arguably adopts something of a Tayloristic approach to sexual improvement: '33 sex tips – all scientifically proven' (December 2000); 'Sex – better and more of it' (January 2001); 'The scientific way to have the best sex of your life' (February 2001), *Cosmopolitan* is replete with the language of continuous improvement: 'Train yourself for really ambitious sex – be the best you can be!' (January 1997); 'Guaranteed – the best sex ever!' (December 2000); 'How to achieve world-class lovemaking' (April 1997). Similarly, *Men's Health* magazine emphasizes an investment orientation to sex: 'The world's greatest sex ideas…to turn you into the greatest lover on earth' (May 2001); 'Get more sex – how to boost your investment in your love life' (June 2006); 'Sex – the best investment you'll ever make' (November 1996). In assessing potential return on one's investment in sexual capital, keeping in mind, of course, that 'sex should always be as wild and exciting as possible' (*New Woman*, May 2001), plenty of investment advice is on offer. *Men's Health*, for instance, regularly encourages its readers to test their sexual knowledge and skill on the 'Orgazmatron', a self-assessment questionnaire that quantifies levels of sexual performance. There is also no shortage of advice on how to reconcile the demands of a time-pressured lifestyle and career with the compulsion to invest effectively in one's love life. This advice largely orientates itself towards 'streamlining' sex, making it as technically skilled, performance-orientated and efficient as possible, advice that is often (reflecting the genre more generally) articulated as an '*n* step' formula: 'Lessons in love – your 15-minute foreplay schedule' (*Men's Health*, August 1998); 'Lazy sex – bedroom shortcuts for the over-worked (or just lazy) lover' (*Maxim*, May 2000); 'Twice the sex, with half the foreplay' (*Maxim*, December 2001); 'How to have the sexiest, most relaxing and most productive hour of your life' (*Men's Health*, November 1998); 'how to deliver in the bedroom' (*Men's Health*, March 1998); '10 minutes to better sex' (*New Woman*, September 2006) and, surely the ultimate in efficiency-driven sex?

'Right first time sex – 20 ways to stop wasting time in the bedroom' (*Men's Health*, September 1997).

So, what might these magazines, and their preoccupation with continuous improvement and 'right first time sex', suggest to their readers? First, as we are repeatedly told how to improve our sexual relationships, readers are likely to learn that such relationships are presently inadequate (otherwise, they would not need improving), or that to constantly strive for improvement in this respect is a natural impulse, if not a moral imperative. Second, readers may learn that they can improve their sexual relationships through the application of a fairly narrow range of techniques, ultimately those that emphasize a managerially orientated sexual efficiency and effectiveness. By apparently pushing back the limits of what can and can't be said, the producers of this 'total quality' sexual discourse are, in many ways, able to present themselves as radical sexual pioneers (much like their sexologist predecessors) when, of course, it could be argued that they are precisely the reverse. In particular, magazines such as *New Woman* and *Cosmopolitan* borrow heavily from feminist discourse, implying to their readership a genuine (emancipatory rather than simply commercial) commitment to the equal sexual worth of men and women. As Hochschild (1994: 15) has emphasized however, what such magazines and advice books appropriate from feminism, as suggested above, are simply the soundbites and buzz-words, so that 'the spirit of commercialism...instrumentalizes our idea of love and commercializes it'. Lifestyle magazines and self-help books certainly propose that sex should play a more central role in the lives of women especially, and that women should rid themselves of anachronistic ideas about the importance of chastity. Yet, at the same time, embedded within the discourse of enterprise which guides individuals in managing the sexual 'career of the self' (Grey, 1994), potentially critical and emancipatory discourses such as feminism are colonized, and incorporated into an instrumental, performance imperative. The self-purportedly ironic tone adopted by magazines such as *Men's Health* and *Maxim* in their coverage of gender-related issues also sediments a discursive sexuality organized largely according to the terms of the 'heterosexual matrix' (Butler, 2000), one that continues to position desire as a largely heterosexual, masculine prerogative. *Men's Health*'s regular column 'Alpha Male', for instance, proffers regular advice on 'all you need to lead in life' including guidance on how to 'triple your sex appeal' and garner insight into 'her secret sex wishes' (October 2008).

On this basis, it could be argued that those currently celebrating the advent of a sexual postmodernization underplay or underestimate the potentially de-humanizing effects of an instrumentalized hedonistic ethic driven more by calculated performance imperatives than a genuine ethic of erotic mutuality or sexual pluralism. Not only do they overlook the arresting effects of our over-investment in sexuality, they also underestimate the extent to which our investment in sexual capital (and of course, our concern to secure a return on this investment), through the pursuit of 'right first time sex', has become something of a marker of distinction (Bourdieu, 1984). In doing so, they underplay the extent to which sexuality has arguably become a way of maintaining a relatively secure position in a consumer-orientated social hierarchy of self and others, rather than a space in which we can escape the pressures to perform. It is in reflecting on the consequences of this, of this managerially orientated cultural preoccupation with short-cut sex, that I wish to turn to the work of contemporary critical theorist Axel Honneth, and his reflections on the importance of erotic intimacy as the basis of ethical relations between ourselves and others.

Management and the colonization of the erotic

Honneth's theory of the struggle for recognition represents a broad continuation of the Frankfurt School's normative critique of capitalist society by linking critical perceptions of social injustice to the negating experiences of having our ethical expectations violated. The roots of his approach are to be found most clearly in Hegel's early writing on the struggle for recognition, from which he takes the idea that human flourishing is dependent on the existence of ethical relations which can only be established through a struggle for mutual recognition. Our relationship to ourselves then, for Honneth (following Hegel), is not simply a matter of a solitary ego appraising itself (for instance, as an entrepreneurial project), but of an intersubjective process, in which our relationship to ourselves emerges only as a result of our encounter with others. On the basis of Hegel's account of the struggle for recognition, Honneth attempts to develop a normative critique of the forms of social misrecognition that negate the possibility of living an ethical life, effectively by precluding this process of mutual recognition and respect. His reworking of Hegel leads to a distinction between three forms of recognition (based on love, rights and social esteem), and three corresponding forms of disrespect (the term used in translation to refer to *Mißachtung* in Hegel's writing, or what is more commonly translated as misrecognition, and which Honneth himself uses to describe 'the withholding or withdrawing of recognition – Honneth, 1995: 132).

The first and most basic denial of recognition in Honneth's account occurs at the level of embodiment, involving what we might broadly term 'interpersonal violence'. As he puts it, 'the forms of practical maltreatment in which a person is forcibly deprived of any opportunity freely to dispose over his or her own body represent the most fundamental sort of personal degradation' (Honneth, 1995: 132), producing a loss of trust in oneself, in others and in the social world more generally. The second form of disrespect he outlines involves the denigration of moral self-respect. Broadly speaking, 'this refers to those forms of personal disrespect to which an individual is subjected by being structurally excluded from the possession of certain rights' (Honneth, 1995: 133). What this denial of rights (and hence of recognition) conveys is that an individual has not been accorded the same degree of moral responsibility as others and in this sense, this type of disrespect typically brings with it a loss of self-respect. The third type of misrecognition involves a denial of social esteem and hence a degradation of a person or group's social value. This typically involves, Honneth outlines, evaluative forms of disrespect that denigrate individual or collective ways of life and their inherited cultural horizons, and which, in doing so, 'robs the subjects in question of every opportunity to attribute social value to their own abilities' (Honenth, 1995: 134). Each of these forms of misrecognition or 'disrespect', Honneth argues, can generate motivational struggles that potentially contribute to the emergence of social conflicts and movements. In his own words, 'the experience of being disrespected can become the motivational impetus for a struggle for recognition' (Honneth, 1995: 138). It is in this aspect of his work that Honneth proceeds from where he feels Hegel left off, namely by asking how the denial or withdrawal of recognition can provide the motivational impetus for social conflict and resistance, and indeed, for a collective struggle for recognition.

Honneth's writing on sexuality, for him the first and most basic form of unification, emphasizes that 'in encountering the desire extended to it *by* the other, the subject experiences itself to be the same vital, desiring subjectivity that it desires *of* the other' (Honneth, 1995: 37, emphasis added). Drawing directly from Hegel's writing on the philosophy of spirit, Honneth emphasizes that only when each subject has also recognized that 'the other knows itself likewise in its other' can it possess a basic trust 'that the other…is for me' (Honneth, 1995: 37). Whereas for Hegel this basic form of recognition is only the prelude to ethical life, an element of it as it were, for Honneth this relationship of recognition is fundamental to the subject's formative process so that 'for every subject, the experience of being loved constitutes a necessary precondition' of recognition (Honneth, 1995: 38), and hence of living an ethical life driven by mutual recognition and respect for oneself and others.

Easily construed as being overly idealistic or romantic, this thesis, as Honneth himself readily admits, becomes plausible only when understood as a claim about the emotional conditions and ethical expectations underpinning the trust relations necessary to engage meaningfully in ethical relationships with others. In this sense, he stresses that it would be a mistake to simply equate sexual love with social bonds; rather, 'what the love relationship does admit is the maturation of preliminary relations of mutual recognition that constitute a necessary precondition for every further development of identity' (Honneth, 1995: 39). In other words, as noted above, intimacy characterized by mutual trust and respect is a prerequisite for intersubjective moral development.

Yet, Honneth's thesis stops short of reflecting on the consequences and types of disrespect that may be experienced in relation to this most basic form of recognition. With this in mind, in the lifestyle media considered above, and taking Honneth's concern to link different types of recognition to the social forms of disrespect through which they are precluded, we might argue that in perpetuating an instrumental, performance-orientated sexuality, such media and the discourses they disseminate limit our potential for erotic recognition and, instead, provide the cultural backdrop to a denial of intimacy, rights and social esteem; the latter particularly so in their continued preoccupation with the prioritization of heteronormativity.

What this suggests is that in the colonization of sexuality by managerial discourses, the freedom to pursue our sense of self through genuinely intersubjective, erotic relations devoid of performance imperatives and the linear purposiveness of rational modes of organization is largely denied us. The idea that contemporary market societies have undergone a process of sexual postmodernization operates, from this perspective, in a narrow historical framework that deflects attention away from the persistence of a performance imperative, and an instrumental concern with sexual efficiency and effectiveness, and its embeddedness in the contemporary cultural landscape. The aggregate effect of this extension of managerialism to sexuality has been to sediment this performance principle and its hegemonic effects, rationalizing yet another of our ways of escape, and leaving little room for an authentic, irrational experience of everyday life.

Sexuality's connection with eroticism, so central to Honneth's account of how we can live an ethical life, from this more critical perspective, is being gradually yet persistently eroded as we become increasingly unable to do other than limit ourselves within the confines of our own individual projects of self. As Gillian Rose (1995) has reflected, echoing the critical tradition on which Honneth draws, eroticism ideally embodies the capacity to reject (albeit temporarily) the linear purposiveness of a rationally ordered social life. Of course, erotic relations are made up of a cluster of rules and role expectations, yet these are ideally formulated and enacted according to a negotiated communicative eroticism, to borrow from Habermas's terminology, which places an important emphasis on an embodied, dialogical multiplicity and self-entrustment. Seen in this light, eroticism is a necessary element in living an ethical life, in finding an escape route from the pressures of our contemporary lifestyles which prioritize work and organization over other forms of existence, yet which seems to have become increasingly subject to a highly performative external mediation, one that serves to arrest its intersubjective potential and close down our ability to find a space for disorder in the seemingly ordered pattern of contemporary life. Such media have become, we might say, strategic interventions into the intersubjective process of becoming the people we are (Hancock and Tyler, 2001, 2004), encouraging us to work and to buy more in order to maintain our social status, and situating the self as a project that requires others to engage in, and to recognize, whilst arresting the intersubjectivity and precluding the kind of mutual recognition on which such projects depend. What this means is that, contra the ideals of critical theorists like Honneth and Rose, eroticism becomes self- rather than other-centred, a process in which the discourse and imperatives of managerialism play a central role.

Concluding thoughts

To summarize, this chapter has argued that the incorporation of management imperatives, discourses and techniques into the contemporary cultural landscaping of sexuality and sexual relations has eroded the ethical potential of the erotic, reducing it to yet another rhetorical aspect of the reflexive project of the self (Giddens, 1992). In erotic sex, as Rose put it, there is much more at stake than simply the pursuit of pleasure; eroticism is fundamentally a way in which we can free ourselves from the confines of the self and, as Marcuse (1955) emphasized, find a release from the fragmenting and alienating effects of an organized society. However, through the incorporation of managerial techniques, imperatives and discourses into those cultural resources that in part guide us through this particular aspect of everyday life, sexuality has arguably become yet another aspect of the lifeworld in which the work ethic reigns supreme. In other words, instrumental rationality and the calculated pursuit of efficiency and effectiveness have intruded into what is arguably, ideally, the most intimate, intersubjective aspect of our everyday lives.

A proliferation of lifestyle media instruct us that it is no longer enough to be simply doing it, or even enjoying it; we should be 'managing it', 'working at it', 'improving it' and so on. Not only does the continued proliferation of 'sexpert' cultures and the corresponding barrage of performative representations of sexuality as a largely aesthetic phenomenon limit our freedom as sexual subjects, when it purports to do precisely the reverse, in terms of their impact on lived experience, such cultures make it difficult for us to engage in the kind of ethic of mutuality on which erotic sexuality depends. This results, as has been argued here, in the perpetuation of a managerial eroticism, a 'total quality' sexuality, underpinned by the instrumental pursuit, in our most intimate encounters with each other, of the entrepreneurial project of the self.

References

Bauman, Z. (1994) *Alone Again: Ethics after Uncertainty*. London: Demos.

Bauman, Z. (1998) 'On Postmodern Uses of Sex', *Theory, Culture and Society*. 15(3/4): 19–33.

Bourdieu, P. (1984) *Distinction: A Social Critique of the Judgement of Good Taste*. London: Routledge.

Burrell, G. (1984) 'Sex and Organizational Analysis', *Organization Studies*. 5(2): 97–118.

Burrell, G. (1987) 'No Accounting for Sexuality', *Accounting, Organizations and Society*. 12 (1): 89–101.

Butler, J. (2000) *Gender Trouble*. First published 1990. London: Routledge.

Comfort, A. (1970) *The Joy of Sex*. London: Quartet.

Coupland, J. (1996) 'Dating Advertisements: Discourses of the Commodified Self', *Discourse and Society*. 7(2): 187–207.

Crook, S. (1998) 'Minotaurs and Other Monsters: "Everyday Life" in Recent Social Theory', *Sociology*. 32(3): 523–540.

Du Gay, P. and Salaman, G. (1992) 'The Cult[ure] of the Customer', *Journal of Management Studies*. 29(5): 615–633.

Elliott, A. and Lemert, C. (2006) *The New Individualism: The Emotional Costs of Globalization*. London: Routledge.

Fleming, P. and Spicer, A. (2004) 'You Can Checkout Anytime But You Can Never Leave: Spatial Boundaries in a High Commitment Organization', *Human Relations*. 57: 75–94.

Foucault, M. (1977) *The Archaeology of Knowledge*. London: Tavistock.

Foucault, M. (1979) *The History of Sexuality, Volume One: An Introduction*. Harmondsworth: Penguin.

Gergen, K. (1991) *The Saturated Self: Dilemma and Identity in Contemporary Life*. New York: Basic Books.

Giddens, A. (1992) *The Transformation of Intimacy: Sexuality, Love and Eroticism in Modern Societies*. Cambridge: Polity.

Grady, D. (1999) 'Sure, We've Got a Pill for That', *The New York Times*. 14 February, p. 1.

Gramsci, A. (1971) *Selection from Prison Notebooks*. London: Lawrence and Wishart.

Gramsci, A. (1988) 'Americanism and Fordism', in D. Forgacs (ed.) *A Gramsci Reader: Selected Writings 1916–1935*. London: Lawrence and Wishart, pp. 275–299.

Grey, C. (1994) 'Career as a Project of the Self and Labour Process Discipline', *Sociology*. 28(2): 479–497.

Habermas, J. (1987) *The Theory of Communicative Action, Volume Two*. Cambridge: Polity.

Hancock, P. and Tyler, M. (2001) 'Managing Subjectivity and the Dialectic of Self-Consciousness: Hegel and Organization Theory', *Organization*. 8(4): 565–585.

Hancock, P. and Tyler, M. (2004) 'MOT Your Life: Critical Management Studies and the Management of Everyday Life', *Human Relations*. 57: 619–645.

Hawkes, G. (1996) *A Sociology of Sex and Sexuality*. Buckingham: Open University Press.

Hochschild, A. R. (1994) 'The Commercial Spirit of Intimate Life and the Abduction of Feminism: Signs from Women's Advice Books', *Theory, Culture and Society*. 11: 1–24.

Honneth, A. (1995) *The Struggle for Recognition: The Moral Grammar of Social Conflicts*. Trans. J. Anderson. Cambridge: Polity.

Jackson, S. and Scott, S. (1997) 'Gut Reactions for Matters of the Heart: Reflection on Rationality, Irrationality and Sexuality', *The Sociological Review*. 45(4): 551–575.

Marcuse, H. (1955) *Eros and Civilization*. Boston, MA: Beacon.

Mintzberg, H. (and Martin de Holan, P.) (2004) 'Management as Life's Essence: 30 Years of *The Nature of Managerial Work*', *Strategic Organization*. 2(2): 205–212.

Plummer, K. (1996) 'Foreword', in W. Simon (ed.) *Postmodern Sexualities*. London: Routledge, pp. ix–xvi.

Rose, G. (1995) *Love's Work*. London: Chatto Windus.

Seidman, S. (1989) 'Constructing Sex as a Domain of Pleasure and Self-Expression: Sexual Ideology in the Sixties', *Theory, Culture and Society*. 6: 293–315.

Simon, W. (1996) *Postmodern Sexualities*. London: Routledge.

Tyler, M. (2004) 'Managing Between the Sheets: Lifestyle Magazines and the Management of Sexuality in Everyday Life', *Sexualities*. 7(1): 81–106.

Chapter 3

Over the limit

The management of drug and alcohol use

Edward Wray-Bliss

Introduction

I am concerned in this chapter with the management of drinking and drug taking – particularly as it pertains to the situation in the UK. Intuitively, intoxication would seem to be a direct contrast to the sober rationality and self-management necessary for the correct performance of organisational or societal roles. One might, therefore, expect today's institutions, 'greedy' as they are for the labour power and cultural alignment of employees (Coser, 1974), to demand moderation or abstinence from these subjects. We might look for organisations to function so as to exclude or manage the intoxicated body, discipline it into different forms of behaviour or supplant the irrationality of intoxication with performative rationality and calculability. In the section immediately following this introduction, I will show moves in these directions through the technology of workforce drug and alcohol testing.

I will also sound a cautionary note against reading into such technologies or wider managerial discourses on drink or drug use, any simple colonisation by management of intoxication. I highlight contradictions, blurred rationalities and inconsistencies in managerial and personal constructions of intoxication. I explore these points through the figures of the 'binge drinker' and the 'recreational drug user'. The reason why I am concerned to draw out such contradictions and confusions in the management of this sphere of everyday life can perhaps profit from some explanation. Clegg et al. (2006), engaging with what they regard as a trend towards presenting management and managerialism as inherently 'bad' and colonising, have argued that such representations of management may become politically disempowering. The critical scholar may unwittingly ascribe a unidimensional and clear headed colonising rationality to management in what is in actuality a contradictory organisational and societal plane. In place of the recognition of 'polyphony' (ibid.) with its spaces for dissent, translation and movement the critic risks reproducing a singular narrative of managerial domination. 'The price', the authors argue, 'for an order erected and maintained through such a unifying grand narrative is the marginalization and silencing of the difference raised by other voices' (Clegg et al., 2006: 16). Clegg et al. are, one might feel, a little too hard on other critics' writings – downplaying perhaps the mobilising effects that some texts may have in drawing a wider audience into debates even if, or perhaps precisely *because*, they may lack all the traditional cautions, caveats and dull moderation of imagination and ire, of more traditionally 'academic' texts (Parker, 2002). They may also be underestimating the subtlety with which some of the colonising arguments are made. I am thinking particularly here of Hancock and Tyler (2008) and contributors to this book, who do not so much represent management and managerialism as dominating the wider lifeworld from without, but rather as spreading through the proliferation of 'expert culture': through the ways we are invited to greater levels of efficiency, self-surveillance and self-management in our putatively private lives. With these caveats in mind, however, the concerns raised by Clegg et al. are important ones. And while an argument may still be made for the clear voiced polemic to mobilise a burgeoning oppositional discourse, the authors are to my mind right to remind us of the unwitting power effects of a continual and persistent repetition of a 'domination' or 'colonisation' reading of management and managerialism (see also Wray-Bliss, 2003). As such my concerns in this chapter are threefold: to question the ways that a narrow managerial rationality is filtering into the leisure time drink and drug consumption of UK citizens; to show the coincidences of interests but also the contradictory and confusing relationships between intoxication, management and self-management; and to thereby s(h)ow confusion in the management of intoxication in everyday life.

Managing drink and drugs at work

The UK has long been fascinated and preoccupied with intoxication, a preoccupation matched perhaps only with that of another bodily, hedonistic and ill-disciplined activity, sex. Both sex and drunkenness were targets for early bureaucratic censure – such as that of the Catholic bishop of Lincoln, Robert Grosseteste in the thirteenth century (Burrell, 1984). 'Rioting, drunkenness, lack of discipline, and sexual activity of various kinds were treated as synonymous in threatening both civil disobedience and those church activities which were taking an organizational form' (ibid.: 104). Such activities were to be managed away, through a process that 'involved both eradication and containment, inside and outside work respectively' (ibid.: 99). Unlike the management of sex, however, moves to eradicate and exclude intoxication from the work organisation, until quite recently, seem to have been pursued with less than wholehearted vigour. Lunchtime drinks and a quiet afternoon of mildly intoxicated production was not (perhaps still is not) uncommon in the British workplace, and it is only within the last few decades that a tacit reliance on the employee's self-management of intoxication at work is being systematically supplanted with a hierarchical codification and dissemination of workplace drug and alcohol policies. The movement from containment to a more explicit policy of intervention would seem to be picking up pace recently, however, with a number of UK workplaces adopting the practice of workforce drug testing – the testing of an employee or prospective employee's hair, blood, saliva, sweat or urine for traces of past illicit drug use or current alcohol intoxication. While still having a considerable way to go before it approaches the 67–80 per cent saturation of workforce drug testing in US organisations (IIDTW 2004), many UK workplaces have such a system in place, with momentum building for wider adoption.

Consideration of workforce drug testing would seem to fit the concerns of this book particularly well. Testing an employee for traces of past drug or drink consumption extends the managerial gaze outside of the working day and into 'everyday' leisure choices and consumption habits. Indeed, the management of everyday life extends to include *yesterdays*: a drug test identifies not current intoxication but the traces, a biological echo if you like, of past consumption. Depending on the type of test, the substance consumed and pattern of consumption, this can range from a few days after consumption (urine and blood testing) up to a year (the testing of hair). An employee can therefore test positive for drug use far beyond the timescale when the substance could conceivably be having any effects on behaviour at work. A positive trace of drug use enables the organisation to instigate other, considerable, disciplinary effects which may include dismissal, compulsion to undergo drug treatment, intensified surveillance or, indeed, initiating criminal prosecution.

In some respects it may seem strange why management would want to get involved with the viscera of drug tests given their demonstrated historical squeamishness in relation to the body (Hassard et al., 2000). Bureaucracy, for instance, may be regarded as the pursuit of the rationalised, sanitised, organisational space, with organisational members divided, *dissected* (Dale, 2001), from their private emotionality, morality and other all-too-human attributes (Weber, 1978; Bauman, 1989). Similarly, though itself anthropomorphised in law (Bakan, 2004) and through the efforts of marketers, the modern corporation tends to prefer its labouring bodies 'without organs' – seeing them instead as factors of production, 'empty vessels' into which love of the product may be poured, knowledge workers (evoking a Cartesian split of mind from body), or disembodied body parts – factory hands for instance (Hassard et al., 2000a). That management would want to acknowledge, let alone extract and meddle in the 'leaky fluids' (Linstead, 2000) of blood, urine, saliva, sweat – even when kept at arms length through the reductive medicalisation of drug testing – may seem out of character.

But *character*, specifically employee's character, is for some the key issue here, with the historical gaze of the drug test signifying a desire to manage this rather than workplace behaviour. Gilliom (1994), for instance, argues that drug testing represents an extension of Edward's bureaucratic control – that it can identify, or deter, those with a wider propensity to break rules and the dictate of officialdom from the workplace. The employee subjected to the (seemingly) biologically exact, and temporally fluid, qualities of a drug test will internalise a self-managing, self-surveilling sobriety and round the clock abstinence from drug use – or be excluded from the organisation. In this panoptic reading of the drug test, we seemingly have a potential for disciplinary effects greater even than those attempted in the aforementioned management of sexuality (see also Chapter 2, this volume). While sex has been the focus of (attempted) exclusion from the site of the organisation those targeting it have had to satisfice with mere containment in the non-work sphere (Burrell, 1984), not least because of the need to reproduce further generations of labour. In contrast, the historical, round the clock gaze of the drug test may seem to offer a seductive promise of prohibiting consumption in work *and* leisure – an aspiration entertained in relation to sex by only the visionary few (Burrell, 1984: 99). Whatever one's views on its claimed panoptic qualities (see Warren and Wray-Bliss, 2009 for a critique), the testing of an employee's bodily fluids or hair for traces of past drug use would seem to have some potential (and signify some desire) to extend managerial control and surveillance further into the non-work time of the employee. Such is the concern on this issue that the Independent Inquiry into Drug Testing in the Workplace felt it necessary to remind readers that 'people are not generally required to organise their lives to maximise their productivity at work' (IIDTW, 2004).

Notwithstanding this cautionary voice, however, a dichotomy between, on the one hand, the managed space of the organisation including the sober self-management of the employee and, on the other, drink and especially illicit drug use is being promulgated by advocates of testing. The editor of the 'authoritative' *Personnel Today* book *Addiction at Work: Tackling Drug Use and Misuse in the Workplace*, for instance, asserted that poor attendance, poor performance, greater absenteeism, clumsiness, increased rates of accidents, more disputes and grievances at work, more frequent job changes, more firings, intimidation, trafficking illicit drugs in the workplace, violence and theft are 'obvious' (though, unfortunately perhaps for the credibility of the author's arguments, unevidenced) consequences of employing people who use illicit drugs (Ghodse, 2005: 5). Similar associations and claims may be found in the publications of the Chartered Management Institute (2003), the Chartered Institute of Personnel and Development (2001) and the Health and Safety Executive (2004) (for a thorough examination of claims that drug use causes harm in the workplace, see IIDTW, 2004; Harris, 2004). What we have in such accounts is a common construction of a class of employees who by virtue of their problematic drinking or illicit drug use per se are unable to manage their own conduct and self at work. Through their addiction, or worse their hedonism and irresponsibility, they demonstrate a lack of the appropriate self-disciplining, self-managing character (Rose, 1990) necessary to trust them in their performance of their sober organisational roles. This construction in turn may be fuelled by, and fuel, what Cavanaugh and Prasad have argued is the particular symbolic threat to the principles of ordered and orderly organisation that drink and drugs pose.

> (D)rug taking signals chaos, a loss of self-control and disintegration, and consequently symbolizes the antithesis of organizational rationality. Habitual drug use by organizational members threatens to undermine organizational rationality by symbolizing an oppositional consciousness rooted in disorder ... Similarly, the drug user also is seen as a deviant who fails to uphold the Protestant work ethic and who shows an immoral disregard for the collective well-being of the organization. (Cavanaugh and Prasad, 1994: 268–269)

The perceived disjuncture between the demands of management/self-management and drink and drug use, of course, may be precisely why drink and drug use has been so consistently favoured as a form of escape from, or anaesthetic for, the stresses and strains of work and the sober identities which work requires of us. We might, therefore, see intoxication as it is constructed in the workforce drug testing discourse as an inherently threatening, anti-organisational practice – one that must be a target for eradication by managed society lest it undermines the necessary sober rationality and self-discipline required of the productive subject. We should look then for managerial rationality to be insinuating its way further into intoxication in everyday life such that the intoxicated subject becomes self-managing, setting limits on their intoxication with an eye to the demands of working life. Mindful too of Clegg et al.'s (2006) arguments in the section 'Introduction', we should also look for the 'others' to this story: for those spaces where tendrils of managerialism have failed to reach or where the effects of managerial rationality are contradictory or confused. I look for both of these elements next through consideration of two modern intoxicated subjects – the 'recreational drug taker' and, first, the 'binge drinker'.

The 'binge' drinker

Simultaneously othered, as excessively hedonistic and irresponsible, and represented as 'everyday', as a routine scourge of evenings in the city centre, the figure of the 'binge drinker' looms large in UK political discourse around youth moralities and the management of cities. Such a figure would seem to be a quintessential embodiment of a Bataillean squander and orgiastic expenditure of excess (Brewis et al., 2007): as can perhaps be illustrated with comparison to the figure of the non-bingeing, 'moderate' drinker. The 'safe, sensible and social' drinker (Home Office, 2007) subordinates their consumption of alcohol to the demands of production and accumulation. Their permissible debauchery ... is definitively reduced, in the intellectual representations *in circulation*, to a concession; in other words it is reduced to a diversion whose role is subsidiary. The most appreciable share of life is given as the condition – sometimes even as the regrettable condition – of productive social activity. (Bataille, 1933 [1985]: 117)

The consumption of drink after work helps them relax for the next day's productive activity – presenting little or no threat to that which they have accumulated; be it family, possessions, salary or their sense of themselves as a controlled, *moderating*, subject. To make a Bataillean reading, their choices and pleasures are reduced to a property of production and accumulation – they, themselves, reaffirm their commodity status in their moderate and sensible drinking. For Bataille, it is precisely in *unproductive* acts of expenditure, acts that are not subordinated to some other judgement of utility or profitability – or what is 'sensible' in terms of the next day's labour – that the 'effervescence of life' is expressed (Bataille, 1967 [1989]: 10). Production and accumulation are therefore not an expression of life as such, but, at best, a means to accrue a surplus that may, and must, be expended – for the sake of pleasure, for the shear exuberance of doing so.

'Binge drinking' fits this Bataillean notion of free expenditure of excess rather well, evoking, as the binge label does images of *violent* (assault and affray), *vulnerable* (uncoordinated, unconscious, vulnerable to attack or accident) and *vile* (vomiting and urinating in public, given to obscene acts or speech) excess. Binge drinking would seem to be a clear abrogation of the self – and intended as such – an abrogation that eradicates self-discipline, the ability to manage one's behaviour, speech, body and discerning mental faculties. As such the binge drinker is out-of-control, a subject who cannot be called upon to manage himself or herself until the alcohol they have consumed works its way through their body. They are the antithesis of self-discipline: a hedonistic subject, unproductive, destructive, revelling in LIFE without thought to the consequences of hangovers, getting up for work, preserving currency, liver or dignity. No wonder then that this subject seems to provoke opprobrium and (jealous? disgusted?) censor by the upstanding, responsible, modern managed society – a society which, according to Bataille (1967 [1989], 1976 [1991]), has tried to forget the need for orgiastic excess.

And yet, considered in the context of a long history of exaggerated fears and fascination with young persons' leisure activities, particularly when they revolve around alcohol or other intoxicants, the out-of-control binge drinker may warrant reconsideration. Two quantitative measurements used in the UK define binge drinking as (i) consuming double the recommended daily 'sensible' drinking volume on one occasion and (ii) half the weekly 'sensible' consumption on one occasion respectively (Measham, 2004: 316). In other words, 8 units for men (just under 3 pints of lager or 3 large glasses of wine in one evening) and 6 units for women (2 pints of lager or 2 large glasses of wine) constitute a 'binge' on the first definition and 10.5 units for men (3.5 pints of lager or the same number of large glasses of wine) and 7 for women (just under 2.5 pints of lager or large glasses of wine) constitute a binge on the second, more generous, definition. Such arguably low volume measures of 'binge' drinking are likely to capture a large number of young people – irrespective of whether these amounts constitute sufficient volume to render their consumers particularly violent, vulnerable or vile.

Leaving aside for the moment, however, questions over the suitability of the rhetorically evocative 'binge' categorisation applied to such levels of consumption and recognising that there are many thousands of young (and not-so-young) people who specifically pursue through alcohol the loss of the inhibiting, disciplining, surveilling self on a night out, what does this tell us about (self)management and its abrogation? Measham (2004: 319) argues that what we see demonstrated here is 'not utterly unbridled excessive consumption portrayed in media images of youth at play', but rather a 'calculated hedonism', a 'controlled loss of control' (Hayward, 2002 and Measham, 2002, cited in Measham, 2004). A measure of 'self regulation' (ibid.) is engaged in, in an attempt to use alcohol to achieve a desired level of intoxication. And while there are certainly casualties of excessive consumption to be found on a night out, they are a reminder for most of 'where to draw the line not only because of the financial, health and safety implications but also the lack of cultural credibility of extreme intoxication' (ibid.: 319).

Introducing the concepts of calculation or self-regulation into practices of self-abrogating intoxication might suggest a profitable shift from considering the 'binge drinker' as a figure of squander and excess and instead begin to evoke subtly different, Foucauldian-inspired, thoughts of consciously cultivated limit experiences. Echoing Bataille's concerns with the way humanity is commoditised when its energies are reduced to a function of utility and production, Foucault is concerned with processes of normalisation, subjectivisation and limitation of the self. For Foucault, power operates not as a top-down force imposing itself on unwilling subjects but rather as a (seductive) net-like structure (Foucault, 1976), inviting subjects to identify, operate and act according to particular sets of knowledge and by so doing, inscribe this knowledge on their self, their 'souls' (Rose, 1990). A significant form of resistance to such subjectivising power effects is to identify the limits of one's current construction of self and to seek to transgress these, to stretch or tear the strands of the web of power within which one is constituted. By so doing, the subject can appreciate, if only temporarily, the arbitrary and foundation-less quality of such power-full constructions of self. At times, transgression and revolt in Foucault's work seems to be celebrated as an end in itself (Foucault, 1981) – like a theoretical justification for Marlon Brando's 'Johnny' in *The Wild One* – even if the consequence is to risk self-annihilation (Simons, 1995: 85). On these occasions Foucault's writing might again remind us of the (indiscriminate) celebration of unproductive expenditure and destruction in Bataille's work. But for this chapter I am more concerned with those movements in Foucault's work evoking a more directed transgression of limits, a deliberate seeking out and cultivation of limit experiences – those moments when the arbitrariness of self is revealed, making other constructions imaginable. Foucault's choice of art as a metaphor for the self that seeks to refuse pre-packaged identity and prescribed subjectivity (Foucault, 1984) is significant here. This metaphor suggests to me not a random or chaotic rejection of limits per se – a rejection that supposes the impossible hope or 'unbearable lightness' (Simons, 1995) of a world outside of power – but rather something a little more crafted, more intentional in its identification and attempted violation of the limits imposed on the self.

So how might 'binge' drinking fit with this picture? The everyday limits of the self, including the physical self, may certainly be breached following the consumption of a significant amount of alcohol. It may penetrate or be penetrated through violence, through wanted and/or regretted sexual encounters and through additional consumption of alcohol, other stimulants or, indeed, food that one may not normally consider wise. Further, some such breaches may be potentially transformative (and not just for the teenager or young adult, but for many an eminent social critic too; see Plant, 1999). Profound experiences of pleasure (or its others), the telling of hidden truths or feelings, the meeting of a temporary or longer-term soul mate may be enabled while intoxication reduces one's normal inhibitions. There is the possibility too for more corporeally transformative effects for some members of the young adult population from a night of drinking – including the consequences of unwise alcohol-laden sexual encounters, (fear) of pregnancy or STD, the effects of assault, accident and longer-term health risks of heavy drinking. In addition to effects for the self, it would appear that, for the managed institutions of the state, the binge drinker is a transgressive subject. The licensing, policing and cleaning of the city centre along with the staffing and security of the accident and emergency ward are, we are told, stretched by the resources having to be called upon to address the irresponsible 'bingeing' night-time population.

Whether the controlled loss of control and calculated excess of 'binge' drinking is personally transformative for the individual – whether it approximates or approaches a kind of Foucauldian limit experience – is perhaps not for a person (thankfully) well out of those teen years, to pronounce upon. I would like to suggest though that such intoxicating behaviour not be dismissed as inconsequential or demonised as mere irresponsibility. The young adult, and especially the teenager, is by definition a fluid category of subject that occupies an *in-between* (Carruthers, 2007) state, one defined by processes of transformation and becoming, emerging from childhood into adulthood. Most teenagers and young adults haven't got the accoutrements of older adults to express (or distract) the self, neither have they yet acquired a seemingly fixed identity, inscribed through repetition of working lives and the continual performance of self (Butler, 1990). The teenager appears more as a desperate rehearsal. Their physical and emotional being is a canvass upon which self-expression is deliberately applied, where identity is carefully crafted according to the sub-cultural style, speech patterns, musical tastes or hair style of their peers. Binge drinking and determined drunkenness might, for such in-between subjects, be a ritualised crossing of limits between the states of childhood and adulthood (Douglas, 1966 [1984]). By removing some of the protective and constraining limits – of the home, of parental supervision and, indeed, of sovereign sober rationality – the drunken teenagers out-on-the-town place themselves in a potentially risky situation in which they must negotiate their own passage and police their own boundaries. For Foucault it is 'in revolt that subjectivity (not that of great men but of whomever) introduces itself into history and gives it the breath of life' (1981, in Bernauer and Matron, 1994: 153). 'Determined drunkenness' (Measham, 2006) might paradoxically be viewed as revolt from the controlled state of childhood to the self-control expected of adults: even though it is expressed in the realm where adults themselves relinquish some self-control and express more childlike behaviour.

This last point is perhaps worth considering a little more in the context of the folding together of self-management, management and intoxication. What is the nature of adulthood mimicked or performed here by the teenager? It might be argued that what we see is the teenager and young adult learning to be a profitable (hyper)consumer. A subject learning to consume to the very edge of incoherence and dissolution while managing, most of the time, to avoid tipping over – remaining therefore able to consume again. Such lessons can then be applied throughout life to the conspicuous consumption of credit, mortgages, food or whatever. To acquire more credence, such a reading would seem to need to show the 'binge drinker' not to be the unambiguously problematic character for managed organisation and the managed state that we have hitherto been given reason to believe.

On this point, whatever 'binge' drinking means subjectively for the teenager or young adult, it can be understood as constituted through a number of deliberate governmental policy moves and commercial decisions. As Measham (2004) documents, the UK rave and dance music scene of the late 1980s to late 1990s was marked by young people's pursuit of pleasure and intoxication outside of the commercial licensed bar and club scene and the dominance of alcohol consumption. Partly in response to the above, and facilitated by the criminalisation of unlicensed raves, local authorities and the drinks industry combined to transform city centres into attractive venues for young adults. Late licensed city centre bars and clubs, decorated or themed to attract young people, proliferated and have proved extremely lucrative both for the drinks industry and for city councils. The nature of the alcohol served changed. High strength bottled lagers, white ciders and alcopops were introduced in the mid-1990s. By the late 1990s a further generation of alcopops, high strength pre-mixed spirit-based drinks, and flavoured spirit based bottled drinks were introduced. By the 2000s shots, aftershots and shooters appeared, often sold at a discounted price for multiple purchases. Together, local and central government and commercial decisions combined to successfully revive the UK's city centre night-time economy through the concentrated consumption of significant amounts of alcohol. As Measham (2004: 318) observes,

current concerns about 'binge' drinking must be tempered by a consideration of this concerted commercial development and official sanctioning of young adult drinking in the UK over the last decade with the transformation of city centres and the deregulation and elevation of licensed leisure to a new peak in young adult 'time out'.

Though some of the excesses of the 'binge' drinker may be more than was bargained for – particularly when this excess spills out of the private body into the body politic (in public urination, vomiting or other anti-social behaviour) – a bargain was struck nevertheless. Intoxication here is not in a relation of exteriority to management or self-management. While the 'binge' drinking subject chooses their own limits at a level that may not directly correspond to those the state and its institutions prefer, self-management of deliberate and determined intoxication and the management of the city centre economy do coalesce rather more than is publicly acknowledged.

If the above suggests a *correspondence*, largely unacknowledged and admittedly uneasy, between *self-management* of intoxication and *managed institutions*, the next subject I consider would seem to suggest a rather different conclusion.

The recreational drug user

The popular media representation and conventional political discourse on illicit drugs in the UK have long centred on images of highly physiologically addictive substances and a widely reproduced conceptualisation of all or most drug use defined by addiction, social isolation, degradation and death. Such a representation is exemplified by the sad and horrible photograph of the discoloured, bloated body of 21-year-old former student Rachel Whitear, slumped forward, on the floor of her bedsit, with syringe in hand. A picture that became iconic after her parents used it in 2002 as part of an educational anti-drugs campaign called 'Rachel's Story'. In this picture the idea of illicit drug taking as waste and destruction, the very real linking of drugs and death, is epitomised. In popular and political anti-drugs discourse such images and linkages, alongside the other couplet of drug use and wider crimes, typically stand as representations of the use of illicit drugs in general. All such illicit drugs are tainted with death, all are linked with the abrogation – permanent as well as symbolic – of the self.

Such taken-for-granted associations, however, are worth re-examining. In contrast to the drug user as a subject mortally addicted to hard drugs, a provocative body of sociological research finds the majority of illicit drugs consumed in the UK to be 'recreational drugs' consumed 'recreationally'. 'Recreational drugs' is a term used to refer to non-physiologically addictive illicit drugs that are consumed as part of a leisure lifestyle. A typical list of recreational drugs would include Cannabis, Amphetamines (Speed), Hallucinogens (LSD, magic mushrooms), 'Dance Drugs' (Ecstasy) and, more recently beginning to figure on such lists (despite the potential that some may develop dependency), Cocaine powder (Parker et al., 2002). Recreational drugs may be differentiated from other substances consumed as part of a leisure lifestyle, such as Alcohol and Tobacco, on the basis of legal classification. While Tobacco and Alcohol have a bounded legality, the consumption and supply of all recreational drugs is illegal, with the criminal penalty ranging depending upon the 'A' (Ecstasy, Cocaine) through 'B' (Speed) to 'C' (Cannabis – at least at the time of writing) classification of the drug.

In addition to being differentiated from legal drugs, recreational drugs are also differentiated from other illicit drugs, such as Heroin and Crack Cocaine, because of the latter's physiologically addictive properties. Thus, where motivation for taking Heroin or Crack Cocaine is understood to likely degenerate into irrepressible (atomistic) physical addiction, the consumption of 'recreational' drugs is understood to remain largely a matter of choice – a deliberate and conscious decision to augment sociability and/or leisure. This differentiation of 'sociable', 'controllable' recreational drugs from 'addictive', 'destructive' Heroin and Crack Cocaine finds further purchase when the consumption choices and attitudes of the populations (adolescent and young adult) most likely to consume illicit drugs are surveyed. Such research strongly suggests that 'dependent or over-frequent drug use, and heroin and crack cocaine taking [is] condemned by [recreational drug] users and abstainers alike' (Parker et al., 2002: 948). Though such populations typically condemn Heroin and Crack Cocaine use, it has been argued that there exists a fairly high degree of 'normalisation' for other recreational drug use (Hammersley et al., 2002; Parker et al., 2002; Parker, 2005). With some suggesting that 'most young people see drug use as fitting into their everyday conventional activities of studying, working, seeing friends, playing sport and so on' (Measham et al., 2001: 12) implying that most users of illicit drugs are 'primarily educated, employed young citizens with otherwise conforming profiles' (Parker et al., 2002: 960).

For normalisation to be explored as a plausible description of young adults and adolescents, relationships with recreational drug use researchers have focused upon two central measures: drug use and attitudes to drug use. Use of recreational drugs in the UK is higher than the European average (Measham et al., 2001). Surveys in 1996 and 2000 showed Scottish and English adolescents to have the highest rates of drug trying of 26 European countries (ESPAD, 1997, 2001). The latest Europe-wide survey data at the time of going to press found the UK to again have above average rates of use for cannabis and other illicit drugs (ESPAD, 2003). Evidence from the North-West England Longitudinal Study suggested up to 47 per cent of 22-year olds had taken Cannabis in the past year. Figures for the other recreational drugs averaged between 11 per cent (Speed) and 16 per cent (cocaine powder), with over half of the population having taken at least one form of illicit drugs in the past year (Parker et al., 2002). Not surprisingly, when lifetime prevalence of illicit drug taking was examined, the figures were higher still, with 70 per cent of 22-year olds reporting Cannabis use, 25 per cent Cocaine powder and 42 per cent Speed. Overall, 76 per cent of 22-year olds reported use of at least one illicit drug in their lifetime. Socio-economic differences do not appear to affect significantly these drug trying or drug consumption rates (Parker et al., 2002; Parker, 2005). Studies of university students, for instance, found up to 60 per cent have some drug experience, with between 13 per cent and 18 per cent using Class A recreational drugs (Ashton and Kamali, 1995; Webb et al., 1996; Makhoul et al., 1998; Birch et al., 1999; see Parker et al., 2002). Such figures are broadly comparable with those of the general (young adult) population. To put the overall picture of drug use suggested here in a wider context, conservative estimates of Ecstasy use alone have suggested that half a million tablets are consumed every weekend in the UK (Feinmann, 2002), other surveys have suggested that 5 million UK citizens regularly use Cannabis, and over 2 million regularly use other recreational drugs (*The Observer*, 2002), even notoriously conservative official UK government estimates suggested that 4 million people in England and Wales used illicit drugs in 2001–2002 (Parker, 2005).

From the above it has been, persuasively, argued that 'the *majority* of young adults have taken drugs and live unscathed to tell the tale' (Measham et al., 2001: 17) and that the behaviour of those on recreational drugs is, in the main, self-managed so that it remains 'benign in respect of friendships, informal parties, romantic relationships, socialising and dancing' (ibid.: 17). It is perhaps to be expected then that there has been found to be widespread accommodation and tolerance in the young adult population towards recreational drug use both by those who take and by those who abstain (ibid.; also Boys et al., 2000; Hart and Hunt, 1997; Hirst and McCameley-Finney, 1994; Perri 6 et al., 1997; Young and Jones, 1997). For example, over 60 per cent of abstainers have been found to hold tolerant or approving attitudes towards those who take recreational drugs, and over a quarter of abstainers reported having close friends who have experiences of taking Amphetamines and Ecstasy (Parker et al., 2002).

Taking both use and attitudes to use into account, the above literature suggests that there appears to be increasing normalisation of 'sensible' recreational drug use amongst young British adults (Parker et al., 2002; Calafat et al. in Drugscope, 2001; though see Shiner and Newburn, 1999). Such normalisation is most apparent for Cannabis and varies somewhat for other recreational drugs. It has been suggested that this differential normalisation principally centres on the drug's potential to impact upon the 'new responsibilities and weekday work demands' (Parker et al., 2002: 960) that the post-adolescent drug-experienced population starts to face. This suggestion helps explain shifts in consumption that have seen an 'increasing focus on substances which do not impact negatively on getting up for work' (ibid.).

Now, we should, of course, treat Parker et al.'s construction of the 'sensible' recreational drug user with the same caution with which we treat any other social science construction. For instance, we need to be mindful that the bulk of the research upon which the above thesis is presented was published several years ago, mainly during the period 2000–2002. While there may be little evidence that drug availability and attitudes to drug use amongst the young adult population in the UK have changed wholesale since this time (Parker, 2005) – indeed there are indications of a grudging governmental recognition of the existence of a settled population of largely unproblematic recreational drug users (ibid.) – there have been, as we would expect, some changes in this picture. For instance, the rise in the potency of Cannabis strains to hit the UK, ongoing shifts towards poly drug use and the greater mixing of illicit drugs with heavy alcohol use (Measham, 2004) suggests that recreational drug use may have the potential for more deleterious effects for the young adult population of today than of even a few years ago.

Further, there may be greater potential for 'slippage' from recreational to more harmful illicit drugs for a small proportion of the recreational drug-consuming population, particularly as more consumers mix their recreational drugs with heavy alcohol consumption, thereby lowering their inhibitions and situational ability to perceive and judge risk in relation to harder intoxicants (Parker, 2005). In addition to these empirical shifts, we can also be reflexive about the rhetorical strategy deployed in the above research. Parker, Measham, Aldridge and others may be read as stressing the calculative, sensible nature of drug use as a deliberate rhetorical counter to prevailing pathologising images of the out-of-control drug abuser. And it *is* an effective political resource and important contribution in this regard, one that I would argue still has a great deal to contribute to policy and theoretical debates. However, we must also not forget the experientially non-rational, non-calculative (Bataillean) pleasures *and risks* of altered states.

Mindful of these cautions, however, the figure of the recreational drug user presented above, like the previous examination of binge drinking, suggests a rather different picture than one of unbridled, uncontained and unmanageable excess. We have here a calculating subject; a subject who attempts to self-manage his/her consumption patterns, contexts and choices of intoxicant according to a complex mix of inherited and experiential knowledge about drugs of choice, personal limits and their social *and work commitments*. It is this latter point which raises further issues for our discussion of management, self-management and intoxication. Should we regard attentiveness to the demands and responsibilities of work as, for instance, indication of the young adult recreational drug user's sophisticated awareness of the *real politick* of their subject location – as evidence of their considerable skill in balancing, or keeping separate, their 'productive' and 'intoxicated' subject status? Alternatively, does this instead represent an effective colonisation of even the realm of illicit intoxication by the voracious demands of the managed organisation? Deciding between these two readings I would suggest is, ultimately, a question of (ethical) choice (Wray-Bliss, 2002) rather than an epistemological necessity – the 'facts' do not compel us to choose either representation. Do we, then, choose to represent the modern consuming subject as capable, knowledgeable, able to negotiate an identity and make choices within a web of competing demands? (Fitchett and Smith, 2001). Or, do we choose to present management and managerialism with the power to colonise all that lies before it?

If we are minded, in the context of this book's concern with the management of everyday life, to lean towards the latter then it is striking that this managerial 'colonisation' is not apparently content with the considerable achievements it has made to date. Namely the production of young subjects whose sense of responsibility – even when faced with the powerful twin seductions of their own youth and easy access to a wide array of illicit intoxicants – leads them to seek to self-manage their consumption to remain productive subjects. Why do I suggest that management is not content with this? While the long-standing UK tradition of the end of the working week alcoholic-fuelled 'binge' (to give it the modern label) is not penalised under a workforce drug test unless the employee is still drunk at work the following week – thereby allowing such subjects the freedom to self-manage their intoxication with relative impunity – use of illicit drugs at the end of working week would be penalised. Recall that it is the trace, the biological echo, of historic illicit substance use that is detected by the test not current levels of intoxication.

On reflection, indeed, the workforce drug test might be regarded as a technology specifically suited to detecting the *self-managing* rather than chaotic or addicted drug user. The user of drugs who is not self-managing, who is not pursuing their intoxication recreationally in a way cognisant of work demands, whose drug use is such that it is clearly affecting performance, would likely come to the attention of the managed organisation in rather more immediate ways than through a microanalysis of metabolites in their bodily fluids. Sophisticated biological surveillance of historical drug use would seem, despite the rather lurid rhetoric of the dangerous drug-using employee running amok, to be specifically suited to detecting those subjects whose drug use is not problematic enough to show up behaviourally.

Compared then to the figure of the 'binge' drinker, whose 'out-of-control' intoxication would, despite a strong rhetoric to the contrary, seem to coalesce with interests promoted by managers of the state and the leisure industry, the work-regarding self-management displayed by the recreational drug user is a target for eradication through workforce drug-testing programmes.

Conclusion

I began this chapter by suggesting that, intuitively, determined intoxication would seem to be the antithesis of managerialism (Cavanaugh and Prasad, 1994). The intoxicated subject stands – a little wobbly, but stands nevertheless – opposed to the soberly responsible, disciplined subject required by work organisations and the managed state. If we can see management's performative rationality creeping into this subject then, the logic might lead us to conclude, perhaps management can indeed colonise everywhere and everyday.

So, is this what we do see in the above exploration? I have attempted to suggest here that the hand of management and the voice of calculative reason do enter the space of intoxication: *but not necessarily in anticipated or consistent ways*. The binge drinker is a target for considerable political critique in the UK precisely for not being a responsible, self-managing subject. Yet the binge drinker is a construction that owes its existence, in large part, to managerial and governmental policy on licensing laws, city centre regeneration and responses to young people's previous choices of intoxication. Regulation and management here goes hand in hand with the proliferation of intoxication. The recreational drug user has been presented as a *self-managing* subject, conscious of the demands of work and social relationships, yet is the target of increasing managerial censor and sophisticated technological intervention with the putative goal of eradication. Indeed, self-management – the hallowed goal of bio-power and the supposed effect of the infiltration of managerialism into everyday life – is itself a contradictory concept here. It can mean both limiting one's consumption to moderate work-regarding levels *and* a determination to consume enough so that the limits of the rational, ordered, disciplined mind are reached, or breached.

Ultimately, therefore, we have an account whereby managerialism, the everyday and self-management *do* all figure in intoxication. But they do not cohere into some seamless discourse of domination or colonisation. They swirl in and out of focus. They are unsteady, confused, befuddled. There are spaces within the work organisation, wider society and in citizen's own pursuit of intoxication that are unlicensed by managerialism. And, I think, we can raise a glass to that.

References

Ashton, C. and Kamali, F. (1995) 'Personality, lifestyles, alcohol and drug consumption in a sample of British medical students', *Medical Education* 29: 187–192.

Bakan, J. (2004) *The Corporation* London: Constable.

Bataille, G. (1933 [1985]) 'The notion of expenditure', in A. Stoekl (ed.), *Visions of Excess Selected Writings 1927–1939 Georges Bataille* Minneapolis: University of Minnesota Press.

Bataille, G. (1967 [1989]) *The Accursed Share, Volume 1* (trans. R. Hurley) New York: Zone Books.

Bataille, G. (1976 [1991]) *The Accursed Share, Volumes 2 and 3* (trans. R. Hurley) New York: Zone Books.

Bauman, Z. (1989) *Modernity and the Holocaust* Polity Press: Cambridge.

Bernauer, J. and Matron, M. (1994) 'The ethics of Michel Foucault', in G. Gutting (ed.), *The Cambridge Companion to Foucault* Cambridge: Cambridge University Press, pp. 115–140.

Birch, D., White, M. and Kamali, F. (1999) *Factors Influencing Alcohol and Illicit Drug Use Amongst Medical Students*. Newcastle: University of Newcastle.

Boys, A., Fountain, J., Griffiths, P., Marsden, J., Stillwell, G. and Strang, J. (2000) *Making Decisions: A Qualitative Study of Young People* London: Health Education Authority.

Brewis, J., Sanderson, C. and Wray-Bliss, E. (2007) 'Interrogating excess: The case of organizational drug policies' *Tamara* 5(5.1): 39–53.

Burrell, G. (1984) 'Sex and organizational analysis', *Organization Studies* 5(2): 97–118.

Butler, J. (1990) *Gender Trouble* London: Routledge.

Carruthers, V. (2007) 'Between lives: Encountering childhood in the early works of Dorothea Tanning' oral paper, presented to the *Association of Art Historians Conference*, Belfast, 2–4th April.

Cavanaugh, J. M. and Prasad, P. (1994) 'Drug testing as symbolic managerial action', *Organization Science* 5(2): 267–271.

Chartered Institute of Personnel and Development (CIPD) (2001) *Alcohol and Drug Policies in UK Organizations* London: CIPD.

Chartered Management Institute (CMI) (2003) *Managing the Effects of Drugs and Alcohol in the Workplace* London: CMI.

Clegg, S., Kornberger, M., Carter, C. and Rhodes, C. (2006) 'For management?' *Management Learning* 37(1): 7–27.

Coser, L. (1974) *Greedy Institutions: Patterns of Undivided Commitment* New York: Free Press.

Dale, K. (2001) *Anatomising Embodiment and Organisation Theory* Basingstoke: Palgrave Macmillan.

Douglas, M. (1966 [1984]) *Purity and Danger* London: Ark Paperbacks.

Drugscope (2001) *Annual Report on the UK Drugs Situation* available from http:// www.doh.gov.uk/drugs/ukdrugsituation2001.pdf

ESPAD (1997) *Alcohol and Other Drug Use Amongst Students in 26 European Countries* Stockholm: Swedish Council on Alcohol and Other Drugs.

ESPAD (2001) *Alcohol and Other Drug Use Amongst Students in 30 European Countries* Stockholm: Swedish Council on Alcohol and Other Drugs.

ESPAD (2003) *Alcohol and Other Drug Use Amongst Students in 35 European Countries* Stockholm: Swedish Council on Alcohol and Other Drugs.

Feinmann, J. (2002) 'Putting the E in health' *The Observer*, 10 March, p. 54.

Fitchett, J. and Smith, A. (2001) 'Consumer behaviour in an unregulated market: The satisfactions and dissatisfactions of illicit drug consumption' *Journal of Consumer Behaviour* 1(4): 355–368.

Foucault, M. (1976 [1980]) 'Two lectures' in M. Foucault (ed.), *Power/Knowledge* New York: Pantheon, pp. 79–108.

Foucault, M. (1981) 'Is it useless to revolt?' (trans. J. Bernauer) *Philosophy and Social Criticism* 8(1): 5–9.

Foucault, M. (1984) 'Politics and ethics: An interview', in P. Rabinow (ed.), *The Foucault Reader* Middlesex: Penguin, pp. 373–380.

Ghodse, H. (ed.) (2005) *Addiction at Work: Tackling Drug Use and Misuse in the Workplace* Aldershot: Gower Publishing.

Gilliom, J. (1994) *Surveillance, Privacy and the Law: Employee Drug Testing and the Politics of Social Control* Michigan: University of Michigan Press.

Hammersley, R., Khan, F. and Ditton, J. (2002) *Ecstasy: And the Rise of the Chemical Generation* London: Routledge.

Hancock, P. and Tyler, M. (2008) 'Beyond the confines: Management, colonization and the everyday' *Critical Sociology* 34(1): 29–49.

Harris, M. (2004) 'Alcohol and drug use in the workplace' in R. Griffin and A. O'Leary-Kelly (eds), *The Dark Side of Organizational Behaviour* San Francisco: Jossey Bass, pp. 341–372.

Hart, L. and Hunt, N. (1997) *Choosers Not Losers?* NHS: Invecta Community Care.

Hassard, J., Holiday, R. and Willmott, H. (eds) (2000) *Body and Organization* London: Sage.

Hassard, J., Holiday, R. and Willmott, H. (2000a) 'Introduction' in J. Hassard, R. Holiday and H. Willmott (eds), *Body and Organization* London: Sage, pp. 1–14.

Hayward, K. (2002) 'The vilification and pleasures of youthful transgression' in J. Mucie, G. Hughes and E. McLaughlin (eds), *Youth Justice: Critical Readings* London: Sage.

Health and Safety Executive (2004) 'The scale and impact of illegal drug use by workers' Research Report 193, HSE.

Hirst, J. and McCameley-Finney, A. (1994) *The Place and Meaning of Drugs in the Lives of Young People* Sheffield: Sheffield Hallam University.

Home Office (2007) 'Safe, sensible, social – next steps for the National Alcohol Strategy' *homeoffice.gov.uk*.

IIDTW (2004) *Drug Testing in the Workplace: The Report of the Independent Inquiry into Drug Testing at Work* York/London: Joseph Rowntree Foundation/ Drugscope.

Linstead, S. (2000) 'Dangerous fluids and the organization-without-organs' in J. Hassard, R. Holiday and H. Willmott (eds), *Body and Organization* London: Sage, pp. 31–51.

Makhoul, M., Yates, F. and Wolfson, S. (1998) 'A survey of substance use at a UK University: Prevalence of use and views of students' *Journal of Substance Misuse* 3: 119–124

Measham, F. (2002) ' "Doing gender, doing drugs": Conceptualising the gendering of drugs cultures' *Contemporary Drug Problems* 29(2): 335–373.

Measham, F. (2004) 'The decline of ecstasy, the rise of "binge" drinking and the persistence of pleasure' *Probation Journal* 51(4): 309–326.

Measham, F. (2006) 'The new policy mix: Alcohol, harm minimisation, and determined drunkenness in contemporary society' *International Journal of Drug Policy* 17(4): 258–268.

Measham, F., Aldridge, J. and Parker, H. (2001) *Dancing on Drugs: Risk, Health and Hedonism in the British Club Scene* London: Free Association Books.

Parker, H. (2005) 'Normalization as a barometer: Recreational drug use and the consumption of leisure by younger Britons' *Addiction Research and Theory* 13(3): 205–215.

Parker, H., Williams, L. and Aldridge, J. (2002) 'The normalisation of "Sensible" recreational drug use' *Sociology* 36(4): 941–964.

Parker, M. (2002) *Against Management* Cambridge: Polity Press.

Perri 6., Jupp, B., Perry, H. and Laskey, K. (1997) *The Substance of Youth* York: Joseph Rowntree Foundation.

Plant, S. (1999) *Writing on Drugs* London: Faber and Faber.

Rose, N. (1990) *Governing the Soul* London: Routledge.

Shiner, M. and Newburn, T. (1999) 'Taking tea with Noel: The place and meaning of drug use in everyday life', in N. South (ed.), *Drugs: Cultures, Controls and Everyday Life* London: Sage, pp. 140–159.

Simons, J. (1995) *Foucault and the Political* London: Routledge.

The Observer (2002) 'Drugs uncovered' *The Observer*, 21 April 2002.

Warren, S. and Wray-Bliss, E. (2009) 'Workforce drug testing: A review, critique and reframing' *New Technology, Work and Employment*.

Webb, E., Ashton, C., Kelly, P. and Kamali, F. (1996) 'Alcohol and drug use in UK University Students' *Lancet* 348: 922–925.

Weber, M. (1978) *Weber: Selections in Translation* Cambridge University Press: Cambridge.

Wray-Bliss, E. (2002) 'Interpretation – appropriation: (Making) an example of Labour Process Theory' *Organisational Research Methods* 5(1): 80–103.

Wray-Bliss, E. (2003) 'Research subjects/research subjections: The politics and ethics of critical research' *Organization* 10(2): 307–325.

Young, L. and Jones, R. (1997) *Young People and Drugs* Liverpool: SHADO.

Chapter 4

Managing health in everyday life

Bill Hughes

> The management of health and vitality, once derided as narcissistic self-absorption has achieved unparalleled ethical salience in the conduct of the lives of so many.
>
> *(Rose, 2007: 14)*

Introduction

It has become commonplace for sociologists of health and illness to note that the vast majority of healthcare work is carried out not by professionals, but by ordinary people. For every prescribed medication there are two incidences of self-prescription. One can invoke the metaphor of the 'illness iceberg' to demonstrate that about one-ninth of illness episodes are reported to healthcare professionals. The rest are managed by lay persons. Stacey (1998: 198) notes that such data are indicative of 'the extent to which people experiencing symptoms look after their own health'. Feminist scholars have described and analysed, in detail, the role of women in the management of informal healthcare systems and have noted its centrality to the domestic economy and the processes of social reproduction that sustain everyday life in the family and community (Abbott, Wallace and Tyler, 2006). Empirical medical sociology has discovered that the patient and the potential patient have devised many ways of taking care of themselves and that the patient is, in fact, a health worker in the division of healthcare labour. This is the case with respect to health maintenance as well as 'restorative and ameliorative health work' (Stacey, 1988: 6–7). In the contemporary world of health and health care there is much more emphasis on people doing things for themselves, making informed choices and using professional services as active consumers as opposed to dependent patients.

For healthcare providers and professionals working in the system, the discourse of patient compliance has gone. It has been replaced by the notion of concordance suggesting 'an open and informed discussion between the patient and the doctor about treatment options' that can lead to 'an agreement about the way in which a condition will be treated' (Gabe, Bury and Elston, 2004: 110). Out of this framework of intensive lay participation in health-related activities has emerged a new 'will to health', a new set of obligations in which every citizen becomes an 'active partner in the drive for health' and takes responsibility 'for monitoring and managing their own health' (Rose, 2001: 6).

It is also commonplace to argue that the struggle for control of the means of production has been displaced by the struggle for the control of information (and its production). The 'information society' – or what Manuel Castells (1996) has called the 'networked world' – has produced a general fragmentation of the locus of information and a massive expansion of the availability of and access to knowledge. In this context 'thought collectives' (Fleck, 1979) like the medical community no longer retain a monopoly with respect to the specialist knowledge that they produce. Information boundaries are fluid and flexible. Re-skilling through information and education brings the lay person – at least partially – on to the terrain of the professional. This represents a challenge to medical dominance and is indicative of the medicalisation of lay persons' relationships to their own bodies and behaviour. Furthermore, medicine has little curative efficacy in this era of chronic and degenerative disease. Its 'heroic' days are numbered. In what the World Health Organisation (WHO) (1986) has called the 'postmedical era' the role of medicine is to provide clinical/moral templates and coaching guides that will help citizens to manage health behaviour, including lifestyle, consumption and risk and to help patients to manage chronic illness. As the responsibility for health and illness moves from professional to lay person then the intellectual tools that underpin this responsibility follow. Discourses of self-care generate a democratisation of medical knowledge and information. In this context, medical power rests not on social closure and the monopolisation of knowledge but on its expansion into and colonisation of everyday life. The professional–patient relationship is restructured. Paternalism is replaced by partnership. The expectation of patient compliance is replaced by the concept of the patient as an active subject, a contributor in the healing and health maintenance process. The patient – once mired in ignorance and subordinated in the hierarchical dyad, that is, the professional–patient relationship – is expected to take on and manage the duty to get better or, in the case of chronic illness and disability, to take responsibility for the efficacious management of symptoms. We have entered the (postmedical) era of the citizen healer.

In this chapter, I will argue that 'postmedical' medicine has become a salutogenic science of self-regulation and an ethical force that influences the everyday decisions and actions of millions of people. The case will be made that the valorisation of experiential knowledge and lay skills, the re-ordering of the patient into an informed and active subject and the medicalisation of behaviour, lifestyle and social space that arises out of the discourse of 'the new public health' transform the life-world into a *preventorium* or a vital space that is indebted to the 'voice of medicine' for the prescriptions that constitute its moral architecture. As medical information proliferates and becomes embedded in everyday life, each and everyone of us is obliged to manage the way we live. Health and betterment become 'everybody's business'. The *preventorium* re-configures life and health in terms of risk, susceptibility and genetic predisposition (Rose, 2007) in such a way that the *lebenswelt* becomes a forum for the management and control of our biological futures (see, for example, Castel, 1991; Weir, 1996).

The valorisation of lay knowledge and labour

In the past couple of decades there has been a valorisation of lay knowledge. According to Lash (2002: 17), 'logical and ontological knowledge no longer have a separate status from trivial everyday or empirical knowledge'. 'Trivial', everyday knowledge about health has manifest itself in the growth of self-help groups and new social movements that challenge traditional centres of power and control and seek participatory and democratic relationships with expertise (Gabe et al., 2006). Lay knowledge is primarily experiential and it is knowledge of this order – personal and subjective – that has demanded epistemological legitimacy within the world of health care. Medicine – dominated by knowledge that is clinical, abstract, impersonal and objective – has had to make room for an epistemological position alien to its scientific basis.

Lay critiques of medicine have, in the past couple of decades, become more widespread (Williams and Calnan, 1996; Prior, 2003) and they are not unrelated to the general growth in scepticism about expertise and the attendant processes of 'lay re-skilling' which Giddens (1991) identifies as an important characteristic of 'late modernity'. There has also been a secularisation of medical mystique and a proliferation of medical information that has made some aspects of medical language and practice more transparent. Certainly, the medicalisation of everyday life that is embedded in the expansion of health promotion has drawn lay and medical perspectives into closer proximity. Once regarded as separate and distinct cultures (Freidson, 1970), contemporary evidence suggests that professional and folk beliefs about health and illness interpenetrate in complex ways. Although 'medical knowledge rests upon the concept of disease and lay knowledge is rooted in the experience of illness' (Williams and Popay, 1994: 120), these distinctive epistemological traditions do not necessarily translate into exclusive paradigms. It is also worth noting that the last few decades have witnessed the transformation of the patient into a consumer, and consumer choice has made a more obvious (and measurable) impact on the hegemony of biomedicine and its monopoly over healing. Lay people have been voting with their feet by seeking alternative therapies (Goldstein, 2003; Furnham and Vincent, 2006; Sointu, 2006). Yet whatever the complexity of these competing forms of knowledge, it seems clear that the growth in the legitimacy of lay and other perspectives in recent decades constitutes an important challenge to the epistemological monopoly of biomedicine.

While it is difficult to understand the reasons behind this valorisation of lay knowledge save in terms of the disintegration and loss of faith in expert culture, there are a number of contemporary processes that, upon examination, clarify the context that has produced it. One could, for example, cite the significant role played by subjectivity and reflexivity in contemporary culture. While this articulates with the experiential knowledge that underpins lay beliefs about health and illness, it is inimical to the positivism and objectivism upon which scientific medicine is founded. Williams and Popay (1994: 123) put the argument in this way:

> The vogue of postmodernism, with its emphasis on the 'contextuality of truth claims' provides a neat legitimation for lay resistance to expert systems of knowledge. Lay knowledge about health and illness thus provides an epistemological challenge to medicine. It offers a view of illness that is subjective and often highly coherent.

The re-skilling of the lay population is partly to do with the postmodern debate about the relative values of different kinds of knowledge. As the prestige of scientific knowledge has declined, the knowledge derived from individual and collective experience has risen in esteem. This reflects the view amongst epistemologists that there is no reasonable means of distinguishing between the worth of different kinds of knowledge. Patients and lay persons – even though they are not schooled in the clinical sciences nor possess professional qualifications – bring valuable knowledge with them to their encounters with professionals. They live in their bodies and know them by virtue of the embodied relation that they have to their physical, emotional and social lives. The idea of the lay expert is a contradiction in terms, but if it means that lay people are 'expert' by virtue of having experiential knowledge of their bodies or their lives, then clearly, this is a meaningful idea (Busby et al., 1997).

The valorisation of lay knowledge is related to the veritable explosion of 'illness narratives' (Bury, 2001); to the stories that lay people tell about their experiences particularly of chronic illness and of the struggles that they go through to come to terms with 'damage' and 'biographical disruption'. Such stories have become commonplace in the media but also in literature and sociological research (Kleinman, 1988). In *The Wounded Storyteller*, Arthur Frank (1995) points out that illness narratives privilege the knowledge derived from experience and take a form in which the struggle for health becomes a story of the transformation of self-identity in which people try to find their way in a context in which they have lost some of the anchors of life. This kind of knowledge about illness is moving, emotive, emotionally rich, personal and subjective. It 'resonates with key features of life and living' (Williams, 2003) and gives patients the opportunity to express their fears and anxieties. It is everything that impersonal clinical notes – the formal story that biomedical professionals tell about illness – are not. Indeed, Blaxter (2004: 68) argues that not only does the decline of biomedicine 'provide the space for lay narratives to flourish' but also that these narratives are therapeutic in their own right: 'Stories do not just describe the experience: they are repair work, creating a new self.' It is not, however, simply a question of lay ideas penetrating medical knowledge (and vice versa). Simultaneously, there has also been a re-configuration of the healthcare division of labour that recognises the patient as a health worker and fuels the idea of a citizen healer who will take responsibility for her own betterment.

One can, for example, illustrate the growth in patient responsibility for healthcare activities and health work by examining [*sic*] the relatively new practice of self-examination. Leaflets about it in relation to breasts, testicles and so on are commonplace in clinics and hospitals and encourage lay people to get to know their bodies by applying the clinical gaze to themselves. It suggests a re-organisation of how ordinary people are expected to relate to and understand their bodies. The frame of reference through which our bodies become known to us is usually regarded as essentially personal and subjective. The idea of self-examination, however, suggests that we bracket our subjective body schema and apply a clinical frame of reference to our corporeal being. In touching our own breasts or testicles, we are expected to adopt a medical/management or objective form of tactility in which we exteriorise ourselves (Hughes, 2000). Through such acts of vigilance, we turn the medical gaze upon ourselves and engage in a preliminary form of self-diagnosis. This is a clear example of what Michel Foucault (1980) called self-surveillance, a moment in which social control and self-control collapse into one another.

In the *preventorium* of modernity, the logic of medicalisation extends into the private world of self-reflection. Medical knowledge 'empowers' us to inspect ourselves. Medical discourse provides us with the tools of vigilance and self-management:

> Bodily manifestations usually considered innocuous by lay people have to be dramatised in order to give them another meaning ie. possible signals of an early cancer. This dramatisation takes place within the dynamics of medicalisation. Its aim is to turn everyone into a sentry, a potential patient looking after his own body and ready to consult his practitioner as soon as he picks up a suspicious signal. The explicit objective is, through adequate education, to medicalise the way that each person looks at his own body. (Pinell, 1996: 13)

The informed patient or lay person is expected to know how to read the body as a medical text, to screen by self-examination and conclude, should bodily norms appear distorted, with a provisional diagnosis. Self-examination or learning to relate to one's body as a medical text, that is, as an object of para-professional self-scrutiny is a clear example of the medicalisation of everyday life and it is clear that the involvement of patients in medical labour restructures the professional–patient relationship. The patient is re-skilled and becomes a producer of health care. The patient in the 'postmedical age' is encouraged to enter into forms of work that were once regarded as the exclusive domain of professionals. Compliance gives way to autonomy. Passivity gives way to responsibility. External scrutiny gives way to self-management.

Another way of illustrating this argument is to examine developments in community care that have brought about the valorisation of informal carers. Those who care in the community for 'dependent' populations have been co-opted 'into a para-professional role' (Biggs, 1993: 141). It is not, therefore, only self-care but care of others which is now deemed to be within the capacity of ordinary people. Ideas about the informed patient/consumer who is an active participant in healthcare partnerships and perhaps even a producer of healthcare knowledge or a 'lay expert' draw heavily on the notion of self-reliance that developed in the 1970s and is sustained by the assumption that new information technologies can help to bridge the knowledge gap between lay persons and healthcare professionals. One should not, however, get carried away with the idea that 'information is empowerment'. There are significant constraints to the democratisation of health knowledge and information sharing between lay persons and professionals and some patients prefer to remain passive and allow the professional to lead the healthcare encounter (Lupton, 1997; Henwood et al., 2003). Most importantly perhaps the rhetoric of empowerment and democratisation is a mask for cost-saving activities.

However, it is clear that people, 'lay people', are, as Meg Stacey (1994: 89) once argued, 'as much producers as consumers of health care'. This recognition begins to undermine the traditional distinction between professionals and patients and recognises that the knowledge of the latter is valuable and valid. Stacey argues that the 'crucial point which flows from this understanding is that unpaid health workers – that is lay people are part of the health care team'. And she goes on to suggest that 'Historically, however, they have been treated as "the other", the people out there, the people that can create a nuisance when they don't conform, when they don't comply with the latest professional ideas' (1994: 89). The contemporary reconstruction of the patient as active is, according to Pinell (1996: 1), part of the 'civilising process' of modernity. He examines, using the work of Norbert Elias, 'the tendency towards the medicalisation of self-control behaviour and the emergence of the patient as a medical auxiliary involved in the division of medical work'. This transformation of the patient from a passive object of medical practice to an active agent is, therefore, grounded in wider historical and social processes:

> Medical organisation nowadays, demands the reintroduction of the patient as an actor. This position of the patient being an actor in his own treatment corresponds to the dominant ideological value of our contemporary society, where the consciousness of oneself as an autonomous and responsible individual has become the dominant expression of one's relation to the social world. (Pinell, 1996: 14)

It has been, as we have seen, the tradition of biomedicine to expect compliance, passivity and conformity from patients. However, the values of individual autonomy and self-determination that have developed incrementally throughout the modern period and have mushroomed in contemporary culture make expert-centred values difficult to sustain. As medical knowledge has become much more available and accessible to the lay community (Nettleton, 2004), the mystique of medicine has declined. Distrust in authority is widespread (O'Neil, 2002) and medical authority is by no means excluded from the so-called 'crisis of trust'. In the new episteme, trust is democratised and the active citizen healer is born. Responsible for her own health and betterment, she stalks the *preventorium* seeking the information that will transform her personal health project into a scientifically informed business plan. In order to manage her health and discipline her lifestyle the contemporary citizen healer requires an adequate Management Information System.

The informed patient

The imperative to inform begins with the management of epidemics. Biomedicine, in its infancy, developed theories of contagion that produced the practice of quarantine – the separation of bodies to prevent the spread of disease. Information was required for the proper management of this process. This is an early example of the tendency of biomedicine to link with public health and to be the source of recommendations about social order and the management of the environment and it marks an early historical stage in the development of the *preventorium*. Rudimentary forms of health education proliferated during the nineteenth century but the imperative to inform and produce the informed patient who can take responsibility for the management of their own health reaches its final chapter with the arrival of the 'information society'.

The networked world of the information society has produced a general fragmentation of the locus of information and a massive expansion of the availability of and access to what used to be esoteric medical knowledge. Chris Shilling (2002: 623) notes that 'globally, it is generally accepted that health-related information is second only to pornography as a subject searched for on the net'. This glut of information is timely for medicine and health care, because more than ever, the patient or potential patient is expected to be knowledgeable enough to act responsibly as a healthy citizen and to cope with the contemporary diseases that are most likely to be encountered. The major killers of the nineteenth and early twentieth centuries were infectious diseases (McKeown, 1979), acute conditions amenable to cure. Today's killers and disablers are of a rather different order; chronic, degenerative and behavioural illnesses amenable to care and prevention but resistant to curative strategies (Locker, 1991b: 251).

Parson's concept of the 'sick role' allocated expectations, obligations and privileges to the parties in the medical encounter in a manner commensurate with acute illness but given that the contemporary epidemiological map is dominated by chronic and preventable conditions, the professional paternalism and patient passivity embodied in the sick role have become anachronistic. Parson's idea of a temporary role is not consonant with the permanence associated with chronic and degenerative conditions. We have entered a 'new biological era' in which the pattern of disease is such that the responsibility for illness shifts markedly from professional to patient: 'The age of heroic medicine has been replaced by the mundane medical management of chronic as opposed to acute illness' (Turner, 1996: 8). Frank (1995) argues that we live in a 'remission society' in which many people are suffering from or have survived serious illness that 'is experienced not so much as disruption but as part of "life's map" or "life's journey"' (Bury, 2005: 70). Patients with chronic illness are (or rather, become) 'professional patients' because the longevity of their illnesses imbues them with considerable knowledge and skills relative to their condition. They become informed about and active in relation to their own treatment. Passivity is inimical to a disease that has become integrated into individual identity:

> For the chronically ill, information is a significant resource for managing their lives. It reduces uncertainty, helps the individual to come to terms with the illness and allows for the development of strategies for managing the illness in everyday life. (Locker, 1991a: 90)

The information need for chronically ill people has become a psychological imperative. With terminal illness, recent evidence points to the same need and suggests that the journey towards death is marked by a managerial imperative (Meredith, 1996: 724). In the information society, information has become a need and, it is frequently argued, should be a right. Concepts of citizenship – not to mention those around consumption and the consumer – are tied into patient demands for information and this makes it much more difficult for professions to put a closure on specialist knowledge. The growth in discourses of patient choice underlines the need for information, since choice, as the saying goes, should be informed. Even (indeed, especially) in the once taboo area of cancer, oncologists, radiologists and radiographers are convinced by the imperative to inform (Meredith, 1996: 724; Paterson and Price, 1996: 117).

This imperative is underlined by a new discourse of patienthood that is inseparable from the development of ideas about prevention and health promotion. In this discourse, the patient is represented as an autonomous, rational subject and his or her health is conceived in terms of his or her behaviour, lifestyle and capacity for the management of self and health. The patient is, as we have seen, drawn into the process of the production of health and becomes an agent of self-surveillance. As Pinell (1996: 1) argues, the 'tendency towards the medicalisation of self-control behaviour' reinvents the patient as a practitioner 'involved in the division of medical work'. The accent on lifestyle and behaviour in the improvement of the population's health stresses the importance of information. In 1976 a DHSS publication entitled *Prevention and Health: Everybody's Business* argued that the responsibility for health lay with individuals and that ergo, the role of the state and professional health services: 'Is limited to ensuring that the public have access to such knowledge as is available about the importance of personal habits to health and, at the very least, no obstacles are placed in the way of those who decide to act on that knowledge' (DHSS, 1976: 62).

This elevation of the patient to the status of 'active subject' and 'citizen healer' arose alongside the financial panic that hit welfare capitalism in the wake of the oil crisis of 1974. The ensuing economic depression strengthened 'new right' political doctrine of individualism and bolstered the notion of minimalism in the nature and scope of state intervention. The re-skilling of patients – completely deskilled during the era of heroic biomedicine – was a device in the battle against escalating healthcare costs. Since the economic crisis of the 1970s there has been massive ideological investment in the construction of the *preventorium* and it has been based on the production of a morality of betterment that demanded the self-management of well-being. The imperative to inform is often set within the context of a new lexicon of self-responsibility. What distinguishes the patient as active subject from the patient as passive recipient of medical care is the availability of information and it is information that provides the gateway to betterment through self-discipline. The citizen healer, in the spirit of rational asceticism that characterises the *preventorium*, is expected to turn the medical gaze upon herself, but in order to do so she needs the necessary tools, the knowledge, the 'facts', the appropriate Management Information System which is made up, for the most part, by the moral prescriptions embedded in health promotion advice.

The 'system' constituted as transformative and empowering provides the basic ingredients of self-control, self-care and self-efficacy. As the patient is transformed into the citizen healer then so too is the health professional. As the patient becomes the 'informed', the professional becomes an informant. The imperative to inform is central to the transformation of both patient and professional roles. It has been driven by – among other things – epidemiological change, the volatile economics of health care that were redrawn in the 1970s in the wake of depression, unemployment and the crisis of welfare, and by the 'civilising process' (Elias, 1978, 1972) by what Michel Foucault called the shift from surveillance to self-surveillance (Johnson, 1993). These arguments describe *la longue duree* of social change and the conditions under which externally governed populations are transformed into self-monitoring and self-managing subjects. In addition to the growth of ideas of self-care in the 1970s, the concept of the 'informed patient' has been boosted since the 1990s with the exponential growth of the Internet and other new media technologies and by the way in which these have been appropriated by health policy-makers in the UK. Policy documents, such as *Information for Health* (Department of Health, 1998) and *Building the Information Core* (Department of Health, 2001), celebrate the possibilities of e-health and the ways in which patients might use new information technologies as consumers and producers of healthcare knowledge (Hardy, 1999, 2001; Henwood et al., 2003).

These developments towards an 'information age health care system' (Eysenbach, 2000) are, in large part, about engineering the more efficient use of healthcare resources. The hope is that 'informed patients' will use accessible information to take more responsibility for their own health care and some enthusiasts for 'health informatics' envisage a 'brave new world' of 'on-line' health in which informed consumers can make informed choices from a menu of possibilities that is selected on the basis of the most up-to-date information (Ferguson, 1997). Indeed, despite reservations about the quality of some of the health information available on the Internet, it is clear that some people use it for second opinions or to challenge professional opinion or to seek help from alternative practitioners (Jadad, 1999), all of which suggest that the knowledge gap between professional and patient is being closed by health consumers or citizen healers who use information to give themselves more control over their bodies and their lives. The Internet is an important source of patient information but it is also a challenge to professional expertise and a growing factor in the redrawing of the relationship between patients and healthcare practitioners (Eysenbach and Diepgen, 1999; Hardy, 1999; Jadad, 1999). Indeed, it has been argued that 'health and medical knowledge are being metamorphosed into information' and that 'medical knowledge has escaped, metaphorically and literally' and 'is now increasingly produced by health consumers and users' (Nettleton, 2004: 673). In capturing the raw data of health surveillance, citizen healers are able to operate as rational managers of their own lifestyles and make the *preventorium* into a productive space for their own betterment.

The rise of the imperative to inform is central to the process in which biomedicine gives way to 'postmedicine' and to a 'regime of total health' (Armstrong, 1993) in which 'knowledges of the biophysical body (hitherto medicine's most sacred object) seep out into cyberspace' (Nettleton, 2004: 674). In the disciplinary space created by this process a reductionist and mechanical concept of patienthood gives way to one in which the patient (and potential patient) becomes a self-regulated rational, autonomous subject who partners the professional in the battle against disease and – most importantly – the maintenance of health. The latter takes priority because the *preventorium* is primarily a salutogenic space. Salutogenic self-regulation puts pressure on lay persons to look after themselves but the information revolution provides them with the knowledge appropriate for so doing. Some argue that postmodern society is primarily an information society that helps to bring about the democratisation of knowledge and the proliferation of expertise. 'At the level of the patient', writes Mildred Blaxter (2004: 136), 'new forms of communication provide wider access to information' and 'privileged access to information is no longer the exclusive mark of the doctor and the internet loosens the boundaries between the person and the professional'. The information that circulates in the *preventorium* and provides the basic techniques for personal regimes of health management is derived from the practices of the 'new public health' which has been described by one commentator as the 'dispensary' (Armstrong, 1983) for contemporary 'surveillance medicine' (Armstrong, 2002).

The new public health

Medicine is omnipresent in the form of information which we use to guide us through the pitfalls and problems of contemporary life. It is the source of the good life, the clue to longevity, health, fitness and the body beautiful. It is our companion in decisions that need to be taken about eating, and sleeping, and drinking and sex and it informs how we run and plan our cities and communities

(Bunton, Nettleton and Burrows, 1995). The growth of what has become known as the 'new public health' is a powerful illustration of the way in which the biomedical model of health is giving way to multiple conceptions about how to tackle the health of populations and the key role that lay people can and (perhaps) should play. It also suggests that the patient is being transformed into the 'health seeker' (Fox and Rainie, 2002) in which one of the central obligations of citizenship is the monitoring and management of one's health (Rose, 2001, 2007).

In the nineteenth century public health had been about the 'sanitary idea' and sanitary engineering: its task, to make habitable the terrible spaces created by the juggernaut of urbanisation. The 'new public health' began in the 1980s. It is interested in health promotion and community strategies for improving the health of neighbourhoods and populations. In the 1970s the stark realities of health economics combined with powerful critiques of biomedical effectiveness to pave the way for the re-emergence of public health. The new public health embraces social change as a strategy for the improvement of health but it is most concerned with the regulation of behaviour in terms of medical knowledge and norms. It seeks to encourage people to adopt patterns of living that are healthy (Ashton and Seymour, 1988; Lupton, 1995) and to make them responsible for their own betterment. Biomedicine challenges disease whilst the new public health challenges people to take responsibility for their well-being. Biomedicine – at the height of its power – demanded ignorance, dependency and absolute trust in health professionals. The new public health establishes an ethical imperative for the management of health lifestyles and healthy self-governance (Rose, 2007).

The centrepiece of the new public health is health promotion. In the last three decades, it has shifted rapidly to the centre of healthcare strategies in all 'advanced' societies displacing *en route* the pillars of pathogenic biomedicine – disease and cure. It foregrounds health maintenance, ideas and information that help ordinary people to take care of themselves and it repositions the relationship between the expert and the lay person. It is based not on an assumption of lay dependency but on the autonomy of the subject. Health promotion advocates healthy behaviour but recognises that rational action requires choice. Biomedicine was grounded in a language of necessity, of decisions taken by experts followed by compliance from patients. Loss of faith in expertise in the latter half of the twentieth century makes the manner of operation of biomedicine incommensurate with the values of autonomy, self-control and self-actualisation. Where the expert stands back – as in health promotion – and offers advice at a distance and in a spirit, which recognises the autonomous-self, it offers a service more in keeping with the contemporary ethic of health self-management. It also rescues health practice from the clinic and makes everyday life the central space for the mundane, ethical management of health lifestyles. It is the key discourse in the moral architecture of the *preventorium.*

Definitions of health promotion abound, but certain key themes are widely accepted to be at its heart. First, health should be regarded not as an end in itself, but as a resource for everyday life. Second, health should be an important objective for societies (not just individuals) and a fundamental human right. Third, health – *contra* biomedicine – is more than the absence of disease or infirmity. Last, that 'promotion' should be regarded as a process of enablement and facilitation, designed to support lay people as they attempt to manage their lives and improve their well-being (Bunton, Nettleton and Burrows, 1995). The rhetoric is fundamentally ethical. It envisages a simultaneous medicalisation and moralisation of the life-world and health is understood in terms of the management of the 'vital forces and potentialities of the living body' (Rose, 2007: 7).

Health promotion provides a new model of theory and practice for health professionals who are moving from hospital to community, who will be working with people rather than disease, who will be more reticent to cure because they will be most focused on encouraging people to look after themselves. Rather than apply medical knowledge to biological subjects, health promotion seeks to release medical knowledge in the form of ethical prescriptions that are designed to encourage change in attitudes, behaviours, communities and cities. Health promotion challenges biomedicine and simultaneously offers it a future as a social practice with an unlimited jurisdiction. In order to do so the new public health has had to help medicine to begin to re-order its uni-dimensional and reductionist conception of causality.

The 'germ theory' of disease that underpinned medical aetiology in the latter part of the nineteenth century arose from the identification of specific bacilli with specific diseases; for example, the tubercle bacillus was isolated and identified as the cause of tuberculosis and streptococcus was identified as the cause of scarlet fever. These scientific discoveries fed into programmes of public health that were based on information about personal hygiene. Conceived as the enemy of the notorious germ, cleanliness became virtuous, a moral imperative and a major behavioural pre-requisite for a healthy life. Mundane, hygienic, body maintenance activities became the ethical and practical solution to the omnipresent germ and formed key disciplinary techniques associated with the infant *preventorium*. Public programmes to clean up the environment existed alongside exhortations to wash, clean and preen. Middle-class Almoners and charity workers preached cleanliness and hygiene to the working-class poor and taught poor women about the relationship between the application of the principles of domestic science and the avoidance of food-, water- and air-borne diseases. This form of 'health education' brought about an increased emphasis on bodily self-control. According to Pinell (1996: 7), 'it was during the nineteenth century that social pressure for self control in everyday behaviour added hygienic care to considerations of decency'. The 'civilising' of everyday activities through the creation of new norms of embodiment had its roots in the discovery and dissemination (in popular form) of medical facts. Manners and 'decent behaviour' were radically transformed by the new discourse of hygienic self-care and the defeat of the germ was no longer the province of the scientific expert. The 'civilised', vigilant citizen would also have an important part to play in keeping the germ at bay.

The dramatic rise of chronic illness in the twentieth century, as we have seen, gave significant impetus to the imperative to inform and drew lay people into the management of illness. While this took place largely on an individual basis within the confines of the medical encounter, health education began to expand beyond its 'handy hints on hygiene' basis. As cancers and heart disease began to emerge as the major killers in the Western world – signalling the impotence of heroic biomedicine – then health education became used, increasingly, as the epistemological basis of self-surveillance. As biomedicine began to recognise that disease can be caused by behaviour and *ergo* prevented by behavioural modification then medicine began to enlist, more frequently, the vigilance of the lay population. As it did so, it put into place the ingredients for its own dissolution into postmedicine and created the conditions for the rise of the disciplinary space that I have called the *preventorium*. In this space the central assumptions of biomedicine are re-configured. In what follows, I will demonstrate this with respect to aetiology and therapy.

The major killers of the twentieth century appeared to be caused not so much by germs but by behaviour. The doctrine of specific aetiology that stood at the centre of nineteenth- and twentieth-century biomedicine has had to be modified, indeed replaced by a multi-causal model of disease causation. People had to be encouraged to change their behaviour and, therefore, take responsibility for the management of their own health. Medical science had to begin to lean on social science and to publicise its findings in the form of behavioural 'prescriptions' about how best to conduct one's self. The technologies of the so-called 'information society' provided the technical means for the widespread dissemination of medico-behavioural information. The boundary between medicine and public health became increasingly blurred and the life-world came increasingly under the jurisdiction of medical prescriptions for healthy options and activities.

'The translation of health knowledge into behavioural change', argued Parish (1995: 14), 'required a more comprehensive approach than health education alone'. Thus in the late 1970s, health promotion was born and medicine entered into the information or 'postmedical age', offering lifestyle advice and mapping out the risks associated with a whole range of behaviours. Health promotion experts mediate between the 'discoveries' of laboratory medicine and a population encouraged to discern between good and bad, pathogenic and salutogenic. The medicalisation of lifestyle transforms patients and potential patients into managers of their own well-being, agents of betterment who are obliged to engage reflexively with available medical knowledge and to survey and implement the possibilities for action in the constant battle between the forces for life and living and those that stand in opposition to vigour and vitality. Each and every one of us is conscripted into a never ending war against the frailties and hazards of human existence. The more total and comprehensive the regime of health becomes, the more urgent becomes both the imperative to inform and the obligation to act upon that knowledge. Lifestyle, objects of ingestion, the environments in which we work, rest and play, indeed the entire eco system, are drawn into the expanding aeteological domains of health, come under scrutiny and are subjected to examination in order to analyse them for their pathogenic and salutogenic properties. Like aetiology, 'therapy' in the *preventorium* acquires a more liquid meaning.

In the not too distant past, 'therapy' meant an action done to a patient by a doctor or some other accredited and formally recognised, usually state registered, health practitioner. It was something done to the body or mind of an individual in order to effect cure, care or elimination of symptoms. Such action was controlled by the medical profession (usually men) and its subordinate semi-professions (usually women) with the approval of a (political) state that recognised the profession as the sole legitimate authority with regard to matters of health, illness and therapeutic practice. In the postmedical world what constitutes the therapeutic is something much more elastic and diverse. It can mean anything that is good for one. Medicine remains the most important tribunal of appeal in terms of making a sensible judgement about what is good but as we sink deeper into a world of 'medical pluralism', what constitutes the therapeutic will continue to expand. It is also important to note that health has attached itself to a host of new 'objects'. Behaviour is the example that I have called upon most frequently in this chapter but 'public policy' is another more esoteric instance. In this example ('healthy public policy') health deserts its traditional locations of body and mind and finds a new home in/ on a discursive object/subject. As it searches for the solutions to health rather than the origins of disease, postmedicine transforms the geography of therapy.

As we produce discourses about healthy cities, healthy eating and care in the community we approach therapy and the therapeutic not so much as clinical action but as a set of adjustments that must be made to behaviour or social organisation in the name of a socio-ethical imperative. As the emphasis shifts from cure to prevention and promotion, therapy becomes much more than an action or process that happens to bodies (perhaps minds) in hospitals. It cannot be separated from the conduct or circumstances of one's life and it is embroiled in everything that we do and don't do as we muddle through in that mundane and crepuscular domain that philosophers sometimes call the *lebenswelt*. In this context, we are encouraged to redefine therapy in ways that might be commensurate with our needs or philosophical disposition. The meaning of therapy moves – seeping like a liquid or a gas – into the community and becomes geographically or spatially diversified (Nettleton and Burrows, 1994). Eating, sleeping, drinking, sex and recreation are all activities that are relevant to our health and we can and we are expected, if not obliged, to choose to do them in such a way that protects us from illness. The life-world therefore becomes saturated with ethical questions of betterment – questions about how one should live one's life and 'therapy' becomes the practical measures that we adopt in order to manage those lives. Salutogenic discourse provides the moral architecture of the *preventorium*.

Concluding remarks

The concept of the self invokes a plethora of affixes which have become a semantic menu for discourses about health and well-being. Self-acceptance, self-care techniques, self-determination, self-development, self-empowerment, self-healing, self-help, self-help groups, self-organising systems, self-realisation, self-esteem, self-recognition, self-renewal, self-responsibility, self-sufficiency and, last but not least, self-management. The ubiquitous hyphen links self with what should be done to it in order to make it be or feel better. Though the concepts can all be read as descriptive, each contains a normative element, a recipe for action, an ethic of responsibility to oneself and a call to manage one's own freedom. In a highly individualised world this language contains both a denigration of dependence on expertise, prescriptions for health and happiness and signposts to a future secured by one's own efforts to prevent the onset of disease by the management of one's health lifestyle. The self, or more accurately, the embodied self, has become a 'project', something to be discovered, actualised, developed, constructed, changed and improved (Shilling, 2004). It is a project that requires information and education and is founded on a quiet epistemological revolution that valorises experiential knowledge and provides ordinary people with access to ideas that were once monopolised by healthcare professionals. It is – above all – an ethical project in which the responsibility to look after oneself has been transformed into an obligation:

> We have seen an intensification and generalisation of the health promotion strategies developed in the twentieth century, coupled with the rise of a private health insurance industry, enhancing the obligations that individuals and families have for monitoring and managing their own health. Every citizen must now become an active partner in the drive for health, accepting their responsibility for securing their own well-being. (Rose, 2001: 17)

The conflation of health and self-management does not seem entirely commensurate with the Habermasian view of New Social Movements and self-help groups as 'new shoots sprouting in the fault lines between system and lifeworld and concerned with the "grammar of life"' (Scambler and Kelleher, 2006: 220) or with self-help as the source of 'the last examples of voices from the lifeworld resisting the dominance of an expert system' (Scambler and Kelleher, 2006: 224). For Habermas the practices of contemporary health seekers are an indication of system – life-world conflicts where a noble laity protect the latter from the former and support the battle against the colonisation of the life-world in the name of communicative rationality. In the case that I have made here, the *lebenswelt* is pretty much saturated with the 'voice of medicine'. Indeed, it provides the ethical, salutogenic prescriptions that map out the choices that are available to people as they construct and enact their health lifestyles. I have called the space in which they enact these choices the *preventorium*. It is a space in which fear, risk and anxiety tread and where freedom and choice are, at least, represented as important protagonists but it is also a sphere that is dominated by the battalions of the system who whisper truths about how to live and offer moral prescriptions to those who may have strayed from the path of prudence and moderation. As one looks around the space one is likely to encounter information that will help one make appropriate decisions and conduct oneself in ways that will harm neither body nor soul, and one is likely to find or be directed to skills that one can utilise in order to act salutogenically and one will experience recognition for one's ideas about health which one will be expected to use to maximise one's chances of becoming an ethical subject. One will also become acutely aware that, in this space, there is no point in looking beyond one's self as far as the responsibility for health is concerned. And, as the *preventorium* becomes increasingly subject to the impact of the geneticisation of life, then its imperative is even more thoroughly embedded in the language of the management of responsibilities (Kerr, 2003; Svendsen and Koch, 2006). The future will be at stake and biology will not be destiny for one will be expected to manage the implications of one's genetic profile and to optimise the vital future by taking action in the vital present (Rose, 2007). Postmedicine or the kind of medicine that is at the core of the moral architecture of the preventorium is, therefore, a form of authority that is active in the everyday, mundane lives of people who wish to manage those lives in order to make themselves better.

References

Abbott, P., Wallace, C. and Tyler, M. (2006) *An Introduction to Sociology: Feminist Perspectives*, London: Routledge.

Armstrong, D. (1983) *The Political Anatomy of the Body: Medical Knowledge in Britain in the Twentieth Century*, Cambridge: Cambridge University Press.

Armstrong, D. (1993) From clinical gaze to the regime of total health, in A. Beattie, M. Gott, L. Jones and L. Siddell (eds) *Health and Wellbeing: A Reader*, London: Macmillan.

Armstrong, D. (2002) The rise of Surveillance medicine, in S. Nettleton and U. Gustaffson (eds) *The Sociology of Health and Illness Reader*, Cambridge: Polity.

Ashton, J. and Seymour, H. (1988) *The New Public Health*, Milton Keynes: Open University Press.

Biggs, S. (1993) *Understanding Ageing: Images, Attitudes and Professional Practice*, Buckingham: Open University Press.

Blaxter, M. (2004) *Health*, Cambridge: Polity Press.

Bunton, R., Nettleton, S. and Burrows, R. (eds) (1995) *Sociology of Health Promotion: Critical Analysis of Consumption, Lifestyle and Risk*, London: Routledge.

Bury, M. (2001) Illness narratives: Fact or fiction, *Sociology of Health and Illness*, 23, 263–285.

Bury, M. (2005) *Health and Illness*, Cambridge: Polity Press.

Busby, H., Williams, G. and Rogers, A. (1997) Bodies of knowledge: Lay and biomedical understandings of musculoskeletal disorders, in M. Elston (ed.) *The Sociology of Medical Science and Technology*, Oxford: Blackwell.

Castel, R. (1991) From dangerousness to risk, in G. Burchell, C. Gordon and P. Miller (eds) *The Foucault Effect: Studies in Governmentality*, London: Harvester Wheatsheaf.

Castells, M. (1996) *The Rise of the Network Society, Volume 1*, London: Blackwell.

Department of Health (1998) *Information for Health: An Information Strategy for the Modern NHS, 1998–2005*, London: Department of Health.

Department of Health (2001) *Building the Information Core: Implementing the NHS Plan*, London: Department of Health.

Department of Health and Social Security (1976) *Prevention and Health: Everybody's Business*, London: HMSO.

Elias, N. (1978) *The Civilising Process. Volume 1: The History of Manners*, Oxford: Basil Blackwell.

Eysenbach, G. (2000) Consumer health informatics, *British Medical Journal*, 320, 7251.

Eysenbach, G. and Diepgen, T. (1999) Patients looking for information on the internet and seeking teleadvice, *Archives of Dermatology*, 135, 2, 151–156.

Ferguson, T. (1997) Health online and the empowered medical consumer, *Journal of Quality Improvement*, 23, 5, 251–257.

Fleck, L. (1979) *Genesis and Development of a Scientific Fact*, Chicago: University of Chicago Press.

Foucault, M. (1980) The eye of power, in C. Gordon (ed.) *Power/Knowledge: Michel Foucault, Selected Interviews and Other Writings*, New York: Pantheon Books.

Fox, S. and Rainie, L. (2002) *Vital Decisions*, Washington DC: Pew Internet and American Life Project.

Frank, A. (1995) *The Wounded Storyteller: Body, Illness and Ethics*, Chicago: University of Chicago Press.

Freidson, E. (1970) *The Profession of Medicine*, New York: Dodd Mead.

Furnham, A. and Vincent, C. (2006) Reasons for using CAM, in M. Kelner, B. Wellman, B. Pescosolido and M. Saks (eds) *Complementary and Alternative Medicine: Challenge and Change*, London: Routledge.

Gabe, J., Bury, M. and Elston, M. (2004) *Key Concepts in Medical Sociology*, London: Sage.

Gabe, J., Kelleher, D. and Williams, G. (2006) *Challenging Medicine* (3rd Edition), London: Routledge.

Giddens, A. (1991) *Modernity and Self-Identity*, Cambridge: Polity Press.

Goldstein, M. (2003) The culture of fitness and the growth of CAM, in M. Kelner, B. Wellman, B. Pescosolido and M. Saks (eds) *Complementary and Alternative Medicine: Challenge and Change*, London: Routledge.

Hardy, M. (1999) Doctor in the house: The internet as a source of lay health knowledge and the challenge of expertise, *Sociology of Health and Illness*, 21, 6, 820–835.

Hardy, M. (2001) E-health: The internet and the transformation of patients into consumers and producers of health knowledge, *Information, Communication and Society*, 4, 3, 388–405.

Henwood, F., Wyatt, S., Hart, A. and Smith, J. (2003) Ignorance is bliss, sometimes: Constraints on the emergence of the informed patient in the changing landscapes of health information, *Sociology of Health and Illness*, 25, 6, 589–602.

Hughes, B. (2000) Medicalized bodies, in P. Hancock, B. Hughes, E. Jagger, K. Patterson, R. Russell, E. Tulle-Winton and M. Tyler (eds) *The Body, Culture and Society: An Introduction*, Buckingham: Open University Press, pp. 12–28.

Jadad, A. (1999) Promoting partnerships: Challenges for the internet age, *British Medical Journal*, 319, 761–764.

Johnson, T. (1993) Expertise and the state, in M. Gane and T. Johnson (eds) *Foucault's New Domains*, London: Routledge.

Kerr, A. (2003) Rights and responsibilities in the new genetics era, *Critical Social Policy*, 23, 2, 208–226.

Kleinman, A. (1988) *The Illness Narratives. Suffering, Healing and the Human Condition*, New York: Basic Books.

Lash, S. (2002) *Critique of Information*, London: Sage.

Locker, D. (1991a) Prevention and health promotion, in G. Scambler (ed.) *Sociology as Applied to Medicine*, London: Balliere Tindall.

Locker, D. (1991b) Living with chronic illness, in G. Scambler (ed.) *Sociology as Applied to Medicine*, London: Balliere Tindall.

Lupton, D. (1995) *The Imperative of Health: Public Health and the Regulated Body*, London: Sage.

Lupton, D. (1997) Consumerism, reflexivity and the medical encounter, *Social Science and Medicine*, 45, 3, 373–381.

McKeown, T. (1979) *The Role of Medicine*, Princeton, NJ: Princeton University Press.

Meredith, C. (1996) Information needs of cancer patients in the west of Scotland: Cross sectional survey of patients views. *British Medical Journal*, 313, 724–729.

Nettleton, S. (2004) The emergence of e-scaped medicine, *Sociology*, 38, 4, 661–679.

Nettleton, S. and Burrows, R. (1994) From bodies in hospitals to people in communities: A theoretical analysis of the relocation of health care, *Care in Place*, 1, 2, 3–13.

O'Neil, O. (2002) A question of trust: The Reith lectures 2002, available online at www.bbc.co.uk/radio4/reith2002 (consulted 12/10/06).

Parish, R. (1995) Health promotion: Rhetoric and reality, in R. Bunton et al. (eds) *The Sociology of Health Promotion*. London: Routledge.

Paterson, A. and Price, R. (1996) *Current Topics in Radiography*, London: Saunders.

Pinell, P. (1996) Modern medicine and the civilising process, *Sociology of Health and Illness*, 18, 1, 1–16.

Prior, L. (2003) Belief, knowledge and expertise: The emergence of the lay expert in medical sociology, *Sociology of Health and Illness*, 25, 3, 41–57.

Rose, N. (2001) The politics of life itself, *Theory, Culture & Society*, 18, 6, 1–30.

Rose, N. (2007) Molecular biopolitics, somatic ethics and the spirit of biocapital, *Social Theory and Health*, 5, 3–29, Available online at www.palgravejournals.com/sth/journal/v5/nl/full/8700084a.html (consulted 8/4/07).

Scambler, G. and Kelleher, D. (2006) New social and health movements: Issues of representation and change, *Critical Public Health*, 16, 3, 219–231.

Shilling, C. (2002) Culture, the 'sick role' and the consumption of health, *British Journal of Sociology*, 53, 4, 621–638.

Shilling, C. (2004) *The Body and Social Theory* (2nd Edition), London: Sage.

Sointu, E. (2006) Recognition and the creation of wellbeing, *Sociology*, 40, 3, 493–510.

Stacey, M. (1988) *The Sociology of Health and Healing*, London: Routledge.

Stacey, M. (1994) The power of lay knowledge, in J. Popay and G. Williams (eds) *Researching Peoples Health*, London: Routledge.

Svendsen, M. N. and Koch, L. (2006) Genetics and prevention: A policy in the making, *New Genetics and Society*, 25, 1, 51–68.

Turner, B. (1996) *The Body and Society: Explorations in Social Theory*, London: Sage.

Weir, L. (1996) Recent developments in the government of pregnancy, *Economy and Society*, 25, 372–392.

Williams, G. and Popay, J. (1994) Lay knowledge and the privilege of experience, in J. Gabe et al. (eds) *Challenging Medicine*, London: Routledge.

Williams, S. (2003) *Medicine and the Body*, London: Sage.

Williams, S. and Calnan, M. (1996) *Modern Medicine: Lay Perspectives and Experiences*, London: UCL Press.

World Health Organisation (1986) Lifestyles and health, *Social Science and Medicine*, 22, 117–124.

Chapter **5**

Managing sleep?

The colonization of everyday/night life

Philip Hancock, Simon Williams and Sharon Boden

Introduction

Throughout history sleep has been thought of in many, often esoteric ways. For those who envisage life as subject to the demands of an increasingly corporatized and administered world it may well be considered a last bastion of freedom; a refuge of refusal, a physical and conceptual space where at least the unconscious, free of the demands of the *performance principle* (Marcuse, 1972), might still express the subject's deepest desires. Granted, healthy sleep might in its own way contribute to the reproduction of the efficient labourer – Gramsci's (1971) 'new type of worker' – but for the most part, in the contemporary Western world at least, it has been seen as a 'private' matter (itself the product of the 'civilising process', as Elias (1978 [1939]) reminds us), stubbornly resistant to corporate values and organizational interventions.

In this chapter we question whether such a view of sleep is still sustainable, however. For it would seem to us, at least, that sleep and the act of sleeping is increasingly an object of managerial and organizational interest. As companies appear evermore concerned to mould their employees' lifestyles according to their needs, sleep has itself become a target of micromanagerial intervention. Often this is in the guise of programmes designed to promote well-being amongst employees. That is, or so it would appear, management consultants and company managers are increasingly starting to look at *healthy* sleep in terms of *efficient* sleep, whereby the nap can become a source of competitive advantage in the frenetic environment of global business. And where companies cannot intervene directly, the growth of an intermediary expert culture around sleep is ensuring that the technical imperatives of managerial rationality continue to permeate our everyday lives as slumber is increasingly organized as the new force to 'unlock creativity' and 'realize life-goals'.

Such interventions should not be seen as restricted merely to the realm of the subject as employee, however. On the broader social stage, sleep as an everyday – or should that be everynight – practice is also facing a myriad of attempts to see it organized and commodified to an unprecedented degree. As the medical-industrial complex generates evermore sophisticated and expensive drugs to put us to sleep and keep us awake, the diagnosis and treatment of sleep-related disorders has itself become a burgeoning economic concern. Combine this with a market in beds, mattresses and pillows which is exceeding all previous expectations, and the idea that sleep remains a somehow private and largely unregulated affair appears increasingly untenable. Rather, it is more the case that when, where and how we sleep is itself becoming not only a highly managed affair, but also a lifestyle issue that is increasingly associated with how we work, play and even identify ourselves; a largely unrecognized aspect of the contemporary 'project of the self' (Giddens, 1991).

In this chapter, then, it is our intention to develop and substantiate this proposition, namely that sleep is not only increasingly managed, organized and regulated, but that integral to this is an emerging reality of sleep that is being marketed as a lifestyle issue, linked as it is to practices not only of work but also of consumption and self-management. In doing so, we aim to touch upon a number of concerns including

- the developing technical interest in sleep amongst both employers and representatives of labour;
- current attitudes of management to the importance of sleep as an organizational resource;
- the growing importance of the 'sleep industry' (including pharmaceuticals and other sleep-related technologies) as a component element of the ways in which everyday lifestyles and corporeal needs are increasingly aligned with corporate interests;
- the potential impact of work-related issues on patterns and experiences of sleep outside of the workplace.
- the increasing significance of an expert-culture of sleep which is making its presence felt through a range of media, including consultancies, popular 'how – to' texts and the mass media.

Organization knows no bounds: The management of everyday/night lifestyles

To suggest that sleep, as an aspect of everyday life, is increasingly subject to an extension of managerial and organizational influence is not, of course, to make a particularly outlandish claim. After all, the proposition that the realm of the everyday – of the mundane, trivial and taken-for-granted aspects of our day-to-day lives – has increasingly come to represent another component of what Giddens (1991) has described as the 'juggernaut' of modernity is one that has a notable history. Certainly, classical sociology can be understood, in many respects, as the primary articulation of this process, concerned as it was with socio-cultural modernization and its relationship to the expansion of capitalism and the industrialization processes that accompanied it. Today, critical scholars such as Habermas (1984, 1987) have observed what they consider to be a *colonization* of communicatively ordered social relations by various manifestations of a technical and largely instrumental rationality which, in many respects, can simply be seen as the inevitable extension of this process.

Yet to propose that sleep might somehow be undergoing such a colonization process suggests that it is something other than simply a base biological function as one might suppose, and is rather a socially negotiated practice. Well, while perhaps only 20 years or so ago such a proposition might have been greeted with a degree of if not incomprehension, then certainly scepticism, today this is increasingly less the case. In part this can be attributed to a growing academic concern with sleep, particularly in the field of sociology (Taylor, 1993; Williams and Bendelow, 1998; Hislop and Arber, 2003; Williams, 2007) and cultural studies (Summers-Bremner, 2007). As Williams (2005: 3 *original emphasis*) has observed, the realization that 'sleep…[is] a complex (learned) behaviour or practice that displays a high degree of *socio-cultural plasticity or variability*' is one that is increasingly gaining credence.

Consequently, studies ranging from the discussion of the relationship between sleep, religion and the protestant work ethic (Finger, 2006) to the social and cultural aspects of sleeping in the Japanese classroom (Steger, 2006) have recently emerged, while the relationship between gender, age and sleep (Hislop and Arber, 2003, 2004, 2006) has pointed to the ways in which shifting socio-cultural and economic expectations throughout the life course have notable impacts upon how, when and where we sleep. As such, they have illustrated the ways in which sleep is often a negotiated process; a process particularly shaped by traditional gender roles with Meadows (2005), for example, demonstrating how a married couple's sleeping arrangements are based upon a dynamic, changing set of requirements over the life course and a range of gendered and other socially established expectations (such as whether the couple should continue to share a bed even during nights when one of them is clearly disturbing the other).

What such research suggests then is that sleep, and the act of sleeping, is in part something which is subject to both private and public expectations and sanctions, which in turn are spatially and temporally negotiated and mediated in a variety of ways. The 'social etiquette of sleep' (Williams, 2007), moreover, pervades every aspect of social relations, regulating the ways in which certain sleep activities and ways and places of being asleep are simultaneously proscribed and/or permitted in a 'civilized' society. This latter observation, for instance, is well illustrated through the work of Canadian visual artist Germaine Koh, whose performance art work of 2003, *Sleeping Rough*, was designed to 'elicit a range of

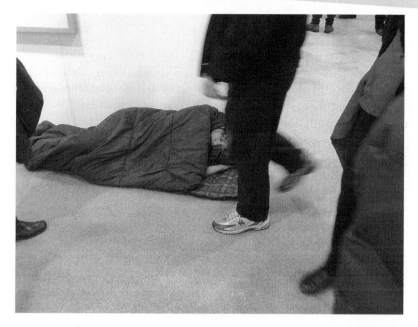

Figure 5.1   Sleeping Rough (2003) – a performance by the Canadian artist Germaine Koh

emotions from revulsion to empathy, and questions of appropriate behaviour and responsibility' (Figure 5.1).

What Koh's work is seeking to do is represent what are in effect the 'abject' qualities of sleep (Kristeva, 1982) when taken out of the context of private, contained activity, a context whose appropriateness is itself a socially constructed and subsequently negotiated actuality.

From a Western perspective, socially negotiated sanctions surrounding sleep are perhaps nowhere more keenly felt than in the workplace, where to sleep is almost exclusively considered to be an inappropriate form of behaviour, as 'matter out of place' to coin one of Douglas's (1966) most notable phrases. Once again, however, the socio-cultural contingency of such an outlook is illustrated well by Steger (2003) and her discussion of the Japanese practice of *inemuri*. Inemuri, according to Steger (2003: 181), literally means 'to be asleep while present', and is an acceptable form of napping in certain parts of Japanese culture. Unlike napping that might take place in a more Westernized culture – that is, away from public view – inemuri is practised not only in full view of other people, but also in the kinds of formal and professional situations that would be unthinkable to the average Westerner.

To sum up thus far then, we are arguing that sleep, and the act of sleeping, is not only a biological but also a profoundly social and a negotiated practice. As such, like so many other quotidian activities it is subject to a range of symbolic, economic and culturally interventions which are mediated through an equally extensive range of socio-cultural and economic resources, and it is the nature and character of these resources that concerns us here.

The sleep-deprived society?

That the citizens of contemporary industrialized societies are either not getting enough sleep or getting sleep of insufficient quality is a concern that is increasingly being discussed both within the popular media as well as more scholarly locations. Sleep, or more accurately a lack of it, has been cited across Europe as the cause of a range of not only localized problems such as higher levels of accidental workplace fatality (Åkerstedt et al., 2002), but perhaps most infamously in the UK, where the fatal Selby rail crash of 2000[1] was directly attributed to a lack of sleep on the part of the car driver involved. In fact, to the casual observer it might appear that a lack of quality sleep, as much as global warming or rising crime rates, is the malaise of our age, undermining everything from personal safety to national economic prosperity. In the UK, for instance, policy reports such as those by Demos (Leadbeater, 2004) and Capgemini (2005) have pointed to a mounting sleep crisis deriving from the pressures of a 24/7 society and the demands made by an increasingly flexible and accelerated economy, with 49 per cent of the UK full-time workforce claiming not to get enough sleep and 43 per cent of UK senior managers saying that staff performance or staff shortages keep them awake at night.

Recent research into the portrayal of sleep matters connected to work within the UK print media has also highlighted similar issues (Boden et al., 2008). In particular, it has identified how sleep is predominately framed as a neglected component of our work and social lives. One that can be all too easily sacrificed to the requirements of the 24/7 society, long-hours culture and the struggle to create a harmonious work-life balance. Not only is the media an information provider on sleep, however. Sleep is also presented as part and parcel of a moral and healthy lifestyle, something not simply to be worked at but 'bought into' through a range of lifestyle choices, goods and services.

And it is not only in the UK and Europe that sleep has become perceived as an increasingly problematic socio-cultural, as well as economic issue. Across the globe a range of high-profile disasters including the Bhopal catastrophe, and the explosion of the space shuttle Challenger (Dement, 1998) have all been directly blamed in some quarters on sleep-deprivation. In the US in particular, in many respects the home of sleep research, organizations such as the National Sleep Foundation (2005) are suggesting that around 75 per cent of the American adult population regularly experience sleep problems, with daytime excessive tiredness having notable consequences for people at work. Similarly, in Australia, a series of internet surveys such as that by the recruitment website *Careerone* (2006) have also reported on, and, in doing so, generated concerns about levels of healthy sleep, once again particularly in relation to the stresses and strains of work, claiming that around 77 per cent of their Australian respondents lost sleep over work-related issues while nearly 82 per cent had woken up feeling nervous about going to work.

How seriously though should we take these claims regarding a sleep-deprived or sleep-worried society? To what extent might they be seen as the first stages in creating a state of emergency (Benjamin, 1999) or moral panic (Cohen, 1972) around the activity of sleep, rendering it more easily amenable to intervention and management? Certainly, there is good reason to be sceptical about the actual extent to which sleep is the problem it is portrayed as. From a sociological point of view (Williams, 2005), the tendency of such reports to rely either upon methodologically spurious quantitative surveys or potentially misleading second-hand statistics, which appear to indicate a reduction in the number of hours actually slept by people today compared with a century ago, merely reinforces this suspicion. Similarly, from a bio-medical perspective the tendency of such reportage to homogenize sleep needs across a diverse population has led the likes of sleep psychologist Jim Horne (2006) to dismiss the view that unless we regularly enjoy at least eight hours a day we are sleep deprived as simply 'nonsense' (*BBC News Online*, 12th April 2007).

Having said that, it would perhaps be churlish not to also acknowledge that, for many people, a lack of sleep is a genuine and distressing problem. Equally, there is also good reason to believe that with the evermore extensive penetration of both work and entertainment technologies into our domestic settings, combined with the insecurities that have accompanied an increasingly flexible economy, for many, quality sleep is also often in short supply. Nevertheless, however one looks at the problem, it cannot be denied that a concerted effort appears to have taken place over the last decade or so to (re)present sleep as far more of a medical and social problem than has ever been the case before.

Sleep and the medical–industrial complex

Now, the fact that there appears to be an increasing effort on the part of certain quarters to construct sleep, or more accurately, a deficit of it, as a significant political and cultural problem in contemporary (post)industrialized societies should perhaps not come as a great surprise. After all, as Foucault (1979) would remind us, a defining characteristic of modernity has been the ways in which the body is ever subject to a regime of discipline which not only locates it in space/time but which, in doing so, renders it an object of both knowledge and control. From this understanding then, it is perhaps only to be expected that the dormant body would be viewed as yet another site of power/knowledge, both an outcome and a victim of such discursive practices. Nevertheless, while such an account is, without doubt, a persuasive one, there is also a range of more specific economic and perhaps organizational influences peculiar to this particular historical juncture that also require taking into account.

Sleep has always represented something of a liminal zone between the realm of economically productive activity (be that production or consumption) and a state of withdrawal from the realm of economic necessity. For the likes of Marx[2] (1939) and Gramsci[3] (1971), for instance, sleep was to be viewed as integral to the successful reproduction of labour, a necessary recuperative process that would allow further surplus value to be exacted from the working subject. On the other hand, as Weber[4] noted, sleep – if deemed to be excessive – was equally decried as antithetical to the spirit of accumulation and asceticism which provided such a powerful impetus to the evolution of modern capitalism. Yet as capitalism has sought to expand its capacity for exploitation it has needed to unearth new sources of value not so much by extending its global reach (which it has already pretty much exhausted) but by delving ever deeper into the everyday, personal components of our daily lives, reducing even the most intimate and personal dimensions of social reproduction – 'the entire realm of life' (Hardt and Negri, 2000: 275) – to an object realm of management and commodification. It is in such terms then that we can perhaps understand in part the attempt to submit sleep to the same level of market discipline that currently affects many other aspects of our everyday lives. Sleep has become something to be negotiated across both consumption and production networks which also implicates the commercial and colonizing exploits of a burgeoning 'sleep industry' (Williams, 2005), alongside the construction of sleep-related images and ideas, discourses and representations, in a variety of media.

Of course, the notion that sleep is now big business is probably something that most of us are already at least intuitively aware of. From traditional pocket sprung beds to mattresses and pillows made out of a range of space-age materials; from complex medical equipment designed to diagnose a myriad of recently defined sleep disorders, including 'shift work sleep disorder' (SWSD), to evermore refined pharmaceuticals developed to either keep you awake or put you to sleep, a vast amount of money is there to be made from sleep. Certainly at the last estimate in 2005 the global pharmaceutical market for diagnosed 'sleep disorders' was estimated to be worth around US$4.3 billion and was forecast to increase 158 per cent to US$11 billion by 2012. Perhaps even more staggering than this is that in the US alone it is reported that between 2000 and 2005, the market value of the wholesale mattress industry rose by 40 per cent to $6.4 billion, while beds that cost up to US$50,000 are being sold to an increasingly sleep-conscious professional-class.

Furthermore, it is often the case that the line between what might be considered to be the legitimate medical use of many of these sleep-oriented technologies and pure lifestyle-based consumption is a fine one to draw. A prime example of this is to be found with the wakefulness-promoting drug *Modafinil*. While originally developed by Cephalon (under the brand name Provigil) for therapeutic purposes in the treatment of narcolepsy, it has subsequently been used by the US military and is now a favourite amongst 24/7 executives and go-getters. As one interviewee in an article in *New Scientist* (Lawton, 2006: 34) commented regarding its illicit use,

> I find I can be very productive at work. I'm more organised and more motivated. And it means I can go out partying on a Friday night and still go skiing early on Saturday morning.

Not that such usage is perhaps all that illicit. Modafinil is easily available over the Internet, and its manufacturers have been criticized by the Federal Drugs

Adminstration (FDA) for misleading promotional material in its direct-to-consumer advertising (DTCA). And while far more effective 'alertness' drugs are currently in the pipeline, when sleep is still required drugs such as *Ambien* (manufactured by Sanofi-Aventis) and its major competitor Lunestra (manufactured by Sepracor) are ready to hand. A new generation of sleeping tablets, meanwhile, are currently in development with the aim of modifying our sleep architecture: the ultimate goal perhaps being the promotion of more efficient forms of sleep (i.e., improved sleep quality) in less time (i.e., reduced sleep quantity).

Until such ambitions are finally realized, however, companies such as *MetroNaps* are ready and able to take up the slack. While perhaps most famous for locating some of their high-tech sleep pods in New York's Empire State Building, *MetroNaps* is an interesting indicator of changing attitudes not only to where we sleep, but also to how we sleep. Designed to create what the company terms a 'semi private acoustical and visual environment', a MetroNaps pod provides sufficient privacy and isolation to allow a limited amount of sleep while, at the same time, proscribing what might be considered to be inappropriate nocturnal activities. Specifically, they have been designed with busy executives and even university students in mind with part of their pitch on their Australian Web site being that it is estimated that 90 per cent of all Australian university students get inadequate sleep and therefore, rather than having them fall asleep in labs and other 'busy common spaces', a better investment would be to provide half a dozen sleep pods. Or alternatively, as they claim on their UK Web site:

> **An Alert Workforce Is an Effective Workforce**
> We have all witnessed it: our colleagues falling asleep at their desks and in meetings, costing your company thousands of pounds in lost productivity.
>
> A mid-day nap has been proven to improve memory, alertness, mood, learning and creativity. Until now few options existed for companies wanting to offer resting facilities. MetroNaps solves the problem of where to nap with the MetroNaps Pod.
>
> Improve your bottom line:
>
> ● Boost workforce productivity.
> ● Improve employee satisfaction.

Thus, while the problem of sleep, be it real or imagined, might be something to be concerned about it is, quite clearly, a manageable one. Providing, of course, we recognize the right products and services.

Managing sleep at work

While the above developments refer largely to macro-level interventions into the economic and socio-cultural spheres, what is also evident is that a similar set of processes are starting to manifest themselves inside the workplace. As we noted earlier, much of the survey work undertaken, especially in the UK, has notably targeted mostly managers regarding their experiences of the effect their work has on their sleep patterns and vice versa. For instance, expanding on some of the figures cited earlier, according to the aforementioned Demos (Leadbeater, 2004) report, 51 per cent of UK managers claim to regularly not get enough sleep while 50 per cent of these also claim to become more irritable and prone to shouting while at work due to tiredness. More generally, around 13 per cent of the overall working population claim to make more mistakes at work as a result of excessive tiredness. Similar results have been publicized in relation to the Capgemini (2005) sponsored *Red Eye Report*, which claimed that around 55 per cent of senior managers who responded to its survey felt that a lack of sleep had led them to make decisions which had had serious repercussions for their business.

One possible solution that appears to have emerged in response to this perceived problem has been to encourage companies to take the sleep needs of all their employees more seriously, providing not only an understanding ear when it comes to a discussion of sleep-related issues, but also concrete polices and, where possible, suitably sleep-friendly facilities. It is within this context that companies such as MetroNaps and their pitch regarding an alert workforce being an effective workforce start to make far more sense, in that it can be seen as part of a broader set of organizational interventions into the usually private sphere of sleep and its associated practices. This has led to a situation whereby sleep, or perhaps more accurately alertness, is portrayed and responded to as yet another source of potential corporate advantage, something which requires managing in the same manner that, say, motivation or diversity might.

It must be admitted, of course, that to a certain degree the notion that the sleep of employees is subject to managerial intervention within the workplace is perhaps too obvious a truism to be worth commenting on. After all, is it not one of a manager's first duties to ensure that his or her charges are not asleep but working, and that when sleep is required it is an activity that is pursued well-away from the workplace? Certainly, according to our own recent survey of senior human resource and personnel managers in the UK, sleep remains largely viewed as an ambiguous and undesired dimension of employee behaviour. While those surveyed professed a concern for employee well-being, and an awareness of its relationship to high-performance, little thought or attention was found to be paid to the sleep needs of employees, or how these might be managed more effectively. Thus, while 97 per cent of respondents considered employee well-being to be an important contributor to effective company performance and 87 per cent believed that all employees perform better after a good night's sleep, only 15 per cent of respondents thought that it was in the company's interest to facilitate short periods of sleeping or napping at work while 72 per cent of respondents thought that sleeping at work projects the wrong image of the company.

Yet while these figures are largely indicative of a predominantly negative orientation towards sleep as an organizational concern per se, there is also evidence that this might well be changing. In an article in the highly influential *Harvard Business Review*, for instance, American sleep scientist, Charles Czeisler

(2006: 58) has urged business leaders to establish clear policies in relation to the management of the sleep needs of employees, arguing that it is not only an issue of social responsibility, but perhaps more tellingly, that 'a good sleep policy is smart business strategy. People think they are saving time and being more productive by not sleeping, but in fact they are cutting their productivity drastically'. Such academic evocations are paralleled not only in the activities of companies such as MetroNaps, however, but also by consultancies such as William and Camille Anthony's US-based *Napping Company*. Claiming to bring 'the science of napping to the workers and the workplace', their self-professed 'evidence based approach' exhorts managers and workers alike to realize simple truths such as 'napping is the no cost, no sweat way to improve worker performance', and 'napping can be good for you and good for your company' (Anthony and Anthony, 2005: 210).[5] In the UK, similar ventures such as the consultancy *Sleep Unlimited*, while perhaps not as successful as their US counterparts, suggest the start of a similar shift in thinking on these issues, especially when related to questions of well-being at work and the work-life balance. Indeed, in relation to this latter concern, they have recently expanded their consultancy services to include families with young children, a group traditionally vulnerable to sleep disturbances and its negative consequences for work and personal well-being.

Despite the obvious cynicism that ventures such as this might arouse, there is no doubt that the idea of napping, or indeed sleeping at work, is one that is starting to find sympathetic ears. Perhaps one of the most unlikely sources of support was the East of England Development Agency who, in 2004, suggested that introducing dedicated sleeping areas and beds might increase creativity among employees (if not indeed pro-creativity). Indeed, it is something that is starting to catch on amongst a number of organizations in the UK, especially those involving what have been described as 'extreme jobs' (Hewlett and Luce, 2006) such as finance, law and areas of public relations. In transport and logistics, we now see the majority of European airlines, including British Airways, allowing pilots to take naps on long haul flights, while even less glamorous companies such as *Feel Good Drinks* are reported to have installed a rollup bed in the corner of one of their meeting rooms for staff to use in order to bolster creative napping (Katbamna, 2006).

The question persists, of course, as to what extent we should welcome such organizational interventions into the sleeping patterns and practices of employees, or conversely, to what extent should we view them as essentially colonizing activities, potentially serving to even further undermine the socially negotiated and/or intimately ordered quality of sleep? Well, there are occasions, perhaps associated with particular industries, when a pro-active managerial orientation towards sleep should not only be welcomed but applauded. A report by the Centre for Sleep Research at the University of Southern Australia (Baker and Ferguson, 2004), for example, set out comprehensive guidelines for the Australian mineral extraction industry in relation to minimizing accidents and fatalities related to fatigue and the consequences of poor quality sleep more generally. Certainly, it might be hoped that considering the hazardous working conditions such an industry might present, that such guidelines would not only be supported by all concerned, but equally, would be adhered to as a moral if not a statutory responsibility.

Yet while we might indeed welcome a genuine concern with the consequences of a poor or disturbed sleep regime for employees working in hazardous industries, particularly when questions of safety are at stake, we should perhaps introduce a note of caution in relation to a more widespread managerial interest in the topic. After all, for companies such as the aforementioned *Feel Good Drinks*, or any other organization for whom the idea that providing sleeping facilities at work might boost creativity or output, then the question of whether or not such interventions represent not only an intensification of managerial control, but furthermore a potentially illegitimate expansion of that control clearly requires asking.

Certainly, one instance of that question being asked is to be found in a paper by Baxter and Kroll-Smith (2005) who question the potential consequences of what they see as the blurring of previous distinctions between public and private space/time implicated in the institutional promotion of workplace napping. Drawing on a range of examples of this practice in the US, they chart the rise of the workplace nap in conjunction with the ever-greater demands of a flexible economy and a competitive marketplace. While they outline a mixture of informal and more formalized napping polices and practices, one thing that is abundantly clear is the link made between the examples they provide and the pursuit of increased productivity and employee commitment. Furthermore, where more formal arrangements are in place, the regulatory and indeed highly disciplined nature of these are extremely high. Take, for instance, *Nova Chemicals* where there exists a 'Controlled Alertness Recovery Programme' that, while allowing employees to choose their own napping times, operates, as Baxter and Kroll-Smith (2005: 46) observe, a policy verging on the micromanagement of employees sleeping practice:

> The program grants employee 10 minutes to find and brief a replacement and prepare for the nap, 20 minutes to nap and 15 minutes after the nap as an alertness recovery period. The purpose of this alertness recovery period is 'to offer a strategy of improving alertness and reducing the risk of fatigue in a safe and controlled environment'.

What we are observing here is the introduction of an organizational logic by which the generally private, though socially negotiated process and practices of sleep are reconstructed as a quantified and regulated adjunct to the more formal labour process. Sleep is itself a source of value, the exploitation of which requires an erosion of the distinction between what Zerubavel (1981) has referred to as *gross* and *net* time,[6] as well as the dissolution between domestic and occupational space. A process which, as Baxter and Kroll-Smith (2005: 51) go on to note, is less about the promotion of balance and care, but rather the expression of a systematic attempt to 'increase mental acuity and amplify efficiency, [while normalizing] a formerly covert practice into rule-governed structures of organizations'.

Sleep and everyday (night) lifestyles

There can be little doubt that the kinds of practices we have encountered above represent a potentially potent set of interventions into the ways in which sleep is both conceptualized and practised in people's everyday/night lives. From the commodification of sleep through the ever-expanding market in sleep-related paraphernalia to the active management of sleeping within the workplace, the inevitable consequence is to fundamentally reconstruct sleep as a problem of organization – be it self-organization or workplace organization. Sleep becomes intrinsically wedded to the requirements of a system's rationality or logos, one that displaces the notion of sleep as a negotiated outcome of both cultural and intersubjective relations and, instead, grounds it firmly in the reproduction of prevalent economic relations and the organizational imperatives that derive from them.

This gradual erosion of distinctions between home and work, and negotiated and organized spheres of activity cannot, of course, be solely identified with the realm of sleep and its associated practices. As has been noted elsewhere (Nippert-Eng, 1995; Hochschild, 1997), this has been a growing and disturbingly observable phenomenon for some time now. Nevertheless, it would seem to us that to witness such a process extending itself to the realm of sleep is a development that still evokes a concerned response. Nor is this a concern that should be confined purely to observing the practices of large organizations such as drug companies, or the activities of companies in relation to their immediate workforces. Beyond the macro and meso, there is another microlevel of activity; one equally concerned with the furtherance of a discursive construction of sleep as both a problem and a resource and which also draws liberally on the language and rationality of management in order to establish a legitimacy it might otherwise find difficult to muster.

As we have already suggested, the idea that the achievement of healthy, or more accurately, productive sleep is an increasingly problematic aspiration for the populations of advanced Western economies – one that 'calls for *ever renewed vigilance*' (Williams, 2007: 152, original emphasis) – is receiving ever-increasing publicity. This, in turn, has resulted in a situation whereby in certain quarters anything other than the experience of such an idealized and potentially highly reified sleeping pattern is treated as indicative of another, and often far more serious pathology; one that requires specialist, medical or material intervention. Indeed, as one critical commentator in the US (cited in Singer, 2007: 9) recently observed,

> Now when people can't sleep for a couple of nights, they think they are part of a national sleep epidemic and there should be something to fix it.

It would be amiss, however, to assume that having potentially created a sleep crisis the sleep-industry, if we might call it that, is only concerned with remedying its consequences post hoc. For as we have suggested above, a more microintervention, one aligned to a discursive ideal of immediate and often preventative self-management has also started to make its presence felt, particularly through the realm of the self-help text and the ever-ubiquitous lifestyle industry of which they are a component part.

While examples of such discursive interventions abound, what are perhaps of most interest to us here are those that clearly reflect the formal and largely quantitatively and performatively orientated imperatives of organizational management. So, for instance, we have *Cosmopolitan* magazine (May 2007) providing us with the '9 Steps to Better Sleep' which includes, amongst other things, arriving at work 20 minutes early so as to undertake the day's internet surfing, scheduling 20 minutes a day in which to worry and closing the day on an orgasm. Similar highly directive articles also appear in such places as *Men's Health* ('Get Good Sleep' – October 2006, '9 Steps to Better Sleep' – January 2007, 'Easy Shut-Eye' – February 2007), and even on the BBC's own Web pages, dedicated to the discussion of all things sleep-related.[7]

Similarly, as the presence of the expert culture that increasingly seems to dominate every aspect of our daily lives persists, sleep has also become the domain of those authors whose lifestyle texts seek to influence not only our ideals but also our physical actions and attributes. From audio books such as *5 Steps to Better Sleep* (Crowe, 2006) which combines music and dialogue in order to help 'identify improvements that can be made to everyday habits', to the somewhat self-evidently entitled *60 Second Sleep-Ease: Quick Tips for Getting a Good Night's Rest* (Currie and Wilson, 2002) or Mednick and Ehrman's (2007) more recent *Take a Nap! Change Your Life*, sleep is promoted not only as a physical, but also an economic and lifestyle good as well. To manage one's sleep is presented as an opportunity to maximize one's lifestyle opportunities, economically, culturally and emotionally.

For Megan Brown (2004) – drawing on particular examples of the work of Foucault (1997) and Deleuze (1995) – such material does indeed threaten what she considers to be an overwhelming example of an increasingly disciplinary society; one that has permitted an extension of managerial control over the behaviours of individuals well beyond the more legitimate confines of the workplace. In particular, she clearly identifies the link between the medicalization of sleep and its increasing vulnerability to the discursive colonization of a managerial rationality:

> There is a parallel between increased medicalization of the human body and enhanced possibilities for constant management of workers. Discourses of self-help, medicine and corporate management all depend, in part, upon appeals to individual self-improvement; people are constantly compelled to monitor and micromanage every possible aspect of their lives. (Brown, 2004: 174)

It is not only a colonization of the body, be it dormant or awake, as an object of managerial self-intervention that appears to be at stake here, however. There is also the question of the status of sleep itself as a spatial and temporally negotiated practice. One that, by virtue of its previously identified liminality, embodies a potential to actively resist the demands of economic performativity and the economies of the production/consumption nexus (witness, for instance, the practice of staging a 'sleep in'). It is not, therefore, purely a question of the extent to which 'people's daily habits be made to fit – and benefit – corporate practices and values' (Brown, 2004: 187), but equally it is one of the political and even ontological status of sleep.

The sleeper awakes – Concluding thoughts

More and more, work enlists all good conscience on its side; the desire for joy already calls itself 'a need to recuperate' and is beginning to be ashamed of itself. (Nietzsche, 1974: 259–260)

The sleepless are on call at any hour, unresistingly ready for anything, alert and unconscious at once. (Adorno, 1974: 38)

In the light of the closing comments of the previous section, it is perhaps interesting to consider one of H. G. Wells's (2005) lesser known dystopian novels of the early twentieth century *The Sleeper Awakes* [1910].[8] In it, a nineteenth-century character, Graham, awakens to find himself at the end of a 200-year sleep during which, in large part due to his own inactivity, he has amassed enough property and wealth to make himself the owner of the world. Thus, while asleep, Graham has been strangely somnambulant, dormant yet active, both external to the animated sphere of value production, yet equally integral to its onward momentum. For us, what this story highlights is the way in which we are all becoming, to a lesser or greater extent, contemporary Grahams. That is, our sleep, which we continue in part to enjoy as a dormant release from the pursuit of economic productivity, is becoming transformed into yet another adjunct of both the relentless cycle of production and consumption, as well as the reproduction of evermore commercially dependent subjectivities.

Now in part this can be understood simply as an extension of the process of commodification which has been a component element of capitalism's evolution from its very birth. Thus sleep, and the pursuit of an idealized notion of sleep, is now something that can simply be purchased in the marketplace. Be it through pharmaceuticals or other medical interventions, sleep technologies such as mattresses, pillows or sleepwear, or the expert advice of those authors and experts who offer ten ways to get a good night's rest; healthy, restful and equally productive sleep is presented as something that we should have not only a right to expect, but also to achieve – assuming of course we can afford to do so.

Yet it is not just sleep as a commodity that appears to be an issue here, it is sleep as a source of value in its own right. That is, from both the corporate and self-management perspectives on sleep, sleep is increasingly envisaged as something that can be exploited in its own terms, valorized as a source of both organizational and individual competitive advantage. Managed and organized properly, sleep can be understood as a form of embodied capital, one that can be cashed in for increased energy, alertness and creativity, all of which are deemed highly desirable in an increasingly intensive and flexible economy. None of this is to suggest that sleep has, or indeed could be, ever fully rationalized. There remains and most likely always will, a stigma and a joy attached to sleep that will never fully allow it to become simply another site of managerial hegemony; sleep will ultimately remain 'excessive', that is, beyond the bounds of total rationalization. Such an observation not withstanding, however, there are clear indications that human sleep patterns and behaviours are not only currently being constructed as an issue of concern and interventions across a range of media, but that the nature of these interventions are deeply organizational in tenor, and instrumental in objective.

In conclusion then, what might we want to say about sleep, organization and the management of everyday life? Certainly, there is sufficient evidence to suggest that sleep is increasingly being viewed as both an organizational resource and a form of individual capital, and it is the connections between its management at a macro-, meso- and microlevel that has been our primary concern here. This is a concern that has led us to argue that sleep, far from being a mere biological process that takes place beyond the bounds of organization, is very much a negotiated social order, a contested site on which the struggle for colonization is played out, and on which managerialism as a mediating social and cultural force can increasingly be discerned.

Notes

1. This accident was widely believed to be the outcome of the inattentive actions of a driver (Gary Hart) who had reportedly spent the previous evening talking throughout the night by telephone to a woman he had met via an internet dating agency. He was then thought to have fallen asleep at the wheel, driving off the M62 motorway, and onto a section of the East Coast Main railway line.
2. ' ... the working-day has a maximum limit. It cannot be prolonged beyond a certain point. This maximum limit is conditioned by two things. First, by the physical bounds of labour-power. Within the 24 hours of the natural day a man can expend only a definite quantity of his vital force. A horse, in like manner, can only work from day to day, 8 hours. During part of the day this force must rest, sleep' (Marx, 1939: 215).
3. 'The employee who goes to work after a night of "excess" is no good for his work. The exaltation of passion cannot be reconciled with the timed movements of productive motions connected with the most perfected automatism' (Gramsci, 1971: 292).
4. 'Waste of time is thus the first and in principle the deadliest of sins. The span of human life is infinitely short and precious to make sure of one's own election. Loss of time through sociability, idle talk, luxury, even more sleep than is necessary for health....is worthy of absolute moral condemnation. ...' (Weber, 2001: 104).

5. If such 'evidence-based' rhetoric should fall short of their desired goals there is, of course, the range of T-shirts, bookmarks and even the national 'Workplace Napping Day' sponsored, not unsurprisingly, by the Napping Company, to help them drive the point home.
6. The former refers to what we might term private time – that concerned with leisure and everyday living. The latter, however, refers to the quantified time of productive labour – that which is prescribed, regulated and monitored.
7. http://www.bbc.co.uk/science/humanbody/sleep/articles/advicetips.html
8. Though it is better known in its movie guise as Woody Allen's (1973) comedy adaptation *Sleeper*.

References

Adorno, T. (1974) *Minima Moralia: Reflections from Damaged Life* (Trans. E. F. N. Jephcott). London: NLB.

Åkerstedt, T., Fredlund, P., Gillberg, M. and Jansson, B. (2002) 'A Prospective Study of Fatal Occupation Accidents – Relationship to Sleeping Difficulties and Occupational Factors', *Journal of Sleep Research* 11: 69–71.

Anthony, C. and Anthony, W. (2005) 'The Napping Company: Bringing Science to the Workplace', *Industrial Health* 45: 209–212.

BBC News Online (2007) 'Why Should We Get Eight Hours Sleep?' http://news.bbc.co.uk/1/hi/magazine/6546209.stm

Baker, A. and Ferguson, S. (2004) *Work Design, Fatigue and Sleep: A Resource Document fort the Minerals Industry.* Minerals Council for Australia.

Baxter, V. and Kroll-Smith, B. (2005) 'Normalizing the Workplace Nap: Blurring the Boundaries between Public and Private Space and Time', *Current Sociology* 53(1): 33–55.

Benjamin, W. (1999 [1969]) *Illuminations.* London: Pimlico.

Boden, S., Williams, S. J., Seale, C., Lowe, P. and Steinberg, D. L. (2008) 'The Social Construction of Sleep and Work in the British Print News Media', *Sociology* 42(3): 541–558.

Brown, M. (2004) 'Taking Care of Business: Self-Help and Sleep Medicine in American Corporate Culture', *Journal of Medical Humanities* 25(3): 173–187.

Capgemini (2005) *Capgemini Red Eye Report: Understanding What Keeps UK Business Leaders Awake.* London: Capgemini Press Office.

Cohen, S. (1972) *Folk Devils and Moral Panics.* London: MacGibbon and Kee.

Crowe, J. (2006) *5 Steps to Better Sleep* (Audio CD). London: Pentangeli Publishing.

Currie, S. and Wilson, K. (2002) *60 Second Sleep-Ease: Quick Tips for Getting a Good Night's Rest.* Far Hills, NJ: New Horizon Press.

Czeisler, C. (2006) 'Sleep Deficit: The Performance Killer', *Harvard Business Review.* 84(October): 53–59.

Deleuze, G. (1995) *Negotiations: 1972–1990.* New York, NY: Columbia University Press.

Dement, W. (1998) *The Promise of Sleep.* New York: Delacorte Press.

Douglas, M. (1966) *Purity and Danger: An Analysis of Concepts of Pollution and Taboo.* London: Routledge.

Elias, N. (1978 [1939]) *The Civilising Process: The History of Manners Vol. 1*. Oxford: Blackwell.

Finger, A. (2006) 'Disciplining the Dormant Body: Sleep, Religion and Work Ethics', paper presented to the 6th ESRC *Sleep and Society* Seminar (Sleep, Worktime and Work Ethics), 14 March, University of Warwick.

Foucault, M. (1979 [1975]) *Discipline and Punish: The Birth of the Prison*. London: Penguin.

Foucault, M. (1997) 'Technologies of the Self', in P. Rabinow (ed.) *Ethics: Subjectivity and Truth*. New York, NY: New Press.

Giddens, A. (1991) *The Consequences of Modernity*. Cambridge: Polity.

Gramsci, A. (1971) 'Americanism and Fordism', in Q. Hoare and G. Nowell-Smith (eds) *Selections from the Prison Notebooks of Antonio Gramsci*. London: Lawrence and Wishart, pp. 277–318.

Habermas, J. (1984) *The Theory of Communicative Action, Vol. 1: Reason and Rationalization of Society* (Trans. T. McCarthy). Cambridge: Polity.

Habermas, J. (1987) *The Theory of Communicative Action, Vol. 2: The Critique of Functionalist Reason* (Trans. T. McCarthy). Cambridge: Polity.

Hardt, M. and Negri, A. (2000) *Empire*. Cambridge, MA: Harvard University Press.

Hewlett, S. and Luce, C. (2006) 'Extreme Jobs: The Dangerous Allure of the 70-Hour Week', *Harvard Business Review* 84(December): 49–59.

Hislop, J. and Arber, S. (2003) 'Sleepers Wake! The Gendered Nature of Sleep Disruption among Mid-Life Women', *Sociology* 37(4): 695–711.

Hislop, J. and Arber, S. (2004) 'Understanding Women's Sleep Management: Beyond Medicalization-Healthicization: A Response to Simon Williams', *Sociology of Health and Illness* 26(4): 460–463.

Hislop, J. and Arber, S. (2006) 'Sleep, Gender and Ageing: Changing Relational and Institutional Constraints from Mid-to-Later Life', in T. Calasanti and K. Slevin (eds) *Age Matters: Realigning Feminist Thinking*. Abingdon: Routledge.

Hochschild, A. R. (1997) *The Time Bind: When Work Becomes Home and Home Becomes Work*. New York, NY: Metropolitan Books.

Horne, J. (2006) *Sleepfaring: A Journey through the Science of Sleep*. Cambridge: Cambridge University Press.

Katbamna, M. (2006) 'Sleeping on the Job', *The Guardian Saturday Work Supplement*, 18 March, p. 5.

Kristeva, J. (1982) *Powers of Horror: An Essay on Abjection* (Trans. L. S. Roudiez). New York, NY: Columbia UP.

Lawton, G. (2006) 'Get Up and Go', *New Scientist* 189(2539): 34–38.

Leadbeater, C. (2004) *Dream On: Sleep in the 24/7 Society*. London: Demos.

Marcuse, H. (1972 [1955]) *Eros and Civilisation: Philosophical Inquiry into Freud*. London: Abacus.

Marx, K. (1939 [1867]) *Capital Volume 1: A Critical Analysis of Capitalist Production*. New York, NY: International Publishers.

Meadows, R. (2005) 'The Negotiated Night: An Embodied Conceptual Framework for the Sociological Study of Sleep', *The Sociological Review* 53(2): 240–254.

Mednick, S. C. and Ehrman, M. (2007) *Take a Nap! Change Your Life*. New York, NY: Workman.

National Sleep Foundation (2005) *Sleep in America Poll: Summary of Findings*. Washington DC: National Sleep Foundation.

Nietzsche, F. (1974) *The Gay Science*. New York, NY: Vintage.

Nippert-Eng, C. E. (1995) *Home and Work: Negotiating Boundaries through Everyday Life*. London: University of Chicago Press.

Singer, N. (2007) 'Hey, Sleepy, Want to Buy a Good Nap?', *New York Times*, 1 February: 8–9.

Steger, B. (2003) 'Getting Away with Sleep – Social and Cultural Aspects of Dozing in Parliament', *Social Science Japan Journal* 6(2): 181–197.

Steger, B. (2006) 'Getting Smart by Napping in Class – Social and Cultural Aspects of Sleeping in the Japanese Class-Room', paper presented to the 6th ESRC *Sleep and Society* Seminar (Sleep, Worktime and Work Ethics), 14 March, University of Warwick.

Summers-Bremner, E. (2007) *Insomina: A Cultural History*. London: Reaktion Books.

Taylor, B. (1993) 'Unconsciousness and Society: The Sociology of Sleep', *International Journal of Politics and Culture* 6: 463–471.

Weber, M. (2001 [1904]) *The Protestant Ethic and the Spirit of Capitalism*. London: Unwin.

Wells, H. G. (2005 [1910]) *The Sleeper Awakes*. Harmondsworth: Penguin.

Williams, S. (2005) *Sleep and Society: Sociological Ventures into the (Un)Known*. Abingdon: Routledge.

Williams, S. (2007) 'The Social Etiquette of Sleep: Some Sociological Reflections and Observations', *Sociology* 41(2): 313–328.

Williams, S. and Bendelow, G. (1998) *The Lived Body: Sociological Themes, Embodied Issues*. Abingdon: Routledge.

Zerubavel, E. (1981) *Hidden Rhythms: Schedules and Calendars in Social Life*. Chicago, IL: University of Chicago Press.

Part **2**

Management and everyday domesticity

Chapter 6

Through the crack in the time bind

From market management to family management   *Arlie Hochschild*

Introduction

How workers handle the lack of time affects how open they are to market understandings of life at home. Some workers passively submit to the time bind (the 'endurer') while others actively resist it (the 'resisters'). Still others actively accept the time bind (the 'deferrer,' the 'busy bee,' the 'delegator') and so welcome any tips on office efficiency that might apply to the home. 'Family 360,' a family consulting service, illustrates how a professional service can operationalize at home metaphors, idioms, and concepts drawn from the market world. Constant busyness is, I suggest, the current 'opiate of the masses,' which can block from view the cultural fissures through which market instrumentality and emotional detachment sometimes seep into life at home.

The December 2002 issue of the *New York Times Magazine* was devoted to 99 of the year's most innovative ideas in America. One of these ideas was a new service called 'Family 360.' Designed by a management-consulting firm called LeaderWorks based in Monument, Colorado, the program offers 'personalized family assessments' to executives at such corporations as General Motors, Honeywell, and Dupont. Based on 'Management 360,' a widely used program for evaluating executives at the workplace. For a thousand-dollar fee, Family 360 offers to evaluate a client's performance as parent and spouse at home.[1] Remarkably, along with the idea of hyper-fuel-efficient cars and genetically engineered featherless chickens, Family 360 is presented to the reader as an idea that seems unusual today but could seem normal tomorrow. The culture of market management can become, it hints, part of the culture at home.

In Karl Polyani's *The Great Transformation: The Political and Economic Origins of Our Time* (1944), he argues that we have moved from being a large society in which there were islands of market life to a large market in which there are islands of social life. In this chapter, I briefly describe social trends which increase the sphere of the marketplace, and argue that the family is itself one such market-surrounded society. I take Family 360 as an example of how market culture challenges – even as it offers to improve – family culture. The degree to which a market culture gains acceptance at home depends, I further argue, on the fit between market culture and an employee's strategy for managing time – that is, hers temporal strategy. The temporal strategies of the busy bee and the deferrer – strategies preferred by those at the top of the corporate ladder serve, I suggest, as market culture's first port of entry into the home. To put it differently, market culture slips into the family through the crack in the 'time bind' at the top.

First, what do we mean by market culture? There are many expressions of market culture but one of the most intriguing recent expressions is found in the service described above. How does such a service work? In a subsection of an essay entitled 'The Year in Ideas,' journalist Paul Tough (2002: 80–82) describes,

> The Family 360 process starts with the executive's spouse, children and in some cases his parents and siblings filling out a detailed questionnaire in which they evaluate the subject both quantitatively – scoring him from 1 to 7 on, say, how well he 'helps create enjoyable family traditions' and 'uses a kind voice when speaking' – and qualitatively listing 'three to five positive attributes' and 'two things you want this person to do less.' The data are then analyzed by LeaderWorks, and the results are sent to the executive in a 'growth summary' report that presents his family's concerns in the form of bar graphs and pie charts and identifies 'focus areas' for such things as 'paying special attention to personal feelings,' and 'solving problems without getting angry.'

The consultants interview the worker's spouse, children, other relatives, and people who see him or her from every vantage point – hence the term, '360.' Then LeaderWorks personnel meet with the family to create a 'Development Plan to Strengthen Family Relationships.' The company also provides, as Tough (2002: 81–82) notes,

> An investment guide with hundreds of specific actions that let you connect with your family *as efficiently as possible:* buy a speakerphone for the home so you can join in on family game night when you're on the road; go for a walk with your child every day, even if it's only to the end of the driveway; create 'communication opportunities' while doing the dishes with your spouse or waiting in line with your child at the store. [italics added]

The premise behind this service is that the executive can be as efficient at home as he or she is at work, with no loss – indeed, with a gain – to his or her family life. Indeed, as the Internet description for Family 360 notes, 'The Family 360 Process is a way to assess how you are doing with the precious time you have to build and strengthen your important personal relations. The Process can help you identify the "high leverage activities" that will mean the most to your important relationships.' In a Web-based promise of a free, quick, report on work-life's best practices, the applicant is asked to answer such questions as, 'if you have children, what specific actions have you taken to teach values, encourage contribution or create memories?' The process, the designers promise, is 'hard hitting' while also 'user friendly,' and can be augmented by other offerings such as the 'Family and Life Success Services.'

The client's scores are totaled up and the evaluators appraise the impact of those scores on the client's desired 'individual legacy' and 'family legacy.' As is done in the business world, the executive can then compare his or her 'person practices' with those of 'other busy people' in order to see if he or she is doing better or worse than they are.

To the newcomer, this service would seem like an unusual, even humorous, idea. Why would a person use it? The consultants offer two reasons. The first is to improve the busy executive's performance as a father, and the second is to make him a better employee – in his role as supervisor of working parents. As the Family 360 Web-page description says, 'Today's tough organization climate demands the most from employees, including ever increasing amounts of their time, energy and commitment.' The idea is to be a good time-bind dad and a good boss to time-bind employees. In the words of a Honeywell Executive quoted in the Family 360 Internet description,

> Being a leader requires a number of leader behaviors, one of which is to manage the entire person that works for you. It's foolish to believe that a person who is unfulfilled in their personal life will be able to turn it off like a toggle switch when they walk in the doors of the company. So, to the degree that you can add fulfillment to the whole life (sic) you're helping them add value to their employer.[2]

Durkheim on the contradictions of 'Family 360'

Family 360 suggests a remarkable contradiction. On one hand, the service appeals to the executive's desire to be an active, participatory dad and this is a new ideal for highly placed businessmen in America. Men, the idea is, should now share with women the task of childrearing (an idea supported by the culture, and welcomed by many women). On the other hand, Family 360 invites men to share childrearing in the manner of the market. Men are going home, so to speak, only to bring the marketplace with them. As Emile Durkheim might note, the introduction of Family 360 into the home would appear to help a father reconnect with his neglected family, and so reaffirm the moral sphere of the family. But the attitude of bureaucratic scientism, rational calculation, and emotional detachment a client is asked to take toward his most intimate bonds seems to undermine the moral sphere of the family. The ends affirm the family.

The means affirm the marketplace. And the means can subvert the ends. Indeed, as John Dewey has cautioned, any ends is only as good as the means used for achieving it.

To put it in other terms, the regime of justification, as Boltanski and Thévenot (1991) theorize, points to the solidarity of the home, but all of the rest – the rules about what to do, how to see, how to experience time and relationship, the *habitus* in Bourdieu's terms – points to the conduct – and solidarity – of business.

So let us take a closer look at the premises of Family 360. First, while the stated goal of the program's sessions is to improve the emotional bonds between the client and his family, the professional advice is aimed, not at what the man feels but what he does. The program evaluates what it calls 'person practices' and advocates what are termed 'high leverage activities.' Behaviors, in turn, are quantified, lending to them an aura of objectivity and science. What becomes most relevant is the amount of a behavior, not the quality of it. A client's score is measured against that of others, so he can see how the competition is doing. Underneath his 'regime of justification' as Boltanski and Thévenot (1991) call it, the executive's relational language remains the language of the market.

To the extent that the program addresses the feelings of the client toward his family, it treats them instrumentally, and calls on the client to do the same. A father is not asked to rethink his relationship with his son, but – as if this were possible – to reach inside the son's head and 'create memory.'

In the same spirit, through his fatherly good works, the client is asked to conceptualize a 'personal legacy' on the model of a personal portfolio. Finally, this service is offered as a 'starter' to be followed by a series of other paid services, proposing, in effect, the idea of the perpetually monitored family, as a means toward the goal of 'adding value' to family life even as through various stages of production, one adds value to a product. If the male executive who signs up for Family 360 is giving more attention to relations with his wife, children, and parents, he is also invited to think of them in market terms.

Still, it is possible and even likely that Family 360 helps fathers pay attention to their families, if only because it borrows from work the sense of seriousness and urgency they associate with work. It may enable workaholic dads to snap out of their workaholism by speaking to them, so to speak, in 'workahol-ese.'

So why does the rhetoric of this program strike us as incongruous? After all, as Christopher Lasch has noted, the servicing of the family is hardly new.[3] A growing number of services – from psychotherapists, social workers, and work-life specialists to radio and television advice-givers – offer to improve life at home. What may strike us as odd is Family 360's language, metaphors, way of thinking.

In order to develop, capitalism depended – Emile Durkheim noted – on pre-contractual moral bonds of trust and solidarity born of a pre-market moral sphere. But once established, capitalism killed them off. 'If,' Durkheim writes, 'in the task that occupies almost all our time we follow no other rules than that of our well-understood interest, how can we learn to depend upon disinterestedness, on self-forgetfulness, or sacrifice?'[4] In light of this key insight, Durkheim might note that the idea behind Family 360 is to help fathers attain their goal of achieving a happy family *without* sacrificing their time.

In short, Family 360 challenges the moral terms by which the family or community understands itself. Despite its stated goal of improving family life, the rhetoric and practices of Family 360 propose a market way of experiencing personal relationships and time. The client and his family are now prepared to live in a totally market world.

Indeed, the application of market terms to family relations implies that the cultural membrane between the two worlds has grown thin. If we can quantify performance at home the same way we quantify performance at work, if we think about our relationships with other people in the same terms, we take a bow to the idea that the family is a branch office to which the special niche of 'relationships' has been subcontracted.

A market worldview is not limited to certain workplaces and families. In the developed world, and especially in the United States, it has become the main worldview. It is the argument of this chapter, then, that as Karl Polyani points out in *The Great Transformation*, we have moved from a world in which the market was inside society to a world in which society is a subset of the market. In some basic sense, modern life *is* market life. Plants, animals, water, gestational motherhood, human organs, nannies' love for the children they tend, bar mitzvah animators who add zest to a party – these are all for sale. As the market has expanded, the sphere of non-commercial life has contracted.

The market is a structure, of course, with a monetary system, a stock exchange, and commercial laws which validate contracts. But the market is also a *culture*. As Harvey Cox (2001) suggests, in the wider society, market culture has replaced religion. If, in the Middle Ages, the church provided people with a basic orientation to life, today the multinational corporation, with its mission statements, its promise of mastery over the vicissitudes of life, and its global power, provides that orientation. The cathedrals of capitalism dominate our cities. Advertising dominates the radio, television, and increasingly the Internet.

Paradoxically the most secular of systems (capitalism) organized around the most profane activity (buying and selling) comes to feel highly sacred. It calls for sacrifice, through long hours of work, and offers its blessings – through commodities. So what began as a means to an end – capitalism as the means, good living as the end – has become an end in itself. It is a case of mission drift writ large. As its promoters portray it, capitalism is a system *in the service of* family and community life. But taken as a religion, the market seeks out ports of entry in various parts of social life. It becomes a dominant discourse. It offers a way of describing reality that feels 'right.' Indeed, like older religions, capitalism partly creates the anxieties to which it also poses itself as a necessary answer. Like the fire and brimstone sermon that condemns 'man the lowly sinner' and then offers redemption through the church, so the market defines the unemployed and poor as unworthy slackers and offers work and wealth as a form of salvation.

The embrace of market culture as a religion suggests the degree to which people feel helplessly dependent on and grateful toward it. But market culture itself is actually a collection of at least four clusters of values – scientism (and its attendant value of quantification, and objective methods of inquiry), bureaucratic standardization (and its attendant premium of objectivity and impersonality), market competition (and an imagery of dog-eat-dog), and commercialism (and its focus on buying, renting and selling). When hitched to any combination of these clusters, or all of them together, any custom or idea can be said to be 'important' or 'legitimate.'

So far Family 360 is a new service, perceived by a prominent source as an idea that might catch on. It has not yet entered the American mainstream. But there were small signs of this mentality in some of the interviews I conducted of employees in a Fortune 500 company for my book, *The Time Bind*, especially among pressured high-level managers. When I asked one hard-driving, ten-hour-a-day executive whether or not he regretted not having more time with his three daughters as they were growing up, he hesitated, and then said, 'Put it this way, I'm pleased with how my kids *have turned out*' (Hochschild, 1997: 67). He spoke of his daughters lovingly, and fondly, but in a sense he also mainly spoke of them as a result – a bottom line.

More generally, Americans commonly use the commercial element of market culture to describe personal relations. Americans might say, 'I don't want to mortgage our relationship.' Or 'If I keep going out with George, I face too many opportunity costs.' Or 'my mother-in-law is a liability.' As George Lakoff and Mark Johnson (1980) note, the metaphor we apply to an experience determines how we see and feel about it. Metaphors guide feelings and feelings guide metaphors.

Closely linked to a market way of seeing human relations is a market way of seeing time. In the marketplace, time is money, and money is a prime 'good.' In the humorous 1950s film, *Cheaper by the Dozen*, a father modeled on the efficiency-minded Frank Gilbreth raises a large brood of children efficiently, the children doing things in batches, and forming assembly lines. Indeed, some spillover of the cult of efficiency from office to home has surely existed for at least as long as industrialism split the realm of work from home. But Family 360 represents a further development of this trend. *Cheaper by the Dozen* was, after all, humorous, and the father devoted long hours to raising his children, and supervised them continually in the manner of a factory manager. In Family 360, the executive is advised in serious tones to squeeze fatherhood into his busy schedule in the same manner.

Such cultural moves often begin at the top of the social ladder, to be emulated later by those lower down, according to the so-called trickle-down effect. And many innovations that gain acceptance into the culture begin as someone's idea for a solution to some problem. There is, as Bourdieu has noted, often a common sense reason that certain ideas or ways of doing things catch on. In this case, we might say that a cult of efficiency catches on as a good way to do things because working parents face practical demands at work, enjoy few social supports, and live in a culture of rush.[5]

Social trends and market culture

Several trends seem to be strengthening the grip of the marketplace over family life. While the effect is unintended, the result influences the mix of prevailing images and practices of parenting in the culture. The first trend is the movement of women into the market. This trend has moved us in the direction of gender equality, and many have argued that women have, to some extent, 'humanized' the workforce. But given the power arrangements in the market world, I would argue that women, like other 'immigrant groups,' have assimilated to the dominant – and in this case male and marketized – norms more than men have been humanized by the newcomers.

Second, for all those in the workforce the workday has, in recent years, begun to lengthen. This is partly due, Schor (1992) argues, to the declining power of labor unions that throughout the nineteenth century 'pushed back the line' on work hours. (With the recent erosion of state support for the non-working, the workplace has also become more essential to those without support.)

Parallel to the growing importance of the culture of work is the growing importance of shopping. The main vehicle for consumerism has been television, which Americans have, over the last 50 years, watched for ever-lengthening periods of time. With 15–18 minutes of every TV hour devoted to advertising, and the average American watching 4 hours a day, television has indeed become an important conveyor belt to the mall. Television has played a role not simply by popularizing the idea of buying things, but – through such shows as Joe Millionaire, Bachelor, Bachelorette, and Hot Date – by applying a commercial paradigm to intimate relationships. (The sexes are portrayed as shopping for a mate, with monetary incentives attached.)

To sum up, the move of women into the workforce, the longer hours of work, and the exposure to commercial culture through television unwittingly combine with the weakening family and sense of local community to increase the dominance of market culture. No one person quite intends this, but the consequences are real and pose an important challenge. The more of our lives we work and spend, the more we feel that is all there is to life. The more working and spending become 'all there is to life,' the more market culture presents itself as the filter through which to see.

Temporal strategies as ports of entry for market culture

All of this has important implications for how we experience time. Most obviously, market life encroaches on non-market life and it does this in various ways.

In my interviews with 130 employees and others associated with the company I have called Amerco (the Fortune 500 Company I studied for *The Time Bind*), I discovered several temporal strategies employees used to deal with overwork.[6]

Each temporal strategy determined the degree to which the individual was trying to maintain meaningful ties with family members or had given up or deferred the effort to do so. For those who kept trying, the issue arose: what shall symbolize my connection to X? Can I change the symbol from here (where it takes a lot of time) to there (where it does not)? So a weekend get-away is replaced by a candle-lit dinner, a camping trip with a game of ball. Some were more open than others to what we might call the 'mobility of symbolism.'

All the temporal strategies I discovered – enduring, deferring, being a busy bee, delegating, and resisting – were commonly used by any given worker at some point in their work life. So, over time, a worker would usually mix one strategy with another, though often one tended to prevail. Only some of these – and this is the central point – served as a 'port of entry' for market culture.

Endurers

Some workers simply endured. One assembly-line worker, who worked a rotating seven-day schedule according to which he worked different hours each week plus several hours a week of involuntary overtime, had this to say:

> I'm just getting through. The other day I was so tired that coming off the shift I bumped straight into my locker door. Last winter I was tired driving home; I ran into a mailbox. I'm not having a great time with my wife and kids. My wife and kids aren't having a great time with me, especially not my wife. We're just getting through. A lot of guys feel the way I do. We joke about it over break. 'Are we having fun yet …?'

He was not trying to sustain meaningful bonds with his loved ones. His family was there. He loved them dearly. But he was in a state of siege. So he was putting his relationships with them on hold. To just get through what he was getting through, he lowered his expectations about having fun or meaningful times with them. He did not focus on a future date after which he would engage with his family. For the time being, he renounced the wish to do that. As one young father of two, a night-shift worker, told me,

> Who promised us a rose garden? Life isn't supposed to be like it is on Lifestyles of the Rich and Famous. The sooner a person recognizes that, the better off he is. I'll be happy not to have this headache.

Another factory worker kept a lowered expectation of family life by comparing his fortunes to those of others still less fortunate:

> My wife is working overtime too, and we have the three kids between us. She has two from her first marriage and I have the one, Jessica, from my first. And I'll square with you. It's a challenge. But we're not as bad off as my brother (laughs ruefully). He's working eight hours plus an hour commute each way, and my brother's wife has a half hour commute. Theirs are older, mind you, but they've

got five kids in the house. He has 2 and the three steps, and I don't think their marriage is going to last.

Endurance or 'just getting through' often turned out to be a temporary state, but to the people in that state, it did not feel temporary. To the extent that they were able to detach themselves from the immediate pressures of work, drinking Cokes around the breakroom table (the room in which workers took rest) during a late night week, they sometimes joked darkly about it: 'just three more brick walls to bump into (laughter).'

Deferrers

While endurers renounced the joy of meaningful or fun times, the deferrer deferred them. Instead of telling themselves, 'this is a hassle but this is life,' they told themselves 'this is a hassle but it's just for now.' As, one junior accountant seen by his superiors as a 'real up and comer' explained,

Jennifer and I both dig in during the week and right now I'm working right through weekends, too. But we're planners and we make sure to get away once a month up to the lake. I always talk about that with my daughter, the fishing we'll do when we get up to the lake.

The deferrer could defer his wish for various lengths of time. 'Later' could be a day later ('we'll have quality time tonight') or a week later ('we'll go to the lake this weekend'), or a production period later ('we'll relax after tax season'). As research by Rakel Heidmarsdottir (2002) shows, a number of long-hours workers keep themselves going by imagining their 'real life' after they retire. Indeed, for the early representatives of the Protestant Ethic, as Max Weber noted, moments imagined to bring the greatest satisfaction came when God rewarded a person for good deeds after death.

The busy bee

While both those who endure and those who defer temporarily gave up the idea of having meaningful connections with people outside of work for now, this was not the case for the 'busy bee.' The 'busy bee' located meaning right where it always was supposed to be – in the daily activities of home life, but condensed them so that they fit into smaller time slots. She did not renounce or postpone fun or meaning. She enjoyed it now, but in a busy, fast-paced way. She took pride in being efficient, effective, and Type A. In essence, she absorbed the time bind *into her personal identity*. What the endurers and deferrers saw as a hassle, the busy bee saw as a challenge. She was energized by pressure. Working under pressure was, many workers told me, like a strenuous hike – good for you, hard, and something you were glad you did afterward. She brought her image of family life close to the reality of it by saying, in effect, 'we *like* it this way.' Often she also persuaded other members of her family, including her children, that hurry was fun for them too. ('Come on kids. Let's see who gets there first!')

Delegators

If endurers were doing without happy or meaningful time, deferrers were deferring them, and busy bees were to some extent hollowing them out, then outsourcers were trying to find someone else to have some part of the happy and meaningful time for them. To be sure, nearly all of the two-job parents I interviewed hired a daycare worker or nanny to look after their children while they worked. A few, in the so-called 'sandwich generation,' also had elderly parents whom they hired care workers to tend or whom they called and visited in nursing homes. Most of them wanted their children and elderly parents to receive excellent care from these care providers but to receive the most basic love from themselves. In other words, they wanted helpers, not substitutes for themselves in these roles. Indeed, some nannies I interviewed reported having been fired when a mother became jealous of a child's love for the nanny. Other outsourcers sought very special caregivers with whom they hoped to share a central place in a child's heart. As one female top executive explained,

> We looked very carefully before we hired Karina, and I'm very glad we did. She is a dream come true. She's a widow, and lives alone. Her children live in Canada now, and she has no grandchildren. So she's alone here and she's fit right into our lives and really clicked with Emily, who is two now. We include Karina at Thanksgiving and Christmas, just like family. And she loves Emily almost as a mother would, even better (laughs).

Resisters

Finally, instead of adapting themselves to a grueling schedule, some workers tried to change the schedule itself. Although deferrers and busy bees tended to be found at the top of the hierarchy – prominent examples to other workers of successful accommodation to intense work pressure, throughout the ranks of Amerco's workforce were some who sought to limit the source of pressure in the objective realities of the job or company. Such 'downshifters,' as they have been called, tried to lead the life Todd Rakoff describes in his book, *A Time for Every Purpose* (2002). They envisioned and tried to allocate time so as to fit the purpose at hand to an optimum amount of time. As one mother of a nine-year-old girl described,

> I work 80 percent and for now this is just right. Like this afternoon I went out with Cheryl's Brownie troop (a girls' activity club) on the bus. We were laughing at a dress I'd tried to make her that just didn't come out any which way. The sleeves were uneven, the neck was too small, and the skirt was too long. It was hilarious. And we were laughing, Cheryl and a bunch of her friends and me. A year ago, I would have tried to make one Brownie meeting a month, sneaking a look at my watch the whole

time, not letting myself really relax and enjoy the occasion. It was a big deal for me just to let myself relax and enjoy it. I told my husband. Now I want him to get the same sort of into-it feeling too.[7]

Conclusion and implications

Our position in life – gender, class, occupational status – may be associated with a favored temporal strategy for keeping life fun and meaningful. This, in turn, may be related to one's predisposition to accept, or not, a market paradigm through which to experience family life. Busy bees and deferrers tended to be the professionals and executives at or near the top of the Amerco job ladder. Endurers were usually the assembly-line workers. Efficiency did not work for them and while they were not against it on principle, they did not think of it as a good thing. Staying cheerful was hard enough. Resisters did not believe in efficiency at home, and many actively disapproved of it, and so tried to change things so they could escape 'that trap.' Many such resisters were middle-level clerical and technical workers neither consumed by the career culture of the top nor overwhelmed by the financial hardships of the bottom. If the endurer succumbed to the pressure of work, the resister escaped it. Neither one adjusted to intense work pressure nor embraced the cult of efficiency as a happy or at least tolerable aspect of life. So they were less likely ports of entry for market culture. Thus, it was most of all the 'busy bee' and 'deferrer' – generally the women and men of the managerial class – who neither changed their schedules nor felt a need to. And it was for them that market culture most seemed to offer itself as the oil and grease, so to speak, that maintained the frictionless machine of work.

Accepting a life of rush and pressure can introduce the need for a covert form of emotion management. The busy bee in particular could seem to be using over-busyness as a way of suppressing feeling. What the busy bee managed away could be a range of feelings – discouragement, anger, erotic feelings, and discontent with 'how things are.'

In the age of the time bind, we might even say that, next to television, constant busyness is the prevailing 'opiate of the masses' – a way of suppressing feelings and ideas that might challenge the status quo or the market culture into which we have unwittingly slid. Continual busyness by its nature inhibits the individual from thinking about non-busy-bee issues – which can, of course, include such issues as why one is so busy, and the purpose behind it, as well as the state of the larger society.

In the end, the 'great transformation' to a market society is the basic story of modern history and there is little likelihood that we will go back. But the daily lives of modern families reveal many clues to an ongoing, muted yet fierce, struggle between the culture of the market and that of the family. Many daily interactions in the lives of American working families today may well involve a tacit struggle between the prevailing metaphors, regimes of justification, and efficiency-oriented practices of the market and those of the home, community, and unpaid realms of life. Each struggle creates, in turn, a cultural collage, which once normalized, and stabilized, enters the general mix of cultural collages of market/home cultures. We call it 'everyday life.' But those mixes are shifting, in a market direction, offering more support for an emotional detachment and instrumentalism suited to market relations. Counter-trends exist – labor struggles for more time and living wages, and the simplicity movement based in the Northwest, for example. But the curious case of Family 360 raises some basic questions: What is our ability to guard a critical space from which to ask of ourselves the very question, what 'culture' am I living in? And what are the alternatives? The deferrer or busy bee who does not crack a smile at the terminology of Family 360 may have lost that critical space.

In the meantime, the Family 360 client may try to improve his 'person behaviors' in order to get a top-scoring '7' in 'memory creation.' But years later, when he grows old and is looking back, his children's most vivid memory may be of those meetings around the dining room table with the expert who coached dad in how to get to the bottom line in love.

Notes

1. 'The Year in Ideas,' *New York Times Magazine*, December 2002: 65.
2. See electronic references http://www.leaderworks.net/coaching.html and http://www.family360.com
3. In *Haven in a Heartless World: The Family Besieged*, Christopher Lasch (1977) criticized the way in which unconfident parents too quickly relinquish authority over the conduct of their personal life. However, Lasch ends up rejecting such services altogether – a position far from my own.
4. Durkheim (1893: 3–4), as quoted in Fevre (2003: 4). Weber, Simmel and indeed all the classical sociologists, Durkheim, Weber, Simmel, Smith, were, in Fevre's words, 'worried that all moral concerns might somehow be forced out of business by the primacy of economic motivation.' Paradoxically, Marx, both the sharpest critic of capitalism and something of a family man himself, did not feel there was much of a nice moral world in family and community that needed protecting, and advocated outsourcing all care and getting to work.
5. Despite the promise of free time made by the early celebrants of industrialism, and despite some early expansions in leisure time since the late 1990s in the United States, according to an International Labor Organization report, work hours are increasing. This report is only the most recent of many conflicting reports. Focusing on different time periods and countries, some scholars see a

30-year trend toward shorter hours (cf. Gershuny, 2000), while others looking at the work and not simply the work unit trend toward larger hours (Schor, 1992; Hochschild, 2003: 271, footnote 10). Still others find a rise for the white-collar worker and decline for the blue-collar one. Still others have argued that however many hours we work, we are enveloped in a culture of *rush* – speed dials, remote controls, fast foods, ever faster computers, email, answering machines, are all so many products promising to save our time. As James Gleick (2000) notes in his book *Faster*, film producers have increased the speed in cutting from scene to scene, and advertisers have done the same. The length of soundbytes by presidential candidates has shrunk, he notes, from 40 seconds in 1968 to less than 10 in 1988. This cultural echo of speed would seem to emanate from the basic idea that time is money and money is 'it.'

6. These strategies were not present in my first analysis of the material gathered for the book, but are based on further reflections on the intersection between market culture and the ways people manage time.

7. Each strategy has its light side. In a humorous essay on not having time to do things oneself, Adam Gopnik (2002) describes overhearing his three-year-old daughter Olivia talking to an imaginary friend she names Charlie Ravioli. Charlie is 'too busy' to play with her because he's working. In fact Charlie, her imaginary friend, hires a personal assistant to answer Charlie's calls because Charlie is too busy to say he's too busy. Gopnik lays this charming but telling story to his daughter's life as a New York child, but as he also notes busyness is an 'art form' well outside of New York as well.

References

Boltanski, L. and Thévenot, L. (1991) *De la justificación: Les économies de la grandeur.* Paris: Gallimard.

Cox, H. (2001) 'Mammon and the culture of the market: A socio-theological critique'. In Richard Madsen, William M. Sullivan, Ann Swidler, and Steven M. Tipton, eds. *Meaning and Modernity: Religion, Polity, and Self.* Berkeley: University of California Press, pp. 124–135.

Durkheim, E. (1893) *The Division of Labour in Society.* New York: Free Press.

Fevre, R. (2003) *The New Sociology of Economic Behaviour.* London: Sage.

Gershuny, J. (2000) *Changing Times: Work and Leisure in Postindustrial Society.* Oxford: Oxford University Press.

Gleick, J. (2000) *Faster: The Acceleration of Just about Everything.* New York: Oxmoor House.

Gopnik, A. (2002) 'Bumping into Mr. Ravioli'. *The New Yorker*, 30 September: 80–84.

Heidmarsdottir, R. (2002) *Retirement Fantasies and Other Coping Strategies of Employees Experiencing Work-Life Conflicts.* Ph.D. dissertation, University of Texas at Austin.

Hochschild, A.R. (2003) *The Commercialization of Intimate Life: Notes from Home and Work.* Berkeley, CA: University of California Press.

Hochschild, A.R. (1997) *The Time Bind: When Work Becomes Home and Home Becomes Work.* New York: Metropolitan Books.

Lakoff, G. and Johnson, M. (1980) *Metaphors We Live By*. Chicago, IL: The University of Chicago Press.

Lasch, C. (1977) *Haven in a Heartless World: The Family Besieged*. New York: Basic Books.

Polyani, K. (1944) *The Great Transformation: The Political and Economic Origins of Our Time*. New York: Beacon Press.

Rakoff, T. (2002) *A Time for Every Purpose: Law and the Balance of Life*. Cambridge, MA: Harvard University Press.

Schor, J.B. (1992) *The Overworked American: The Unexpected Decline of Leisure*. New York: Basic Books.

Tough, P. (2002) 'Dad's performance review. Sub-essay in "The year in ideas."' *The New York Times Magazine*, 15 December: 80–82.

Chapter 7

Metamanagement and the outsourcing of domestic life

Craig Lair and George Ritzer

Introduction

Outsourcing is commonly talked about in terms of macro-economic phenomena such as the shipping of 'American' jobs to 'foreign' locations (e.g. Dobbs, 2004) and generally involves companies' decision to buy goods or services, once performed in-house, from external suppliers. For example, when a car manufacturer decides to purchase parts for an engine from an outside supplier instead of building these parts themselves, this would be a case of outsourcing. However, a number of works have begun to explore how 'outsourcing' is taking place in the context of the family and domestic life (Conover, 1997; Sheth and Sisodia, 1999; Sharpe, 2000; Winslow, 2000; Sandholtz et al., 2002; Chatzky, 2005; Hochschild, 2005; Palmer, 2006). These works explore how individuals and families are increasingly purchasing goods and services, once performed within the circle of family membership, from sources outside of the family. The three most common examples of this type of outsourcing are the use of food sources away from the home (e.g. the use of take-out food), child care (e.g. the use of daycare centers), and the hiring of housekeepers, though, as will be seen below, the variety of outsourcing services available today 'is limited only by one's imagination' (Winslow, 2000).

The emergence of this type of outsourcing is important for a number of reasons,[1] not the least of which is that it represents a significant shift in how domestic affairs are managed by individuals and family members. In particular, we want to show how as individuals and families outsource more and more of their affairs, they are coming to resemble what Mowshowitz (1997: 36) refers to as a 'virtual organization,' that is, an organizational structure that links together a number of *independent entities* into a *functional whole* for the purpose of performing a goal. In this case the goal that links these independent entities together is the performance of an individual's or family's domestic affairs. But since this organizational structure contains entities that are outside of an individual's or family's membership, a different form of management is required than in cases where these types of affairs are performed by individuals or families themselves, or when an individual or family is involved in the direct management of those who take on such affairs (e.g. the direct supervision of a domestic worker). This is because with outsourcing what is managed by the client is the 'linkage' between an individual's or a family's needs (i.e. its 'requirements') and those employed to meet these needs (i.e. the 'satisfiers'), not the actual performance of these affairs. Mowshowitz refers to this process of evaluating the linkage between requirements and satisfiers as metamanagement. Thus, our argument is that with more and more individuals and families using outsourcing services, the structure of the domestic activities is coming to resemble a virtual organization with the corresponding need to metamanage the linkage between the needs of a family and those employed to satisfy them.

As will be seen, the metamanagement of domestic affairs is not only a unique way to order one's domestic affairs; it is also a very rational and highly efficient means of doing so. But a general feature of highly rationalized systems is that they lead to outcomes that are less than rational. Outcomes of this nature are what Ritzer (2004) refers to as the 'irrational consequences of rationality' and a number of them can be seen as being introduced into the domestic sphere as a result of outsourcing and metamanagement. In particular, we will show how some domestic activities are disenchanted as a result of the process of outsourcing. But Ritzer (2005) has also shown how rationality can also be used as an enchanting mechanism, that is, that highly rational systems can have the appearance of being something that is magical or fantastic, and we will show how some cases of the outsourcing and metamanagement of domestic affairs can take on an enchanted appearance as these activities appear to magically happen. But the magical quality of these services opens the door to another irrational consequence that is more closely associated with Marx's analysis of commodities: fetishization. We will end by providing a general conclusion and inquire into the future of the 'core' of the family if this type of outsourcing increases.

Metamanagement

At a general level, metamanagement refers to the 'arrangement of satisfiers to requirements' (Mowshowitz, 2002: 30). In the context of business this does not sound like anything new; managers have long calculated what the best resource is, be it a specific person, piece of equipment, process, and so on, to use in a specific task. What makes metamanagement unique, however, is the fact that this calculation of means to ends no longer takes place solely in relation to the internal resources of a company. Rather, metamanagement is premised on an organizational structure whose 'philosophical foundation … is a categorical distinction between needs and the means of satisfying them' (Mowshowitz, 1997: 374). This stands in contrast to conventional management strategies where there is 'no clear distinction between a requirement and a way of satisfying it' (ibid.: 376) so that a company may come to rely on internal resources to satisfy a specific requirement even though more effective resources are available outside of the company. Metamanagement's emphasis upon the distinction between, and separation of, means and ends 'makes it possible to manage activities in a way that insures systematic efforts to find the "best" match between requirements and satisfiers at all times' (ibid.) whether this match be found internally or, as is increasingly the case as evidenced by companies outsourcing, from outside sources. For example, if an automobile manufacturer is in need of a specialized component and the best supplier of this part is an outside company, then the automobile manufacturer operating under the principles of metamanagement should not attempt to have this part built in-house but instead acquire it from the outside company.

Mowshowitz links the development of metamanagement to the rise of 'virtual organizations.' Indeed, Mowshowitz (ibid.: 376) defines a virtual organization as any 'goal-oriented enterprise operating under metamanagement.' In practice, this means that virtual organizations are a group of companies that are linked together for a specific purpose (i.e. a goal) whose linkages, from a functional point of view at least, give the grouping the appearance a single entity (Secord, 2003: 453). For example, the world-famous athletic shoe company Nike actually produces no shoes of its own. Rather, they concentrate their efforts on the designing of shoes and other goods and then contract with one of nearly 700 factories to have these goods produced for them. Nevertheless, from a functional point of view this network of factories can be seen as comprising a single whole even though this 'whole' is actually and legally comprised of a number of independent entities. Moreover, the organizational structure of Nike and other similar enterprises is 'virtual' since the linkages between these separate organizations could be severed or changed at any time since there is no binding or organic relationship between these different companies. In fact, one of the central benefits of virtual organizations is that they allow couplings and decouplings between separate organizations to take place rapidly as the goals, needs, or preferences of different companies change. Mowshowitz (ibid.: 377) refers to this as 'switching' and shows how this process can take place in the automobile industry:

> Automobiles are complex machines made up of many different components, produced by a variety of suppliers. The abstract requirements in this case may be seen as the components required to put together for an automobile. Concrete satisfiers are the suppliers of the various parts. Since components may be available from a number of different suppliers, it is possible for management to switch from one to another to take advantage of dynamically changing opportunities in the marketplace – for example, a new player may come along offering lower cost, etc.

The practice of switching between various external suppliers instead of supplying goods and services in-house may seem like a simple shift in business operations. However, it actually represents a significant departure from what was the historically prevailing corporate norm – that is, a vision of a self-sufficient, vertically integrated business model where companies would own and operate virtually everything needed for business operations (e.g. the means for procuring raw materials, transporting goods, performing payroll and accounting in-house, the operation of pension funds, research and development, etc.). A vivid example of this can be seen in the history of the Ford Motor Company:

> The vertical integration at Ford eventually reached all the way to Brazil, where the company bought rubber plantations in the 1930s. Ford ships brought iron ore from the company's mines in Michigan and Minnesota, across the Great Lakes, up the Detroit and Rouge rivers, and right to the docks at the Rouge complex. Lumber came from Ford forests in Michigan. Coal miners in Kentucky and West Virginia were Ford employees, as were glassworkers in Pennsylvania and Minnesota, and woodworkers in Michigan lumber areas. The company even owned rail lines, including the 90 miles of track that criss-crossed the Rouge site and connected its various structures. (Gordon and Malone, 1997: 336)

However, beginning with the economic stagnation of the 1970s and increased global competition this business model began to be attacked as being unwieldy, inefficient, and not viable in an increasingly global market. In this new, hypercompetitive market, speed and expertise are seen as the two main factors delivering economic success (Corbett, 2004: 5) and any business operations that are not seen as directly contributing value to these areas are increasingly viewed as a drag on an organization. And in situations where companies are performing so many activities for themselves, there is much potential, if not actual, sources of 'drag' in this type of business structure. An increasingly common solution to this situation is for organizations to concentrate on their 'core competencies' (i.e. what they do better than anyone else and what adds the most value to their product) and to shift all other 'peripheral' activities to others to perform (Prahalad and Hamel, 1990). Management consultant Tom Peters summarizes this new business model nicely: 'Do what you do best and outsource the rest' (Peters cited in Corbett, 2004: 9). But outsourcing the rest to external suppliers requires not only that this company be linked-up with a series of others, but also that these linkages are monitored to see if the requirements are being fulfilled in a satisfactory manner. In other words, this organizational structure requires metamanagement in Mowshowitz's sense of the term.

Mowshowitz's concepts of metamanagement and virtual organization were developed to take account of changing businesses practices, particularly those of multinational corporations that outsource their operations to various suppliers to take advantage of the cost-differentials of different companies and countries. But when individuals and families outsource their domestic affairs they can, in many fundamental aspects at least, be seen as metamanaging their affairs by arranging a series of satisfiers that fit their requirements. This is a relatively new and unique means of ordering domestic affairs; it is also a very rational and highly efficient means for doing so. The problem is that a number of irrational consequences can be seen as resulting from this highly rational means of having domestic affairs performed. To see this, however, it is first necessary to see how families are coming to metamanage their domestic affairs and to highlight some of the unique features of this practice.

Outsourcing and the metamanagement of domestic life

Today an increasing number of families are using businesses to help in the performance of a variety of domestic tasks.[2] In other words, they are outsourcing. For example, one husband noted how '[he and his family are] outsourcing just about everything – cleaning, laundry, house maintenance and lawn care' (Palmer, 2006). A wife said something similar to *Regional Review*: 'I outsource everything I possibly can' by hiring people to do her and her family's housecleaning, yard work, grocery shopping, dry cleaning, film developing, and other errands. Moreover, she often orders take-out or buys prepared meals to cut down on her time spent in the kitchen (Wasserman, 1999). Sandholtz et al. (2002: 58) have even identified a group they call 'outsourcers' who 'strive to get control of their overstuffed lives' by 'farming out certain tasks and obligations (usually in their nonwork lives), then focusing more attention on the activities, relationships, and causes they care most about.' And what types of activities are being outsourced so as to free up time and energy so that individuals and families can concentrate on the areas they care most about?

As was mentioned above, the three most common forms of domestic outsourcing are the outsourcing of food preparation, childcare, and housekeeping. This, however, is just the tip of the outsourcing iceberg as there are other companies that will pooper-scoop one's yard (Stefanini, 2006), organize the homes of their customers (Gardner, 2006), transport children to and from the places that they need to be (so-called 'kiddie cabs') (Conover, 1997), assemble one's photos for them (Hochschild, 2005: 79), and deliver groceries to one's home (Green, 2006). There are also lawn care companies (Kahlenberg, 2005), birthday party planning companies (Barker, 2006), personal shoppers (Thiruvengadam, 2005), and personal concierges who will provide any variety of services for their clients (e.g. run errands, wait in their client's home for a repair man, shopping for their clients, etc.) (Krischer, 2006). As can be seen from this, the range domestic tasks that can be outsourced is quite expansive.

All of these industries are growing, in some cases quite rapidly, thus indicating that these types of services are in high demand. Though there are a number of factors that are making these types of services increasingly popular, we will focus on two of the most prominent ones. The first is the fact that more and more women are participating in the labor force. In 1948, only 32 per cent of women age 16 and old were employed. As of 2006, this number has increased to approximately 60 percent[3] while during this same period, the comparable figures for men actually decreased from nearly 87 percent of men age 16 and over being employed in 1948 to a little less than 74 percent in 2006.[4] One major consequence of the fact that an increasing number of women are working is that there are more and more two-income families. However, as Jacobs and Gerson (2004) have shown, dual-income families face a 'time deficit' as a result of the fact that both partners in these relationships are working so that there is less overall time available for families, and in particular mothers, to spend doing the domestic tasks they have traditionally performed (e.g. caring for children, preparing food, cleaning the house, etc.). These time pressures are a significant factor in increasing the desirability of outsourcing domestic tasks.

However, another factor making these time pressures even more significant, and hence outsourcing more desirable, is that family ties are increasingly taking the form of what Giddens (1991: 6) refers to as a 'pure relationship' – that is, a type of relationship that 'exists solely for whatever rewards that relationship as such can deliver.' In other words, family life is increasingly being reoriented around issues of emotional ties and intimate bonds, as opposed to relationships based on ties of obligation and/or dependence. As Beck and Beck-Gernsheim (1995: 192) put it, '[i]nstead of justifying love along traditional or formal lines, we do so along emotional and individual ones. It originates in what we experience, in our personal hopes and fears rather than in any superior power.' One of the major results of this shift in the conception of the family is that issues such as spending quality time together as a family are of increasing importance to more and more families, and one measure of this is how empirical studies have found that families are spending more time together despite the decrease in the overall amount of family time mentioned above (Bianchi et al., 2006). Families have been able to spend more time together despite less available time for this by concentrating their efforts around the family itself either by foregoing certain domestic activities (e.g. performing lesser amounts of housework [Bianchi et al., 2000] or, increasingly, by transferring these affairs to others. That is, a growing number of families are outsourcing their 'peripheral' domestic functions in order to free time up in order to spend time together as a family. Slater (cited in Winslow, 2000), commenting on this trend, notes that '[e]ven people not making a lot of money pay someone else to do [domestic activities] instead of fighting over who will do it. If you have a limited amount of time to spend, why spend it on housework when you could spend time with family.' Similarly, Kahlenberg (2005) profiles a family that outsources its lawn care so that they can spend more time together. As the mother of this family notes, '[i]f we had to take care of the lawn ourselves, our weekend would be much more about chores' and less about spending quality time together. Potomac Concierge, a personal concierge service located near Washington DC, uses this as a selling point by offering to 'help busy people obtain more balance in their life. Let us take care of your growing 'to do list,' so you can focus on family, work, friends and what you enjoy' (http://www.potomacconcierge.com/).[5] Indeed, one of the most common themes expressed by both customers and providers of various outsourcing services is that by employing these services customers are able to concentrate their efforts on what they care the most about, which often includes spending time together as a family (see Chapter 6, this volume).

These two forces – a decrease in the overall amount of family time available due to the increased labor force participation of women in the face of the desire to spend more time together as a family – have been two of the most powerful forces driving the trend of domestic outsourcing. But, of course, this is not the first time that outsiders have been used in the performance of domestic affairs. For example, domestic workers were commonly employed by middle class families from Colonial times all the way to World War II. Similarly, laundresses were once a major occupational category and, though much less frequent and popular, services that look like some of today's outsourcing offerings (e.g. the delivery of cooked food) have been tried in the past. So while it is true that outsourcing is not categorically new, it is also true that there are a number of elements that make the outsourcing and metamanagement of today unique, two of which are of particular importance.

In particular, metamanagement and outsourcing are a more *indirect* and *organizationally mediated* form of managing one's domestic affairs than was common in the past. This is due to the fact that, with outsourcing and metamanagement, one transfers both the labor involved in performing a domestic affair and the direct responsibility of managing this labor. The result is that the outsourcer of domestic affairs is left only to manage the linkage between his/her needs and the satisfiers contracted to perform these affairs. For example, when clients hire a maid service, they are hiring an organization, and not particular workers, that is responsible for cleaning the house and for managing the workers involved in this. As such, the employment relationship between the client and the workers is mediated by the contracting organization. This mediation of employment relations through an organization is one of the central features that Weber (1946: 196–240) identified with bureaucracy. Bickham Mendez (1998: 119) describes this situation specifically in terms of large housecleaning organizations: in a 'bureaucratized organization structure workers and managers become representative of the agency. The owner of the home to be cleaned is no longer an employer, but a client, and is relieved of the responsibility of managing the domestic worker.'

However, it is also the case that when domestic affairs are outsourced and metamanaged they are often *spatially mediated* as well is the sense that these affairs are performed outside of the home. This is in contrast to the past where, though outsiders were used to help with domestic affairs, this help normally remained within the home (e.g. domestic workers worked and often lived in their employer's home). With outsourcing, in some cases at least, the outside sources of labor that are used are located physically outside of the home. Daycare is the most prominent example of this, but other services (e.g. 'kiddie cab' services, food sources away from home, the running of errands by personal concierges) fit this pattern as well. Outsourcing services allow domestic affairs to be structured in such a manner by allowing individuals and families to have their domestic affairs performed by sources physically absent from them which make them very efficient from the point of view of those outsourcing them. This may occur on a local scale as when, for example, a family gets take-out food from a local restaurant or a personal concierge is hired to run errands in one's community. However, in some cases this type of outsourcing can take a highly distanciated form as, for example, when one uses a virtual assistant located in another country (Jacobs, 2005).

But distanciated relationships are not only found when domestic affairs leave the home. Rather, they are also produced when domestic tasks, while still being outsourced to others, remain in the home when those who outsourced them are not. In other words, distanciation comes in the form of the absence of the outsourcers from the domestic environment while the outsourcees are present within it. An example of this type of distanciated relationship can be seen when one hires a housekeeping company that cleans one's house while one is at work: service providers come into the domestic environment to do their work, while those who hire them are not there. Bickham Mendez (1998) found this situation to be quite common in her study of a corporate housekeeping company but this situation of a client-free environment is quite common in a number of outsourcing services. For example, personal chefs commonly cook meals for their clients while their clients are not there (Winslow, 2000; Anderson, 2005). Similarly, many of the services that personal concierges provide are necessitated by the fact that their clients are not at home to do these activities themselves (e.g. being at home waiting for a repairman to arrive) (see the services offered by the personal concierge company, Everything But Time – http://www.time-less.com/aboutus.html).

These are just some of the unique facets of the outsourcing and metamanagement of domestic affairs that we are witnessing today. But while these unique aspects are important in and of themselves, they are also important in terms of the new wrinkles that they add to an enduring issue in social theory: rationalization.

Outsourcing, metamanagement, and the rationalization of domestic life

Studies of rationality have been a staple of sociological thought since Weber's seminal work in this area. For example, this topic has been important to the critical theorists and their study of instrumental rationality, including Horkheimer and Adorno (1998 [1944]), Braverman (1974), Bauman (1989), and, more recently, Ritzer (2004). As we will show here, outsourcing and metamanagement are rationalizing how domestic affairs are being performed. In doing this, however, we will keep in mind a finding by Weber (1946) and Ritzer (2004) that highly rational systems tend to produce a number of irrational consequences. In fact, we will show how a number of such irrational consequences are present in the case of the outsourcing and metamanagement of domestic affairs. One is a consequence that was identified by Weber: that is, that formally rational systems tend to *disenchant* the world by stripping it of its magical and fantastic qualities (Gerth and Mills in Weber, 1946: 51). This process of disenchanting, or at least the potential for this, can be seen to apply to at least some examples of domestic outsourcing. But it needs to be noted that Ritzer (2005) has shown how rationality can also be used as an enchanting mechanism, that is, that highly rational systems can have the appearance of being something that is magical or fantastic. We will show how some cases of the outsourcing and metamanagement of domestic affairs, especially those where there is a distanciation between the service provider and his/her client, can take on an enchanted appearance as these activities, and from the client's view at least, appear to magically happen while they are away. But the magical quality of these services to seemingly be performed in such an effortless manner on the part of the client opens the door to another irrational consequence that is more closely associated with Marx's analysis of commodities: fetishization.

From a family's point of view, the outsourcing of domestic affairs is a very rational and efficient means of having these types of tasks performed. As Ritzer (2004: 43) defines it, efficiency involves choosing the optimum means for a given end and if one's end is to have certain intimate affairs performed, outsourcing, especially for people who are very busy, is very efficient because it allows for the labor involved in performing domestic affairs to be divided up and distributed over a network of providers outside of the family. That is, outsourcing is efficient for those who do it because transferring these tasks to others frees up time and energy that can then be spent doing other things. In a very real sense, this type of outsourcing is like having another set of hands at one's disposal, though there is also the further advantage that with outsourcing, one set of hands need not be in the same physical location as the other.

Also, since outsourcing and metamanagement involve the transfer of both the labor used in the performance of a domestic affair and the responsibility for managing those who perform these tasks, it is, again from the client's perspective, a more efficient system for having one's affairs performed than in cases where clients are forced to monitor and directly manage workers. Moreover, by freeing clients of the need to directly monitor the labor of the workers to whom they transfer their domestic affairs it allows these affairs to be distributed in a distanciated manner as was noted above (i.e. either the tasks can be removed from the home or the workers can perform these tasks while the workers are not there). This increases the efficiency of outsourcing services that can be organized in this manner.

But while outsourcing may be a very rational way to have one's domestic affairs performed, the problem is that some of the dangers that relate to highly rationalized systems in general can be seen as being evident when domestic affairs are outsourced and metamanaged. In particular, there is the possibility of disenchantment coming in the wake of cases where very intimate or sentimental domestic affairs are involved. One area where this can clearly be seen is in cases where symbolic or emotional exchanges such as gift-buying are given over to others to perform. While outsourcing is a very rational and efficient means for providing these exchanges, the logic involved here runs counter to the type of social action that Weber sees as lying at the base of such activities: affectual action (Weber, 1964 [1947]: 137). As Weber (ibid.: 115) conceives of it, this type of action is defined 'in terms of affectual orientation, especially emotional, determined by the specific affects and states of feeling of the actor.' Moreover, it is a form of action that 'stands on the borderline of what can be considered 'meaningfully' oriented, and often it…goes over the line' (ibid.: 116) in the sense that these actions are rooted in sentiment and not reason, and thus are more nonrational than rational in nature (e.g. it may be more rational and time-efficient to buy a cooked meal, but these issues may have little relevance when one wants to demonstrate one's love by cooking for one's family) (Kalberg, 1980: 1161). The problem is that with many of the activities associated with the outsourcing of domestic affairs, and particularly those involving the exchange of emotional or symbolic goods, the affectual basis of action which Weber saw as being concentrated in family life is, if not replaced, then at least challenged, by a means-ends form of rationality. Take, for example, the case of gift-giving which one can now outsource to a variety of service providers. Arguably gift-giving is an activity that is motivated by sentiment and this can be seen in the popular notion that it is the idea, and not the actual gift, that 'counts' in these exchanges. In other words, what makes a gift meaningful is not actually what is received but rather the thought and care that went into making and/or obtaining it. This means that the 'enchanted' nature of a gift is rooted in what the giver put into it, not in the actual gift itself.

Though there is no way to directly measure the extent to which shopping for gifts is being outsourced, two types of service – personal concierges and personal shoppers – that are rapidly growing offer these services for their clients. For example, in an advice book on how to start your own personal concierge business, Addison (2003: 4–5) describes how a personal concierge 'is not employed by a hotel or corporation. Instead, they market their services directly to clients who pay them for running errands, *buying gifts*, making travel arrangements, or myriad other tasks' (emphasis added). Similarly, in an article entitled 'How to be a Personal Concierge' Tiffany (2001) lists 'Gift-buying' as one of the services offered by people doing this kind of work. Giovanni and Giovanni (2002) also note in their book *The Concierge Manual* that shopping for gifts is one of the services that a personal concierge can perform. However, they not only offer to shop for the gifts ('Why not let us buy that special gift for your friends and relatives?' they ask [op cit.: 81]), but also to wrap and/or return gifts if need be.

Personal shoppers are also ready and willing to buy gifts for their clients. In a book on becoming a personal shopper Kim-York (2005: 6) notes that '[y]ou'll also need to be creative. Many times a client will need a gift for someone. The client gives you a description of the person, and then it's up to you, the personal shopper, to find the gift to fit that person.' Similarly, in describing the work of Samantha von Sperling, Flaherty notes that '[a]s a personal shopper, [von

Sperling] is paid to find perfect, heartfelt presents for everyone on someone else's list' (Flaherty, 2003).

So why are personal concierges and personal shoppers being used to buy gifts for others, including their family members? The principal reason appears to be that a lack of time, energy, and/or desire on the part of the gift-givers creates the impetus to outsource this activity. As Harrison McBride et al. (2005: 9) describe it, '[t]oday, people have less time for leisure, including shopping for clothing, gifts or even food' and, as such, are willing to pay others to perform this task for them. Kim-York (2005: 2–3) echoes this same point: 'With the fast-paced, high pressure professional lifestyles of today, more and more people have limited time to do their personal shopping. Holding down a full-time job, raising children, and maintaining a household doesn't seem to leave enough hours in the day to get everything done. That's why more people are now opting for a "service" to do much of their personal shopping for them,' including the purchasing of gifts. For others, a lack of time might be coupled with a lack of desire and/or interest. One client of von Sperling 'typically puts off Hanukkah shopping until the last minute' so that she ends up doing a lot of catalog shopping and purchasing gift certificates. The ironic development is that when this woman outsources this task her friends and family 'probably end up with more personalized gifts' than would otherwise be the case (cited in Flaherty, 2003).

While very rational and efficient, this type of outsourcing seemingly undermines the traditional and affectual basis of gift-giving. In other words, the nonrational act of gift-giving is displaced by a rational and efficient means of providing for it. Of course, given that many other types of shopping have also been outsourced it should not be too surprising that the specific kind of shopping involved in gift-giving has been outsourced as well. And while Miller (1998: 23) notes that 'love is not only normative but easily dominant as the context and motivation for the bulk of actual shopping practice,' the fact that even the emotionally laden activity of gift-giving is being outsourced cannot tell us whether or not the actual sentiment involved is being outsourced as well. But if shopping is a loving activity, when it is outsourced it is love from a 'paid proxy' (Hochschild, 2005: 82), and if the presence of such a proxy in a sentimental act is exposed, it can be very disenchanting (i.e. it empties the gift of its magical/sentimental qualities leaving it as just a thing). Of course, many of the businesses engaged in this kind of work know that their services have this potentially disenchanting nature to them and consequently try and hide their involvement in this process. This can best be seen in two other types of intimate outsourcing: the outsourcing of card-writing and remembrance services.

Greeting cards can be seen as an early forerunner to the type of intimate outsourcing discussed here in the sense that they represent the transfer of expressing sentiment to an outside entity. The result is that the customer does not create the (printed) sentiment on the card, but rather selects the best expression for the occasion and then personalizes it with a note and/or signature. But it was not always like this: as Gillis (1996: 78) notes, '[t]he first holiday and greeting cards that circulated among kin were homemade.' This, however, began to change by the end of the nineteenth century as 'bought cards accounted for an increasingly greater share of family correspondence as people took advantage of this relatively cheap form of symbolic interaction to extend their family worlds…' (ibid.). But while bought cards, as opposed to their handmade counterparts, may represent an early form of intimate outsourcing, new services are developing that take this kind of outsourcing to a whole other level.

This can be seen in the sprouting number of professional thank-you note writing companies who will, for a fee typically between $3 and $5 per note, handwrite cards for any occasion (e.g. newlyweds thanking their guests for their attendance and/or gifts) (*The Montana Standard*, 2005; Chatzky, 2005). Says Chris Hagan, co-founder of the Baltimore, MD-based That's Gratitude, of this service, it 'is discreet … Unless somebody knows your handwriting, they're not going to know [that the cards have been written by someone else]' (*The Montana Standard* 2005). Storybook Cards, who provides a similar service, advertises on its webpage that '[w]ith our thank you services, your cards will get done with *the same personal attention and accuracy you would devote*' (http://storybookcards.com/services.php – emphasis added).

The Minneapolis, Minnesota-based company Red Stamp Cards similarly offers to handwrite for their clients. However, they also offer something more: after filling out an initial calendar of important dates throughout the year (e.g. birthdays, anniversaries, holidays, etc.), Red Stamp Cards will send you email reminders as this date approaches so that you can get an appropriate card selected from their offerings to the recipient on time with the option of having Red Stamp Cards write out the card for you. In other words, what Red Stamp Cards offers is the *outsourcing of remembrance* in the sense that customers pay this company to be their memory bank of important and/or sentimental dates and to remind them of these. As an article that ran on Scoop du Jour[6] featuring Red Stamp Cards describes the benefit of this service:

> They say as we age, the memory is the first to go … We have a hard enough time remembering how old we told people we were on our last birthday … *how can we possibly be expected to remember other people's milestones,* faux or otherwise? *Thanks to Red Stamp Cards, we don't have to.* Not only will this gem of a site send us a nifty little note prompting special occasions like birthdays and anniversaries per our own personal calendar, they also happen to have an amazing assortment of cards to boot. (emphasis added)

A similar, though cruder and male-oriented, version of a remembrance service is offered by Save My Ass.com. This is a service that you can sign up for and pre-schedule the delivery of flowers in a 'combination of "special dates" and "just because"' (http://www.savemyass.com/public/faq).[7] In other words, this service will set it up so that flowers are delivered not only on specifically sentimentally laden days such as Valentine's Day or his/her birthday, but also on a 'semi-random' basis to feign romantic spontaneity of the part of the client. This website reassures clients that even if it comes out that the flowers are the result of a service as opposed initiatives on these different occasions that this will not detract from the significance of the flowers. For example, one testimonial of a client states that 'I thought my wife would be pissed if she found out about this service. In fact, she told me I better not quit!' (ibid.). That may be the case, but this website also takes several precautions against their involvement in this process being revealed. For example, 'SMA Flowers' is the name that appears on the credit card statement because even though this company has 'found that most recipients don't mind being signed up for [this] service, even when they know about it' they have 'added this privacy feature just in case' (ibid.). Why is there this need for privacy, even if it is just in case? This is because the value of a gift is, in part at least, based on the appearance of a nonrational motivation for it, and if they are exposed as actually being the product of a rationalization system for the delivery of these gifts, the value of the gift is undermined as the gift-giving process is disenchanted.

Disenchantment is always a potential of very rationalized systems. However, Ritzer (2005) has also shown that, despite the potential to act as agents of disenchantment, highly rationalized systems can at times act as enchanting agents as well. That is, part of the allure of these systems may be in the fact that they can have enchanting qualities. As Ritzer (op cit.: 89) puts it, while '[t]here is no question that ... rationalized systems lead in various ways to disenchantment, they paradoxically and simultaneously [can also] serve to create their own kinds of enchantment' (Ritzer, 2005: 89). For example, '[p]eople often marvel at the *efficiency* of rationalized systems; their ability to manage things so effectively can seem quite magical' (ibid.: 90 – emphasis in original). Most, if not all, of the services that take on intimate affairs are, from the client's perspective at least, very efficient systems and are able to both deliver and manage these affairs very effectively which can give them a magical quality. This is particularly the case when these affairs are performed in a manner that is physically distant from those who outsource them.

Indeed, one of the unique aspects of outsourcing and the need to metamanage these services, as opposed to directly managing those to whom one transfers one's intimate affairs who are in close proximity, is that clients and service providers are often physically distant from one another. In some cases this is because intimate affairs are transferred to locations outside of the home (e.g. daycare), though, in a growing number of cases, this is because service providers work in the homes of their clients when their clients are not there (e.g. a housekeeping service that cleans one's house while one is at work).

Certainly from a division of labor perspective, having a number of one's affairs performed away from home and/or at home while one is at work is very efficient. Moreover, the performance of these affairs can also seem quite magical in the sense that they appear to simply happen while one is away. That is, since these activities are performed out of the sight of the client, it is easy to forget that these are often time- and energy-intensive tasks that require a great amount of effort on the parts of the people performing them. And to the extent that clients do not recognize and/or appreciate that these services are the result of actual human labor and is instead something that just happens when one pays for them is the degree to which they are fetishized in the Marxian sense of the term. Marx (1976 [1867]: 163–177) argued that material goods were fetishized when they were turned into commodities and appeared to have properties such as value, independent of the human labor that went into the production of the good. In other words, a commodity is fetishized when the real forces that generate it – the labor of workers congealed in it – becomes mystified and is made invisible in the process of capital exchange. When Marx spoke of fetishization he was thinking particularly of how this concept applied to material goods. However, when intimate affairs are outsourced in a manner where a client does not see the actual performance of these tasks, we can extend this idea and apply it to these types of services. In fact, one of the benefits of these types of services is that necessary tasks get done without the client having to do the work or be involved in monitoring those who do.

For example, in contrast to past research on domestic work which found that most clients 'preferred an individual, female worker to either a household service agency or to a male employee' because they could develop a personal relationship with the person cleaning their home, Bickham Mendez (1998: 123) found the situation to be quite different today:

> Domestic workers and managers [of a nationally franchised housekeeping company] told me of employer/clients who were too busy to establish personalistic relationships with employees. These women specifically requested that housecleaners clean while they were not home and expressed a desire to escape time-consuming and emotionally-draining personal relationships with them … [C]lients often hire a household service agency precisely in order to achieve distance between themselves and housecleaners, thereby avoiding the emotional work involved in personalistic management of domestic workers.

Many personal chefs also note that most of their clients are not home when they perform their work. For example, one personal chef notes that

> I do all of the work in their [i.e. the client's] home. I'm using 99 per cent of my own utensils. I clean up. *Most often people don't know that I've been there* except for the smell in the house or the food in the fridge or they realized the kitchen is really clean. (Cited in Winslow, 2000 – emphasis added; cf. also Cone, 2005)

There is certainly a magical and enchanting quality to such services – domestic affairs appear to just get done – but, in the absence of seeing the actual labor involved in their performance, the potential is readily there for these types of intimate affairs to be fetishized.

Conclusion

As was shown above, there are many unique elements to outsourcing and metamanagement that make them both a very rational/efficient means for having these types of affairs performed and a means that has the potential to introduce a number of irrational consequences into the domestic context. One such consequence is the potential for outsourcing and metamanagement to disenchant domestic affairs that are emotion or sentiment-laden. Another is that they open the door for these types of services to appear as things that simply happen, and while this may appear as magical from the client's perspective, it also creates the conditions for these services to be fetishized in the manner that Marx spoke of.

There is another consequence of the outsourcing and metamanagement of domestic affairs that is worth mentioning as well. This is that while it is true that many families employ these services so that they can concentrate their resources around their family, they do so by transferring domestic tasks from the family to others. But if outsourcing is commonly employed by businesses so that they can concentrate on their 'core competencies' by shifting 'peripheral' tasks to others, what are the corresponding 'core' and 'peripheral' activities for families? That is, while it is true that many would not consider yard work or perhaps even laundry as being a 'core' family activity, what of gift-giving and remembrance services? Are these at least not closer to the core than many of the chores that people are willingly giving to others to perform? But if they are closer, what is to stop future businesses from encroaching further into core family functions? This is another way of asking, from a family's point of view, is there anything that 'is "too meaningful" to outsource' (Hochschild, 2005: 78). What exactly this limit is is an issue that only time will tell. But as more and more families face time pressures the desire of families to outsource more and more domestic affairs will undoubtedly increase and the boundary of this 'core' will be pushed further and further back. One can wonder if at some point those who outsource their domestic affairs, even if they are doing so in order to try and preserve their family life, will come to empty the very thing that they are trying to save. One can also wonder if this is what a virtual family will look like?

Notes

1. See Lair (2007) for a review of some of these.
2. This definition is a variation of the one used by Lair (2007). In this work, Lair applies the idea outsourcing to 'intimate affairs' or the activities necessary to reproduce what Habermas (1991 [1962]: 46–47) calls the 'intimate sphere.' See this work for a more extensive discussion of how outsourcing should be defined in relation to affairs of the intimate sphere.
3. http://data.bls.gov/PDQ/servlet/SurveyOutputServlet?data_tool=latest_ numbers&series_id=LNS11300002&years_option=specific_years&include_ graphs=true&to_year=2006&from_year=1948
4. http://data.bls.gov/PDQ/servlet/SurveyOutputServlet?data_tool=latest_ numbers&series_id=LNS11300001&years_option=specific_years&include_ graphs=true&to_year=2006&from_year=1948
5. This website was accessed on 12 January 2008.
6. 'Seeing Red' http://www.scoopdujour.com/scoop/archives/000157.html
7. Accessed on 26 February 2008.

References

Addison, Lisa. 2003. *How to Start Your Own Personal Conceirge Service.* Irvine, CA: Entrepreneur Press.

Anderson, Carol. 2005. 'Carlin Had a High-Paying Job … But She Wanted to Have a Life.' *Personal Chef Magazine* July 1, 2005.

Barker, Olivia. April 19, 2006. 'Coming-of-Age Grows Lavish; Parties Become a Competition in Extravagance.' *USA Today*, 1D.

Bauman, Zygmunt. 1989. *Modernity and the Holocaust.* Ithaca, NY: Cornell University Press.

Beck, Ulrich and Beck-Gernsheim Elisabeth. 1995. *The Normal Chaos of Love.* Malden, MA: Polity Press.

Bianchi, Suzanne M. and Lynne M. Casper. 2000. 'American Families.' *Population Bulletin* 55(4).

Bianchi, Suzanne, Melissa Milkie, Liana Sayer, and John Robinson. 2000. 'Is Anyone Doing the Housework? Trends in the Gender Division of Household Labor.' *Social Forces* 79(1):191–228.

Bianchi, Suzanne M., John P. Robinson, and Melissa Milkie. 2006. *Changing Rhythms of American Life.* New York, NY: Russell Sage Foundation.

Bickham Mendez, Jennifer. 1998. 'Of Mops and Maids: Contradictions and Continuities in Bureaucratized Domestic Work.' *Social Problems* 45(1):114–135.

Braverman, Harry. 1974. *Labor and Monopoly Capital: The Degradation of Work in the Twentieth Century.* New York, NY: Monthly Review Press.

Chatzky, Jean. October 18, 2005. 'Finding Good Help These Days.' *CNN Money.Com.*

Conover, Kirsten. August 11, 1997. 'At Your Service.' *The Christian Science Monitor.*

Cone, Laura (2005) 'Personal Chef Cooks Up Convenience.' *Tampa Tribune* August 29, PASCO; p. 3.

Corbett, Michael. 2004. *The Outsourcing Revolution: Why It Makes Sense and How to Do It Right.* Chicago, IL: Dearborn Trade Publishing.

Dobbs, Lou. 2004. *Exporting America: Why Corporate Greed Is Shipping American Jobs Overseas.* New York, NY: Warner Business Books.

Everything But Time. n.d. [Web page] http://www.time-less.com/aboutus.html

Flaherty, Julie. December 14, 2003. 'Long Christmas List? You Can Outsource It.' *The New York Times* 3, p. 10.

Gardner, Marilyn. 2006. 'Professional Organizers Help Fight "Battle of the Bulging Files"' *Christian Science Monitor* March 29, 2006, p. 14 (http://www.csmonitor.com/2006/0329/p14s01-ussc.html).

Giddens, Anthony. 1991. *Modernity and Self-Identity: Self and Society in the Late Modern Age.* Stanford, CA: Stanford University Press.

Giddens, Anthony. 1992. *The Transformation of Intimacy: Sexuality, Love and Eroticism in Modern Societies.* Stanford, CA: Stanford University Press.

Gillis, John R. 1996. *A World of Their Own Making: Myth, Ritual, and the Quest for Family Values.* Cambridge, MA: Harvard University Press.

Giovanni, Katharine C. and Ron Giovanni. 2002. *The Concierge Manual.* Wake Forest, NC: NewRoad Publishing.

Gordon, Robert B. and Patrick M. Malone. 1997. *The Texture of Industry: An Archaeological View of the Industrialization of North America.* New York, NY: Oxford University Press.

Green, Frank. July 2, 2006. 'Online Express Lane: County's Big Grocers Are Finding that Web Offers Growth Market.' *The San Diego Union-Tribute*, p. H1.

Habermas, Jurgen. 1991 (1962). *The Structural Transformation of the Public Sphere: An Inquiry into a Category of Bourgeois Society*. Cambridge, MA: MIT Press.

Harrison McBride, Laura, Peter J. Gallanis, and Taq Goulet. 2005. *FabJob Guide to Become a Personal Shopper*. Seattle, WA: FastJob.com, Ltd.

Hochschild, Arlie R. 2005. ' "Rent a Mom" and Other Services: Markets, Meanings and Emotions.' *International Journal of Work Organisation and Emotion* 1(1):74–86.

Horkheimer, Max and Thodor W. Adorno. 1998. *Dialectic of Enlightenment*. New York, NY: Continuum.

Jacobs, A. J. 2005. 'My Outsourced Life.' *Esquire*, September 1, 2005. (http://www.esquire.com/ESQ0905OUTSOURCING_214)

Jacobs, Jerry A. and Kathleen Gerson. 2004. *The Time Divide: Work, Family, and Gender Inequality*. Cambridge, MA: Harvard University Press.

Kahlenberg, Reebecca R. April 2, 2005. 'Saying No Mow; More People Outsource Lawn Care.' *The Washington Post*, F01.

Kalberg, Stephen. 1980. 'Max Weber's Types of Rationality: Cornerstones for the Analysis of Rationalization Processes in History.' *American Journal of Sociology* 85(5):1145–1179.

Kim-York, Sophie. 2005. *Career KNOWtes Personal Shopping (How to Have Fun and Make Money)*. Irving, TX: Sparklesoup Studios, Inc.

Krischer Goodman, Cindy. August 23, 2006. 'No Time for Chores? Just Call Your Personal Concierge.' *TheMiamiHerald.Com*.

Lair, Craig D. 2007. 'The Outsourcing of Intimate Affairs.' Ph.D. dissertation, Department of Sociology, University of Maryland, College Park, MD.

Marx, Karl. 1976. *Capital: Volume 1*. New York, NY: Vintage Books.

Merry Maids. n.d. 'About Us' [Web page] http://www.merrymaids.com/company

Miller, Daniel. 1998. *A Theory of Shopping*. Malden, MA: Polity Press.

Mowshowitz, Abbe. 1997. 'On the Theory of Virtual Organization.' *Systems Research and Behavioral Science* 14:373–384.

Mowshowitz, Abbe. 2002. *Virtual Organization: Toward a Theory of Societal Transformation Stimulated by Information Technology*. Westport, CT: Quorum Books.

Palmer, Kim. April 25, 2006. 'Outsourcing Comes Home.' *StarTribune.com*

Prahalad, C. K. and Gary Hamel. 1990. 'The Core Competence of the Corporation.' *Harvard Business Review* 68(3, May–June):79–93.

Ritzer, George. 2005. *Enchanting a Disenchanted World: Revolutionizing the Means of Consumption*. Thousand Oaks, CA: Pine Forge Press.

Ritzer, George. 2004. *The McDonaldization of Society: Revised New Century Edition*. Thousand Oaks, CA: Pine Forge Press.

Sandholtz, K., Derr, B., Buckner, K., and Carlson, D. 2002. *Beyond Juggling, Rebalancing Your Busy Life*. San Francisco, CA: Berrett-Koehler Publishers.

Save My Ass.com. n.d. [Web page]. Available at www.savemyass.com

Secord, Hugh. 2003. *Implementing Best Practices in Human Resources Management*. Toronto, ON: CCH Canadian Limited.

Sharpe, Rochelle. September 18, 2000. 'Nannies on Speed Dial.' *Businessweek Online*.

Sheth, Jagdish N. and Rajendra S. Sisodia. June 28, 1999. 'Manager's Journal: Outsourcing Comes Home.' *The Wall Street Journal*, p. A26.

Stefanini, Sara. 2006. 'DoodyCalls: Finding a Gold Mine in Dog Poop.' *Azcentral.com*

Storybook Cards. n.d. 'Our Sevices' [Web page]. Available at http://storybookcards.com/services.php

The Montana Standard. 'Thank-You Cards, Outsourced.' August 27, 2005.

Thiruvengadam, Meena. October 16, 2005. 'Turning Retail Therapy into a Living.' *San Antonio Express-News*, 1G.

Tiffany, Laura. 2001. 'How to Be a Personal Concierge: Make Every Client Feel Like the Most Important Person in the World With a Personal Concierge Service.' Entrepreneur.com, February 22, 2001.

Wasserman, Mariam. 1999. 'Beating the Clock.' *Regional Review*. vol. Quarter 3. (http://www.bos.frb.org/economic/nerr/rr1999/q3/wass99_3.htm.)

Weber, Max. 1946. *From Max Weber: Essays in Sociology*. Ed. H. H. Gerth and C. W. Mills. New York, NY: Oxford University Press.

Weber, Max. 1964. *The Theory of Social and Economic Organization*. New York, NY: Free Press.

Winslow, Olivia. June 7, 2000. 'Busy Consumers Are Hiring Personal Errand Services to Handle an Increasing Array of Household Chores.' *Newsday*.

Chapter 8

Ideal homes?

Managing the domestic dream   *Karen Dale*

The unlikely but enduring marriage between management and the home[1]

In much of the social analysis of industrialised capitalist societies, the two protagonists of this chapter – 'the home' and 'management' – appear to be incompatible, moving in entirely different social circles and with completely different interests. The ideal of the home has been commonly portrayed as the antithesis of the managerial domain: a 'haven in a heartless world'. This idealised home has been seen as a space of the personal and the private, as opposed to the public world of employment usually associated with management. However, the argument of this chapter is that there has been a close and enduring relationship between 'management' and 'the home'. Management as a specific set of techniques and values developed within the medieval household long before these practices were applied within industrial capitalism and came to be related with a particular class of employees who utilised them, thus becoming described as 'managers'. Recent work has been significant in pointing out the much broader influence of 'management' in everyday cultural and social life (e.g. Parker, 2002; Hancock and Tyler, 2004). And the practices and values of management have continued to influence domestic life too. In this chapter I consider one aspect of this: the use of managerial rhetorics and techniques in the shaping of home renovation and decorating projects.

The ongoing relationship between management and the home is significant, but not because it is a simple and superficial transfer of the language of management into spheres of life other than that of production. Rather it is because the techniques and ideologies of management come to constitute an important element of social relations and identities. These are not limited to discourse, although this is important in the framing and interpretation of social action, but the effects of management can be seen in material and embodied practices. In the example given below, management techniques and values are embedded into the actual physical construction of the house. Thus even the most private social spaces are shot through with the medium of management. Therefore, conceptually, it is important to see private and privatised spaces such as the home as not separate from social relations, and not even solely about the immediate embodied social relations that take place within them, but also those social relations that are embedded in the very construction of the spaces themselves (cf. Lefebvre, 1991). It is these management techniques and ideologies that create ways in which capitalist structures and values can become embedded in every social and material relation. They allow the underlying structures of capitalism to adapt flexibly to contemporary cultural and social patterns, since they are implanted into taken-for-granted aspects of everyday living.

In order to explore in detail this largely obscured but surprisingly long-lasting alliance between management and the home, we begin with a consideration of the particular characteristics of management as a form of interaction with, and indeed transformation of, the material and social world. The perspective that is taken in this chapter is that management is both a *practice*, a specific way of acting upon the world, and an *ideology*, a particular way of looking at the world. Grey argues that 'the ascription of the term "management" to various kinds of activities is not a mere convenience but rather something which has *certain effects*' (1999: 577, emphasis added). Management is in essence a combination of techniques and discourses that make things happen, and make them happen in particular ways. Of course, this is not to suggest that 'management' when taken in conjunction with the home has been a monolithic entity, but rather has changed and adapted over time, just as managerial techniques and discourses within the industrial organisation are also dynamic. The characteristics of management that are brought out below are threads which can be seen through its historical vicissitudes, although manifest in different specific ways depending on context. The specific forms of management practices and ideologies that will be focused on in this chapter are contemporary ones which relate to the analysis of home decoration and renovation discussed in the following section.

This chapter, then, considers management from a sociological perspective. That is, it argues that management plays a role in the forms that society takes and the social relations engendered. Reed (1989) distinguishes three analytical perspectives on management: the technical, the political and the critical. The technical perspective sees management as a set of rationally designed tools for achieving certain objectives. In this view it is conceived as a 'neutral social technology' (1989: 3). In contrast, the political perspective sees management as a social process which is related to power, and especially the use of power to achieve the aims and values of certain interest groups in society. Thus the political view analyses the assumptions which underlie management techniques, how these techniques form a system of social control, and how they are obscured under the guise of rationality (Alvesson and Willmott, 1992). The critical perspective is an extension of this, in that it sees management as a form of social control which perpetuates the capitalist system of production and its ideology. Although this categorisation was devised by Reed to organise existing analysis of management theory, its three elements, taken together rather than as mutually exclusive, can be used for the purposes of this chapter to consider the relations between management and domestic life.

In considering how 'management' has a much broader currency than simply referring to certain tasks performed by a particular set of people in work organisations, Parker sees its wide dissemination today as 'both a civilising process and a new civic religion' (p. 2), a universal solution against chaos and inefficiency. Willmott suggests that '"management", in the sense of reflexive social action, is intrinsic to human agency' (1984: 350). It is particularly a sense of agency, the implication of being able to exert influence over events and surroundings, as well as in social relations that makes management such a potent concept. Parker (2002) argues that management is essentially about a belief in control: control over nature, over human beings, and of our organisational abilities (p. 3). 'Management is one of the ways in which we articulate this control over things by making them manageable, subject to the control of human beings' (ibid.). Yet it is a form of control which has its own effects. Its techniques are presented as rational and objective, as the most efficient ways of achieving the desired goals, and not limited by personal whim, social relationships or emotion. Thus the practice of management can be related to a certain form of detachment from the objects of control, be they human or material.

Ultimately, this also becomes a form of control over self, perhaps at the present time seen most overtly, as Parker (2002) comments, in the proliferation of self-help manuals based around the idea of self-management: manage your emotions, manage your career, manage your time, and so on. These have a resonance with Foucault's 'technologies of the self':

> which permit individuals to effect by their own means or with the help of others a certain number of operations on their own bodies and souls, thoughts, conduct, and way of being, so as to transform themselves in order to attain a certain state of happiness, purity, wisdom, perfection, or immortality. (1988b: 18)

Self-management is a particular way of working on the self that focuses on an impetus for self-mastery, rational techniques, making calculable and visible, weighing up options and making decisions based upon efficiency and effectiveness.

The ideology and practices of 'household management', in their historical and contemporary contexts, demonstrate an enduring, although adaptive, power of 'management' in the construction of what Miller describes as 'calculating selves and calculable spaces' (1992: 78–79). Thus the practices and ideologies of (household) management bring together the technologies whereby we work upon our selves and those technologies that enable our openness to a wider 'governmentality' within society (Foucault, 1991; Rose, 1996: 152). Rose (1989: 10–11) expresses this cogently when he explains that

> citizens shape their lives through the choices they make about family life, work, leisure, lifestyle, and personality and its expression. Government works by 'acting at a distance' upon these choices, forging a symmetry between the attempts of individuals to make life worthwhile for themselves, and the political values of consumption, profitability, efficiency, and social order. Contemporary government, that is to say, operates through the delicate and minute infiltration of the ambitions of regulation into the very interior of our existence and experience as subjects.

This means that just as management in relation to organisation is not neutral but perpetuates certain interests, so too is 'household management' political as well as personal, and contributory to the reproduction and flexibility of class and gender relations, and of capitalism as a dominant societal 'mode of organising'.

There is a 'materiality of ideas' (Braidotti, 1994: 126) achieved through household management, that solidifies whilst it obscures the political nature of household management. This material management of the home produces an ordering which embodied and spatialised social actors then 'live through' or 'enact' (Dale and Burrell, 2007). This everyday repetitive 'performance' of the relations of capitalism, with its stratifications of class and gender, is a much more powerful form of reproduction than one that solely takes place at the level of the ideational.

Yet the home is commonly seen as the antithesis of management. Rather than a place dominated by hierarchy, impersonal functional relationships and rational decision-making, it is meant to be a place of nurturing relationships and free expression of personality and emotions, of leisure, pleasure and regeneration from productive work. As Wajcman (1991: 85–86) argues: 'The split between public and private meant that the home was expected to provide a haven from the alienated, stressful technological order of the workplace and was expected to provide entertainment, emotional support, and sexual gratification.'

This dichotomised 'imaginary'[2] between home and workplace is derived from the physical separation of spaces for production and reproduction that accompanied the Industrial Revolution, although never in as linear and complete a way as conjured up the ideological construction of these 'separate spheres'. Indeed, the rupturism between the household and the industrial enterprise that dominates accounts of the development of modern capitalism might be regarded as a mode of institutionalised discrimination. The pre-industrial revolution household is regarded through the lens of the post-industrial revolution construction of separate spheres between 'home' and 'work', between production and reproduction, where the private domestic sphere has become associated with a gendered division of labour and a lesser value. Thus accounts of the development of capitalism concentrate on the significance of a separate space, a separate organisation, separate ownership and a productivist focus. The influence of commerce and finance often becomes seen as secondary (cf. Fulcher, 2004: 27), whilst the requirements of mass production in moving out of the household are seen as paramount defining characteristics.

What this ignores is that ongoing work of capitalism which continues throughout all aspects of everyday social life, including the domestic home.

Within the discourse of 'separate spheres', management has become associated almost exclusively with modern Western industrialised capitalism. Parker links management with democratic market liberalism (2002: 4) and Grey argues that management 'carries irrevocable implications and resonances which are associated with industrialism and modern Western forms of rationality and control' (1999: 577). Although many writers on management pay a nodding acknowledgement to the root of management in the household, this tends to be briefly dealt with at the level of etymology and then quietly dropped (Mant, 1977: 7–8; Parker, 2002). There is little consideration of how and why it developed from household economic strategies, nor how it might continue to exert an influence on everyday domestic life. The contemporary form of this deliciously clandestine relationship provides the focus of this chapter, but before turning to this it is useful to trace earlier stages in the partnership, to appreciate how it has adapted to the demands of changing times and contexts, forming a relationship which is surprisingly stable and resilient.

As Mant (1977: 7–8) and others have commented, the very origins of 'management' are to be found in housekeeping (French: *menager*) and horse-handling (Italian: *maneggiare*). Yet this should not be taken as some quaint apple-pie trivia, but as a significant challenge to the compartmentalised categories of much social analysis of management. In contrast to a separation of public and domestic spheres, the roots of household management may be seen in the confluence between the household and the economy. The modern word 'economics' comes from Aristotle's idea of the 'oikos nomos'. *Oikos* is the Attic word for dwelling, and *nomos* means laws or management. This refers to the careful administration of the home and its goods in order to provide for the whole family or community. Both economy and management have become transposed to more explicitly public arenas, and their exposition has moved to the stage of the state and the institution (particularly the capitalist organisation). Nevertheless, it is worth returning to the household both to understand the development of management and economics and to argue that the household, despite its symbolic status as the 'other' of public and economic life, remains centrally permeated by capitalism, due, in part, to its covert but long-standing relationship with management.

The recent interest in looking at management in 'everyday life' seems to suggest a narrative whereby management left behind the ill-lit confines of its liaison with the pre-industrial household for a more glamorous partnership with the bright lights of public organisational life and, with its success assured, is now returning to once again seduce hearth and heart. Part of the reason for this underlying story-line is the potent ideology of the home as a private, autonomous realm, a 'separate sphere'. Within this sanctified and sealed off space the individual is seen as possessing choice, freedom and power: lord of all he or she surveys, pulling up the metaphorical drawbridge on the outside world. This dichotomous narrative is one of the themes this chapter is to question. Of course, there are many empirical and theoretical accounts that illustrate a multitude of ways in which the idea of the separation of spheres is problematic. Political economists and geographers have pointed to the role of homeownership in the production of an indebted and thus docile citizenry (e.g. Harvey, 1983), whilst those who analyse consumer culture show how the home is key to many aspects of the perpetration of that (e.g. Miller, 1987). Feminist writers have pointed to the home as the place of gendered work, every bit as much a place of labour as that described as the 'workplace'. Socialist feminist writers have additionally pointed to the home as integral to an understanding of capitalist dynamics, through its reproduction of the workforce on a daily and generational basis, through the care and nurturing of labour both for the next day's work and for its continuance through the next generation of workers. In this, domestic reproduction was seen as in some form of articulation with production and consumption, rather than as a totally autonomous segment of the 'circuit of capital'. Yet this in itself does not go far enough in dismantling the association of the domestic solely with reproduction. Thus, throughout this chapter, it is argued that the home is not the place only of the relations of reproduction, but that it brings together production and consumption with reproduction in multiple and flexible ways. The home is not a castellated edifice, with protective battlements separating it from the wider structural influences of capitalism. Rather, it is a place where these social relations have their very constituency. It is not that the home has been 'invaded' by management but that the home has had an enduring close liaison with management: it has borne and nurtured management practices and ideology, both historically and today. By taking a longer historical perspective on 'household management' it is possible to see that management in and of everyday life pre-dates what key theorists such as Weber would actually classify as modern capitalism, and that it was central to its development and its continuance. This is not to suggest that it exhibits today the same characteristics as it did in the fourteenth century, but that household management is itself adaptive and flexible, and the more powerful for that.

There are particular periods in history where the partnership that might be described as 'household management' has become more explicit and visible. This is especially the case where it has been promulgated in textual form, which of course has left us its traces. One of these periods, during the fourteenth century, was the development of a widespread use within the propertied classes of gentry and merchants of the household account book. Accounts clerks were commonly employed to oversee these nascent management techniques and formularies were written to disseminate the best practices. The problems of organising and maintaining households are even a common topic within poetical romances of the medieval period (Smith, 2003: xv). At a time where mercantile capitalism was taking off, the household, as the key site of economic and social relations of the time, including its role as the unit of state taxation, became a space of calculation and control (Starkey, 1981; Smith, 2003). Another significant period of activity can be perceived during the Victorian period where writers such as Isabella Beeton in the UK and Catherine Beecher in the USA, popularised a rationalised form of household management to be run along industrial lines. Beeton's *Household Management*, serialised from 1859, for example, included a rational hierarchy of servants, specifying their wages, roles and tasks. It also rationalises the siting, layout and provisioning of the kitchen, as well as advocating careful accounting. Beeton (1961) is innovative in including precise amounts and costings of recipes even though the recipes themselves are often seen as highly derivative of the work of better cooks! As Hughes comments: 'The labour is specialized, repetitive, and, more often than not, mechanized. Kitchen equipment is described and illustrated as if it were industrial plant' (2005: 52). This move was intensified at the height of mass production, where proselytes such as Christine Frederick and Lilian Gilbreth explicitly brought the principles and techniques of scientific management into the home, and especially into the design of the kitchen. In this, a specialisation of space to function and a standardisation of processes into routines were afforded centrality. Frederick even conducted her own time-and-motion studies into various household tasks in order to minimise unnecessary movements and steps – the result of which is still seen today in the concept of the 'work triangle' around which the efficient kitchen is designed. Although I do not have space to examine this hidden history of 'household management' here (see, however, Dale, 2008), it is important to highlight this ongoing relationship whereby management techniques have been developed in conjunction with the shaping of the home.

In order to explore this relationship further, this chapter examines the discourses used in contemporary accounts of home design and decoration: the construction of the 'ideal home'. In contemporary times the domestic space has become enrolled within the larger project of identity expression. The plethora of television programmes, magazines and self-help books on the topic indicate that interior design is no longer the sole province of aristocratic domiciles, or of expensive professionals. In exploring the ways that this 'project' of the home is constructed, it is argued that the dominant discourses of aesthetic pleasure and expression of identity are underpinned by the discourse of management.

Management and the construction of the 'Ideal Home'

In the UK, as in many industrialised capitalist economies, there has been a huge growth in the area that might be described in the broadest terms as 'home interest'. The conscious design and manipulation of the domestic interior has, of course, a long history, but in recent decades this has become evermore democratised. Once, the customised items of the luxury goods market and the exclusive professional expertise would have been only available to the wealthiest in society. Now mass produced consumer goods, mass media expertise especially disseminated through magazines and the television, and the development of a 'do it yourself' approach to design have made the creation of an 'ideal home' open to almost anyone. Indeed, the societal pressures may be said to be such that there is an expectation that people will engage in expressing themselves through their homes and that this will not constitute a one-off event but will involve a cyclical process of updating.

This 'home interest' sphere provides fertile ground for examining how management practices and ideology underlie everyday life. A large number of studies have explored the relationship between social actors and their homes and possessions (e.g. Csikszentmihalyi and Rochberg-Halton, 1981; Forty, 1986; Gullestad, 1992; Carsten and Hugh-Jones, 1995; Attfield, 2000; Miller, 2001; Pink, 2004). These provide an important insight into the centrality of the home to social and material relations, as opposed to the peripheral role it is sometimes accorded in social theory:

> A house generally has many aspects and meanings. It is a tool with a practical utility, and with economic, social, aesthetic, cosmological, and symbolic aspects. A place to live in is created by people and functions as a framework for their lives. The house and the inhabitants are in this way mutually constituted. (Gullestad, 1992: 62)

The significance of management practices and ideology within the relationship of people to their homes is thus only one aspect of the complex and diverse web of ways in which people are linked to their homes and possessions, but it is one that has barely been touched upon.[3] Further, I would argue that it is central to the ways in which the 'private' domain of the home is intimately linked to the 'wider' reproduction of economic and social relations.

In looking at the relationship between management and everyday domestic life, I have explored in detail the discourses surrounding 'home interest'. In particular I have considered one of the many magazines on the market. This is '*25 Beautiful Homes*', published monthly by IPC Media since 1998. Issues of the magazine from 2000 to 2008 have been analysed. According to the ABC results on the circulation of home interest magazines July–December 2006, it has a circulation of 116,521 and from the NRS survey from July 2006 to June 2007, it has a readership of 408,000 (www.ipcmedia.com/mediainfo/25homes. pdf). From its own media information (ibid.) its average reader age is 46, is 77 per cent female and 71 per cent from occupational groups ABC1. From readership information it states that 'readers are twice as likely to change the decoration at home regularly'.

25 Beautiful Homes has been described as 'the voyeurs' guide to beautiful homes' (www.magforum.com/magpubs1.htm)! Each issue presents, as the title suggests, 25 homes from the point of view of their owners' stories and with pictures of the main rooms in each house. The narrative is presented from the point of view of the home-owners' experience in bringing their home to its current state. The stories are diverse. They may have built it from scratch, renovated it completely or simply moved in and re-decorated and re-arranged it to a greater or lesser extent. Reading between the lines, the motivation for inclusion in the magazine is also diverse. Reasons would seem to vary, from those houseowners who appear to be about to put the houses on the market thus perhaps seeking to generate interest in potential purchasers; people who have lost partners who were involved in the home's evolution and might be interpreted as seeing the magazine article as a type of memorial; the occasional Bed and Breakfast proprietor; and a large number of owners who occupy various roles in the interior design business, including producers and retailers as well as designers. The style of these stories has evolved over the time-span of the magazine such that they currently include a potted history of the previous house-owning experiences of the owner(s), a description of the number and composition of the rooms of the house, and (optional to the owner) the cost of the house, the cost of renovations and current value of the house. Snippets of advice from the home-owners are extracted as enlarged portions of text arranged around the images, thus presenting the owners as 'experts'. Consumption advice is also presented. Text and images frequently have sources of objects included, a final panel on each house gives examples of where similar objects may be purchased, and a separate page answers readers' letters asking for information on where to obtain items viewed in previous issues.

It must be acknowledged that the narratives presented as quotations from 'interviews' with the home-owners are not comparable with conventional research interview data. This acknowledgement, however, is not to suggest that conventional interview data is somehow 'objective' in comparison; as Stanley and Wise (1983) succinctly put it, there is no data that does not go through the medium of the researcher. But these are interviews as portrayed by the magazine for a particular purpose in selling the magazine to both readers and (potential) advertisers. It is impossible to know what house-owners actually said, how much has been adapted to fit 'house style' [*sic*!] or otherwise given a particular interpretation by journalists and editors. In addition, as with all interviews of any source, the data is a post-action reflective account, and hence subject to those processes of being made coherent, rational and socially acceptable. Nevertheless, these accounts of the processes involved in the creation of a 'beautiful home' still influence a huge market of purchasers and readers, whether the discourses are derived directly from the home-owners or mediated by the media. For example, in a Mintel study on the market for kitchen furniture (August 2007), 42 per cent of respondents agreed that magazines gave them ideas for improving their home and 37 per cent agreed that they were always looking for new ideas to improve their home (from a TGI survey of 25,000 adults, Mintel, 2007).

Throughout this chapter I have been emphasising that management is both about ideology *and* practices, and I would like to maintain this dual awareness through the analysis of the 'ideal home'. The home 'projects' are presented in the magazine through a series of discourses, in word and picture form, which can be analysed in terms of their rhetorical strategies and ideological framework. The work of Gowler and Legge (1996) alerts us to some key aspects of managerial rhetorical strategies which are as relevant to the analysis of household management as they are to organisational management. They argue that the very potency of management relies upon a deployment of a mixture or multiplicity of rhetorical strategies. Management combines both a rationalistic rhetoric ('techno-social' order) with an emotive ('moral-aesthetic') one. It is this combination of twin rhetorics that creates the possibility for things to be done, and it also creates the particular perspective and consequences of managerial control. They argue that the apparently 'plain-speaking' aspect of management discourse, that which is aimed at goals, objectives, plans, budgets, timetables and so on, is also a rhetorical strategy aimed at 'the arousal and direction of behaviour' (1996: 36). Gowler and Legge identify three themes of management rhetoric that can also be usefully distinguished within the analysis of home design projects below. The first is the idea of the 'sovereignty of management', this is that management has a legitimate right to power, to get things done and done in a particular way. This allows management to be a process which is not questioned and which takes precedence over other potential priorities. It also conveys power on those who use its language. The second theme is that of management as accountability. According to Gowler and Legge this combines management as competence with management as possessing a moral superiority, because it is careful, efficient and responsible; it is a 'form of moral and technical reckoning' (1996: 41). It emphasises careful husbandry, especially through the use of accounting language, something which was a feature of the early medieval treatises on household management. The implications of this are articulated by Miller:

> Far from being neutral devices for mirroring the social world, the calculative technologies of accountancy are complex machines for representing and intervening in social and economic life. Along with allied expertises, the creation of calculating selves and calculable spaces enables a normalization of individual lives that is cast in financial terms. (Miller, 1992: 78–79)

This combined technical and moral superiority facilitates the extension of management into greater areas of control: 'the hierarchical ordering of roles and relationships is equated with the responsible conduct of human affairs, and where "the right to manage" is extended to become "the right to manage power and exchange relationships"' (Gowler and Legge, 1996: 42). These themes are combined with that of a third: 'management as achievement'. Management here is about getting results. This in turn is closely related to a complex of meanings around success that Offe characterises as 'the achieving society' (1976: 40 in Gowler and Legge, 1996: 47). Again, power and identity accrue to those who are able to invoke management.

However, it is also important to remember that the houses presented in the magazines and television programmes and discussed below have *also* been constructed in material form. The discourses do not relate to abstract ideas, but to ideas which have been made physical and spatial. The houses are not stage sets, but are habitations within which 'everyday life' is lived. They are social spaces that have been constructed through particular relations of power and ideology, including those embedded in management ideology. These material arrangements have just as significant effects in political and personal terms as do the discourses. People 'live through' these places and spaces as simultaneously social and embodied beings. By 'living through' various social spaces, the constructions of both physical and imaginary space embedded in them become linked to processes of identity construction.

Through the analysis of *25 Beautiful Homes* and other media on home renovation and design, I would suggest that three main discourses are in play that can illuminate the management of everyday life. At the present time the two 'dominant discourses' (cf. Gilbert and Mulkay, 1984) around home design are those of the aesthetics of 'style' and of the expression of identity. The rhetoric of management techniques and control is more *sotto voce*, but as the following analysis indicates it underpins the ideology and practices of the 'ideal home'.

An example of the power of the underlying managerial ideology is shown most overtly in the television programme *Grand Designs* (Channel 4, UK). This is a long running programme, with a spin-off magazine of the same name, which features unusual self-built and renovation projects, predominantly focusing on those projects which start from scratch. Its presenter is Kevin McCloud, himself a lighting designer of some note. He is also the programme's consistent voice of 'authority' and the most vocal and explicit in the use of management rhetoric in relation to house design. He is interposed as interlocutor, 'expert' and interpreter of the process that the home-owners are going through. He consistently poses two narratives to the building projects: first, its aesthetic 'integrity' which frequently consists of an appeal to the expertise of the architect (underpinned by the assumption that the professional opinion on aesthetic matters is superior to that of the layperson). The second is the management rhetoric. His overlaid commentary is often used to interpose a dramatic pessimism and suspense into whether the subjects of the programme will complete their home on time, on budget and to a particular quality. These elements may very well be desired or required by the home-owners themselves, but also a seemingly 'objective' and 'neutral' standard is imposed on the project by this external managerial voice. Throughout this is the assumption of the fundamental need for control: of people, of processes, of material, of time and of cost, and that this constant management of the project is essential to and the only possible route to achieve the aesthetic style and expression of identity that are sought.

The control relationship becomes central to every aspect of the management of everyday life, and it governs relations with materials, space, time, people and self. The following example is typical of the accounts given: 'I'd meet the builder on a Monday morning to plan the week ahead, and every night I'd be on the computer working out a schedule of who had to be working where the next day. I knew almost to the hour who would be doing what, so we never had electricians hanging around waiting for plumbers' (July 2003: 18). Sometimes this is overtly recognised as a set of skills which links employment and 'everyday life', as in this quotation from a couple whose 'day jobs' are as a retail director and a managing director: 'Colin and I organise the opening of large retail stores for a living, and applied the same strict countdown of what we had to do each day to our house', Sally explains. 'The builders thought we were joking at first when we said we were going to be in by Christmas', she smiles, 'but when the carpets were laid on December 22nd, they realised we'd been serious all along' (February 2008: 130).

The most prominent discourse about house design is that of aesthetic style. Homes or rooms are often designed with a particular style in mind, often one which 'fits' with the period of the house or with aspects of the owner's lifestyle. This can be linked with the idea of 'theming' (Gottdiener, 2001). One owner comments that 'I like the idea of decorating each room differently in order to evoke various moods' (July 2003: 14). Another says that she would like to have four houses, so she could decorate each in a different style! Some owners favour an eclectic mix of styles, although these are then held together by a notion of aesthetic taste. The aesthetic management of the ideal home is about creating an effect, an image: '"You need strong elements to anchor a space," explains Harriet. "I didn't want everything to be "olde worlde". There has to be a balance"' (July 2003: 78) or

> 'I've always had a good eye for detail and feel comfortable about making decisions,' she explains, 'It's not so much about set dressing as looking at the complete frame. I tend to concentrate on the way a room is balanced in terms of foreground and background, on how certain objects can enhance the space. I have a passion for texture and adore opulent textiles, and I'm not afraid to use bold designs and patterns. At work or at home, I've learned that if a gamble doesn't pay off, it can always be rectified.' (November 2005: 141–142)

This desire to arrange the space of the home such that it communicates a particular narrative is debated in depth by Baudrillard in *The System of Objects* (1996, originally published in 1968). He argues that items of furniture have been detached from the significance of a 'moral dimension' (p. 14), they are no longer the personification of 'human relationships' (p. 14). He argues that there has been a reorganisation of space which emphasises 'maximum functionality' (p. 14) and a liberation from the relationships between object and social relations (p. 15). Gottdiener argues that from the 1930s, home interiors became commodified 'spaces of consumption' by the design ethos of modernism, such as the Bauhaus. 'Idiosyncratic furnishings were replaced in the home by the norms of modernist interior design with its systematic consuming of modules – kitchen sets, dining-room sets, living rooms sets – that synchronically reinforced compatible ambience' (Gottdiener, 2000: 268). It is this systematised materiality, arranged for consumption, that Baudrillard exposes. Although in some ways Baudrillard's arguments seem to be located within a specific historical period and 'style', and its contrast to a previous time, perhaps demonstrating elements of nostalgia, some points he makes are particularly relevant for understanding the 'ideal home' as a managerial project:

> Traditional good taste ... constituted a poetic discourse, an evocation of self-contained objects that responded to one another; today objects do not respond to one another, they communicate – they have no individual presence but merely, at best, an overall coherence attained by virtue of their simplification as components of a code and the way their relationships are calculated. An unrestricted combinatorial system enables man to use them as the elements of his structural discourse. (1996: 23)

This points to a particular mode of aesthetics, which is very much about an aesthetics of control and ordering. It is also an aesthetics which is to do with social ordering and communication: it is expressive rather than being an end in itself, and it signifies an identity, lifestyle or achievement.

To take the first point, the discourse around aesthetic style is revealed to be ultimately bound up with the manageability of objects. This need for control, which as we have seen, Parker (2002) links intimately with management, is also evident through the overt use of managerial discourses within home design which are considered in more detail below. ' "The best tip I have for a project like this is to plan well, install up-to-date equipment and make your contractors aware of those small but vital details" says William. "We have, and now our household runs like clockwork" ' (November 2007: 168).

This aesthetics of control and communication is achieved and sustained through a close relationship with consumption practices. Indeed, it requires the extension of consumption into an ongoing cycle, rather than as a one-off action whilst a renovation is underway. The following quotations illustrate three different modes of this accelerated consumption: 'I can't resist swapping ornaments and pictures around, or even putting them away and buying new ones' (January 2008: 104); 'We enjoy de-cluttering and starting again, so we were really keen to find our next home, and my next decorating project' (November 2007: 93) and 'The use of neutral shades is key, as this allows for the introduction of fashionable seasonal colours and accessories' (November 2007: 95). As Lefebvre says 'change is programmed: obsolescence is planned. Production anticipates reproduction; production produces change in such a way as to superimpose the impression of speed onto that of monotony' (1987: 10).

The combination of aesthetics, consumption and managerial control is shown in the often expressed need to bring in an 'expert', an interior designer: 'We needed someone to guide us through the huge choice of products out there' (November 2007: 172). This is sometimes because aesthetics has become closely related to brand: 'I was given a pair of David Linley candlesticks, and my love affair with his designs snowballed from there' (November 2007: 173). The very narratives of choice, desire and pleasure that construct the consuming self as supreme, simultaneously obscure the forms of power inherent in these narratives.

The management of the aesthetics of the ideal home, however, is not *just* about ordering an abstract sign system. The domestic sign systems are also social spaces, lived spaces (Lefebvre, 1991). It is important that whilst recognising the significance of the creation of an aesthetic effect and a vision of identity – the 'representational positioning' of the home (Ewen, 1988; Gottdiener, 2000) – we do not allow the materiality of these managed spaces to be leached out. These homes may be represented in the magazines as words and pictures, but they are lived through by the families who inhabit them, and thus the material objects fold back from being solely abstract sign systems to become material surroundings that in turn affect the practices and embodiment of those who 'manage' them. Thus the control and choice represented through management discourses is an illusion, as the material objects and their arrangements, even in the most personalised and private realm of the home, mutually enact with us as we enact with them (Dale, 2005). Thus when one home-owner says, 'I hope I don't sound smug...but this is my dream home, and it does all I want it to do. We use it, it doesn't use us; and it's so easy to maintain' (November 2007: 140), they are articulating a desire, but also an illusion, of managerial efficacy. In the context of the interwoven nature of home renovation and management, the sub-title of Paul Grimaldi's self-help book – 'Getting the Builders in...and staying in control' (2003) – says it all. Just as a number of writers on management have demonstrated that managers are also influenced in terms of their identity and beliefs by their role as managers (e.g. Watson, 1994; Pahl, 1995), so too does the management of everyday life produce the 'certain effects' that Grey comments upon. In the rest of this section, these 'certain effects' become more apparent as we explore the relationship between the management discourse and the articulation of identity bound up in home design.

The home 'project' becomes part of the narrative of the self, as the following representative quotations illustrate: 'We really wanted to make our mark on the house' (July 2003: 42) and 'we wanted a place of our own that reflected our lifestyle and taste' (November 2005: 90). The modern self has come to be seen as something to be worked upon and achieved through this identity-labour (cf. Foucault, 1988a, 1988b; Rose, 1989; Giddens, 1991). As Giddens articulates, the modern self can be seen as 'a reflexive project, for which the individual is responsible. We are, not what we are, but what we make of ourselves ... what the individual becomes is dependent on the reconstructive endeavours in which she or he engages' (in Waters, 1999: 176). In order to construct this coherent self, a narrative structure is required, which, as Giddens recognises, takes creative labour. This can be clearly linked to the conscious projects which many people engage in to create a particular environment, style and ordering of materiality, in their homes, and perhaps is most likely to be demonstrated in those home-owners who reflexively engage in making this project public through the inclusion of their homes in magazine such as *25 Beautiful Homes*. As with the extension of the project of the self to body-work, which Giddens also points to, the home provides a material setting in which to project [*sic*] outwards this inward narrative, making it concrete. It is also interesting that it is open to being a joint identity project, where many other aspects of self-construction are more individualised. This enables couples – and both heterosexual and homosexual couples feature within the magazine – and families to construct collective identity narratives. Both in the accounts that home-owners featured in the magazine give about their domestic 'transformations', and in the very material arrangements that they have achieved, home redecoration forms a way in which people can enter into the 'games of truth' that Foucault talks about. It enables them to not only 'confess' or speak out a 'truth' but produce a form of lived and material discourse that is intended to be the 'truth' about themselves: 'an exercise of self upon self by which one tries to work out, to transform one's self and to attain a certain mode of being' (Foucault, 1988a: 2).

The ordering of the material of the home is closely linked with the organisation of this identity project. Giddens comments that 'The self forms a trajectory of development from the past to the anticipated future. The individual appropriates his past by sifting through it in the light of what is anticipated for an (organised) future' (1991, in Waters, 1999: 176). We can compare this to one of the accountants interviewed by Grey (1994), who explains: 'It's all about ladders, I mean, not just work but getting married and having kids, or houses and cars and things like that. You're always trying to make yourself get one stage further on. You have to have something to aim for, don't you?' (Grey, 1994: 496). This 'organised future' includes the ordering of the materiality of the home:

> Now, with the work complete, Sam and Steve can concentrate on the next part of their plan – raising a family. 'I'm so pleased we decided to tackle the work on the house straightaway,' concludes Sam, 'as with the birth of our twin daughters last year, it was a relief to have everything just as we wanted it.' (January 2008: 98)

The language of the management of career and home is very much bound up with the management of identity as something which is worked upon, is developed and achieved rather than something which is natural or simply part of being (Rose, 1989).

This re-organisation of the identity narrative can also be seen in relation to the management of the objects that are associated with past and future selves, either in relation to the attachment and retention of them, to become differently arranged within new settings and new narratives, or the disposal of them, and the desire to start a new phase of the identity narrative with a new set of material objects and arrangements (cf. Hecht, 2001; Marcoux, 2001): 'The objects are given new meanings through recontextualisation, actively interpreted and arranged in new compositions' (Gullestad, 1992: 78). Examples of this, even to the extent where home-owners completely dispose of their possessions and purchase an entirely new collection, are to be frequently found in *25 Beautiful Homes*: 'Once they had a moving-in date, they put most of the furniture from their previous home up for auction. "Starting from zero again was a great adventure," says Jane, "here we were in our 50s, with no possessions – there was no looking back"' (November 2005: 116). Part of this ability to reconstruct material and social identity in this way comes from the distancing effect of managerial control ideologies, whereby the control of one's lifestyle and its material components can be manipulated for the efficient achievement of rationally presented goals.

Ideologies of the home as identity project are brought together with an ideology of investment and ownership, as the following examples show. One home-owner talks of the cost of a designer kitchen: 'it was a considerable investment' (November 2007: 50). The interconnections of the 'investment' of money, time and energy are shown when the same owner says: 'we have a special fondness for this house because we've put so much into it' (ibid.). Another home-owner in the same issue says: 'I see development as both a cash generator and a pension plan' (November 2007: 119). However, this calculative approach to the home is not separate from but closely integrated with the achievement of aesthetic style and of a pleasurable sense of identity, as another quotation illustrates: '"I think of renovation in terms of painting a beautiful picture. We start with an empty canvas that we gradually paint and eventually sell, hopefully to be loved by someone else. That gives us great pleasure"' (June 2001: 24).

Although this is an approach to life that we tend to take for granted in today's consumer culture, it is one that is premised by a managerialism rooted in economic exchange – the concept of a 'return on capital' (whether money, time or energy is expended) is extended right into the heart of the home, and illustrates the particular sort of connection there is between social agent and material 'resources'. The home is not solely assessed through its suitability for living, but with an eye to how value may be added to it. Private possessions, place of habitation and even one's very self become transformed into assets which can be made to yield up profit of various kinds, including the traditional sort of profit which may be made by the sale of one's home: 'This particular area of South London offers great value for money because there's no tube station, and it has transformed itself in the last 5 years into a fantastic upmarket village[4]' (November 2007: 171). Home-owners in the UK are encouraged to see the home as an investment by such television programmes as Channel 4's *Property Ladder*, which features property development projects as a source of income and often an alternative career; and *Location, Location, Location* and *Relocation, Relocation*, which often factor-in to house choices a consideration of which locations are likely to increase in value and which houses are suitable for generating letting income. Even underlying the most privatised relationship of self and home, there is a calculation and a rationality. If 'alienation' originally comes from the concept of the peasantry being separated from their connection with the land (Dale and Burrell, 2007: 150), modern techniques of 'household management' bring this full circle as we enter into 'technologies of the self' which can be seen as performing this separation or alienation on our own selves, through the medium of managerial practices and ideologies in everyday life.

Thus one's own time and skills become something to be calculated in to a rational and efficient management of the project of the home. One owner explains this cost-benefit analysis: 'I'd decided to do the project management myself, which was saving us £50,000 on a contractor, and that was always some consolation if ever we felt a bit stressed about the cost of renting' (November 2007: 64). Equally, there is a rationalisation of time and space: a home-owner in Los Angeles explains this equation: 'I had to wait nine years to start the remodelling, and even then I only added 90 square feet to a house which, at 1,400 square feet, is still pretty small, but the experience of living here has been radically improved by reorganising the layout' (November 2007: 143–144).

The intertwining of management practices and ideologies within the production of the 'ideal home' produces a language of calculating selves and spaces, as Miller so aptly puts it, which indicates the posited value of people, things and relationships.

In this section I have tried to illustrate how managerial practices and ideology are intimately embedded in even the most supposedly private spaces of the home. These techniques and discourses produce 'certain effects', particular material relationships, forms of governmentality and self-construction which in turn link the domestic sphere and privatised selves tightly into the calculative and commodified forms of social life which produce and sustain capitalist relations on a much wider scale.

Conclusion

> The everyday can therefore be defined as a set of functions which connect and join together systems that might appear to be distinct. Thus defined, the everyday is a product, the most general of products in an era where production engenders consumption, and where consumption is manipulated by producers: not by 'workers', but by managers and owners of the means of production (intellectual, instrumental, scientific). The everyday is therefore the most universal and the most unique condition, the most social and the most individuated, the most obvious and the best hidden. A condition stipulated for the legibility of forms, ordained by means of functions, inscribed within structures, the everyday constitutes the platform upon which the bureaucratic society of controlled consumerism is erected. (Lefebvre, 1987: 9)

Thus it is that Lefebvre, one of the first social theorists (and activists) to focus on the significance of everyday life, points to the complex interrelations between the seemingly separated aspects of society, economy and culture. It is notable that he specifies the part of management in this, although he confines it to the role of managers as social agents, perhaps not surprising, given how difficult it can be to entirely abandon the productivist locus of Marxism, rather than looking at the broader effects of the values and practices of management.

In this chapter I have tried to trace some of these connections that may be more clearly seen by studying everyday life. Through exploring the largely neglected relationship of management and the domestic home, it is possible to develop a broader context for understanding both. In looking, albeit briefly, at the historical development of 'household management' practices, it is possible to appreciate the potency of management as a specific way of relating to the social and material worlds that go beyond its practices within large-scale organisations and limited to a particular group of people designated as 'managers'. At the same time it brings into sharp focus how significant it is to recognise that the home is not a separate, bounded aspect of social life in spatial, social or economic terms.

In considering in more detail the vision of the 'ideal home' portrayed in accounts of home renovation and decorating projects, it is clear that management rhetorics and techniques are central to practices which initially appear to be more about identity and lifestyle construction. As Miller has argued, in studying the home as a primary site of contemporary consumption, it is important to resist the tendency to link this solely to agency and choice, but to also look at 'what the home does with us' (2001: 4). As he states, 'the transformation of the home is integral to the transformation of social relations', but these are messy and contradictory processes (ibid.). Through looking at this particular aspect of everyday life, the project of the 'ideal home', I would argue that there is an enduring relationship between management and the domestic house. It is, of course, a liaison which has changed and developed over time. However, this confluence, which might still be described as 'household management', enables the reproduction of capitalism, with its stratifications of class and gender, in flexible and adaptable ways.

Notes

1. A metaphor inevitably inspired by Heidi Hartmann's classic essay 'The Unhappy Marriage of Marxism and Feminism' (originally published in *Capital and Class* in 1979) and the subsequent collection of essays of the same name edited by Lydia Sargent (1981).
2. There are obviously a range of discussions over the use of the term imaginary in psychoanalytic, philosophical and social theories. What I am trying to capture here is the importance of the sense of meanings and images attributed to the construction of the categories of 'home' and 'workplace' that whilst not empirical nevertheless have a material effect on how they are lived.
3. One exception being Pahl's (1989) book, *Money and Marriage*, which examines the relationship between men and women over household resources and decisions in the light of management and control, which are not necessarily seen as being the same thing nor carried out by the same partner.
4. For me, this has resonances with the design of many modern workplaces, which centres on the rhetorics of collective sociability such as the 'village pump', the 'street' in the British Airways HQ etc. (see Dale and Burrell, 2007), and yet which is closer to the 'street sociability' of modern consumption, with others in the process of consuming, but not with others in the sense of a collective cohesion or community.

References

Alvesson, M. and Willmott, H. (1992) 'Introduction', in Alvesson and Willmott (eds) *Critical Management Studies*, London: Sage.

Attfield, J. (2000) *Wild Things*, Oxford: Berg.

Baudrillard, J. (1996) [originally published 1968] *The System of Objects*, London: Verso.

Beeton, I. (1861) *Beeton's Book of Household Management*, London: Beeton.

Braidotti, R. (1994) *Nomadic Subjects*, New York: Columbia University Press.

Carsten, J. and Hugh-Jones, S. (eds) (1995) *About the House: Levi-Strauss and Beyond*, Cambridge: Cambridge University Press.

Csikszentmihalyi, M. and Rochberg-Halton, E. (1981) *The Meaning of Things: Domestic Symbols and the Self*, Cambridge: Cambridge University Press.

Dale, K. (2005) 'Building a Social Materiality: Spatial and Embodied Politics in Organizational Control', *Organization*, 12, 5, 649–678.

Dale, K. (2008) 'The Hidden History of Household Management', University of Leicester unpublished paper.

Dale, K. and Burrell, G. (2007) *The Spaces of Organisation and the Organisation of Space: Power, Identity and Materiality at Work*, Basingstoke: Palgrave Macmillan.

Ewen, S. (1988) *All Consuming Images*, New York: Basic Books.

Forty, A. (1986) *Objects of Desire*, London: Thames and Hudson.

Foucault, M. (1988a) 'The Ethic of Care of the Self as a Practice of Freedom: An Interview with Michel Foucault on January 20, 1984' in Bernauer, J. and Rasmussen, D. (eds) *The Final Foucault*, Cambridge, Mass.: The MIT Press.

Foucault, M. (1988b) 'Technologies of the Self', in Martin, L., Gutman, H. and Hutton, P. (eds) *Technologies of the Self: A Seminar with Michel Foucault*, Cambridge, Mass.: MIT Press.

Foucault, M. (1991) 'Governmentality', in Burchall, G., Gordon, C. and Miller, P. (eds) *The Foucault Effect*, Hemel Hempstead: Harvester Wheatsheaf.

Fulcher, J. (2004) *Capitalism: A Very Short Introduction*, Oxford: Oxford University Press.

Giddens, A. (1991) *Modernity and Self-Identity*, Cambridge: Polity.

Gilbert, N. and Mulkay, M. (1984) *Opening Pandora's Box*, Cambridge: Cambridge University Press.

Gottdiener, M. (ed.) (2000) *New Forms of Consumption*, Maryland: Rowman and Littlefield.

Gottdiener, M. (2001) *The Theming of America*, Boulder, Colorado: Westview Press.

Gowler, D. and Legge, K. (1996) 'The Meaning of Management and the Management of Meaning', in Linstead, S., Grafton Small, R. and Jeffcutt, P. (eds) *Understanding Management*, London: Sage, 34–50.

Grey, C. (1994) 'Career as a Project of Self and Labour Process Discipline', *Sociology*, 28, 2, 479–497.

Grey, C. (1999) ' "We Are All Managers Now"; "We Always Were": On the Development and Demise of Management', *Journal of Management Studies*, 36, 5, 561–585.

Grimaldi, P. (2003) *Getting the Builders in . . . . And Staying in Control*. London: Right Way Books.

Gullestad, M. (1992) *The Art of Social Relations*, Oslo: Scandinavian University Press.

Hancock, P. and Tyler, M. (2004) ' "MOT Your Life": Critical Management Studies and the Management of Everyday Life', *Human Relations*, 57, 5, 619–645.

Harvey, D. (1983) 'Class-Monopoly Rent, Finance Capital and the Urban Revolution', in Pipkin, J., LaGory, M. and Blau, J. (eds) *Remaking the City*, Albany, NY: State University of New York Press, 334–363.

Hecht, A. (2001) 'Home Sweet Home: Tangible Memories of an Uprooted Childhood', in Miller, D. (ed.) *Home Possessions*, Oxford: Berg, 123–145.

Hughes, K. (2005) *The Short Life and Long Times of Mrs Beeton*, London: Fourth Estate.

Lefebvre, H. (1987) 'The Everyday and Everydayness', *Yale French Studies*, 73, 7–11, trans. C. Levich, 'Quotidien et Quotidiennete', from *Encyclopaedia Universalis*.

Lefebvre, H. (1991) *The Production of Space*, trans. D Nicholson-Smith, Oxford: Blackwell.

Mant, A. (1977) *The Rise and Fall of the British Manager*, Basingstoke: Macmillan.

Marcoux, J-S. (2001) 'The Refurnishment of Memory', in Miller, D. (ed.) *Home Possessions*, Oxford: Berg, 69–86.

Miller, D. (1987) *Material Culture and Mass Consumption*, Oxford: Blackwell.

Miller, D. (ed.) (2001) *Home Possessions*, Oxford: Berg.

Miller, P. (1992) 'Accounting and Objectivity: The Invention of Calculating Selves and Calculable Spaces', *Annals of Scholarship*, 9, 1–2, 61–86.

Mintel International Group (2007) *Kitchen Furniture – UK*, August, London: Mintel International Group.

Pahl, J. (1989) *Money and Marriage*, Basingstoke: Macmillan.

Pahl, R. (1995) *After Success*, Cambridge: Polity.

Parker, M. (2002) *Against Management*, Cambridge: Polity.

Pink, S. (2004) *Home Truths*, Oxford: Berg.

Reed, M. (1989) *The Sociology of Management*, Brighton: Harvester Wheatsheaf.

Rose, N. (1989) *Governing the Soul*, London: Routledge.

Rose, N. (1996) *Inventing Our Selves: Psychology, Power and Personhood*, Cambridge: Cambridge University Press.

Sargent, L. (ed.) (1981) *The Unhappy Marriage of Marxism and Feminism: A Debate on Class and Patriarchy*, London: Pluto Press.

Smith, D. V. (2003) *Arts of Possession: The Middle English Household Imaginary*, Minneapolis: University of Minnesota Press.

Stanley, L. and Wise, S. (1983) *Breaking Out*, Oxford: Routledge and Kegan Paul.

Starkey, D. (1981) 'The Age of the Household', in Medcalf, S. (ed.) *The Later Middle Ages*, New York: Holmes and Meier, 225–290.

Wajcman, J. (1991) *Feminism Confronts Technology*, Cambridge: Polity.

Waters, M. (1999) *Modernity: Critical Concepts*, London: Routledge.

Watson, T. (1994) *In Search of Management*, London: Routledge.

Willmott, H. (1984) 'Images and Ideals of Managerial Work: A Critical Examination of Conceptual and Empirical Accounts', *Journal of Management Studies*, 21, 3, 249–268.

Part **3**

Managing lifestyle and the lifecourse

Chapter 9

From 'My First Business Day' to 'The Secret Millionaire's Club'

Learning to manage from early on   *Alf Rehn*

Introduction

Management is normally perceived as the quintessentially serious, adult activity. At the same time, the themes of business and management are not unknown in children's culture, and closer scrutiny shows that such themes are actually quite prevalent. From classics such as Scrooge McDuck and Richie Rich, to modern examples such as the game 'School Tycoon' and the cartoon 'The Secret Millionaire's Club,' the ethos of managerialism has found a multitude of ways to present itself as normal, natural and fun to children. In this chapter I will discuss the ways in which notions of management pervade children's everyday life, with a particular emphasis on the ways in which popular culture functions as a kind of business pre-school. Of special interest here is the way in which management is presented as a normal and moral activity, and how the accouterments of the business world are positioned as a natural development path for the budding organization man. However, I will also try to point out that the forms of management discourse and phenomena that can be observed in the sphere of children's culture do not represent a one-way affair, and that we also need to take children's own agency into account when discussing management. In the end, what looks like indoctrination might simply be our view of a phenomenon that might be much more complex, and much more fun.

When people talk about management, they talk about adults. In fact, they are quite monomaniacal about it. Even though management is an ever- and omnipresent phenomenon, those writing about it have normally worked from the adult-centric assumption that one has to be at least some 16 years to really be touched by the world of business, and subsequently all of management studies is written by and about adults. Even in those few cases when someone inquires into how organizations are represented in children's cultures (see e.g. Ingersoll and Adams, 1992; Grey, 1998; Rhodes, 2002) this is done mainly in order to find out how organizations are represented, not in order to think about the children (Cue Helen Lovejoy: 'Will someone please think of the children?!?') – let alone in order to think about children's management. Children are, of course, used to this kind of marginalization and one might even say that the experience of being ignored is one of the fundamental aspects of kids' identity-work. Despite (or perhaps thanks to) this, there exists an entire un-researched world of management, namely that of how the processes, images and symptomatics of management exist, play out and mutate in children's life-worlds. I will in this chapter discuss some of the forms this might take.

One could argue that children are not only subject to management, they are in fact inundated by/in it. Whereas most adults live their life in such a way as to have a manager hovering over them for some set amount of time of the day (increasing, but not yet at full coverage), children mostly have not one but several people enacting management-like powers over them and doing so during all hours of the day. Most visible are of course the parents, who will not only drag you out of bed at too early a time, but also force you to go to bed way too early, thus clearly extending normal management powers quite forcibly into the realm of biopower. Often these same powers of management will also tell you when to eat, decide what you're allowed or not allowed to eat, and tell you to go urinate before you go out the door regardless if you feel like it or not. Despite all the talk of subjugation in the workplace, most (but not all) companies will still allow for unguarded bio-breaks and only very rarely control bedtimes (see, however, Hancock, 2008). And if this wouldn't be bad enough, parents are only one layer of management in the lives of children – the other layers being things such as grandparents (well known for enacting highly confusing compensation-systems), teachers (with their outdated knowledge management regimes), and a sundry bunch of coaches drilling them in either individual excellence (e.g. the violin) or team-work (e.g. football). Further, one of the most challenging things a child has to do is to manage the complexities of the contemporary social scene among children, one where affiliations and friendships are constantly renegotiated and reshaped ('unfriending' each other on Facebook and so on) and where both the material culture of childhood and the increasing time pressures of modern life have to be factored in. I mean, do *you* know who should be picked first when putting together a war party in WoW (World of Warcraft), particularly when mom said you can only play for two hours? To this we also have to include the financial constraints of being a kid in a consumption society, where the buying power of pocket money is constantly challenged and where the collectable cards which were worth a fortune 2 weeks ago might be uncool and worthless today.

To an extent, this could be understood as just playing with words. Mom and dad are not managers, going to the bathroom before a long trip is just common sense, and football-practice is not part of the labor process (but then again, who's being naïve here?). However, this does not mean that management is absent from the life of children, nor that management (in different guises) isn't becoming more and more important. While part of my telling might be seen as merely throwing the discourse of management onto something much more innocent, there is in society today a strive for increasing management in all areas of everyday life, so it seems only logical that childhood and children's culture should also be affected. I will in the following point to a number of ways in which this is happening, and also show how the adult-centric worldview of management studies has created a number of lacunas in our understanding of how management and business are becoming evermore embedded into our lives. But before this is done, a few clarifications may be in order.

When we talk about children and management, we need to separate the notion of children being managed from children managing, and further from management as an element in children's culture. It is particularly this last thing I am interested in here, and even more specifically I am interested in the ways in which management becomes *children's* culture and not only an adult interjection into an assumed pure field. The dynamics that is created between how management is introduced into this culture and the ways in which children through their cultural consumption create a hybridized form of management is thus the main theme in writing this. My underlying assumption here is that children do in fact learn about management from a very early age, and that both this learning and the way in which this learning inevitably includes translational effects (i.e. making management more 'childish') affect society more broadly – as children do have a nasty habit of growing up.

I will in the following discuss how the world of business, of work, of management and of global market capitalism can be learnt by consuming children's culture. This will be done by engaging with a series of popular culture artifacts, and seeing how these can be read to give us a more multifaceted view of what management might mean in the everyday life of children. I will in doing so try to show how the meeting of the child and the management discourse must be read as a dynamic process, and will engage with techniques of critical reading such as those suggested by people like Slavoj Žižek (1991, 1992), Martin Parker (2002, 2007), Carl Rhodes (2001, 2002) and Damian O'Doherty (2007).

Learning about business

Although there is a sometimes baffling amount of work done on management education, and a lively and interesting ongoing discussion about how we learn to become managed subjects, very little attention has been paid to how early socialization plays into this (see, however, O'Dell, 1978; Grey, 1998). The implicit assumption in most of the debate is that the areas for learning about management are primarily two – business school and working life. While it is doubtlessly true that these spheres have a huge impact on both our discourses, our way of being, and our way of living, I want to argue that we actually enter these already equipped with a tremendous amount of images and ideas about management, and that this has been insufficiently studied (cf. Hancock and Tyler, 2004).

Let us start by asking a very simple question: As we learn about money, business and management, who is the archetype and iconic figure through which we come into this? Is there a *primus inter pares* among management icons, one that would meet us before we are socialized into management? My very serious answer would be Scrooge McDuck. The Disney corporation is without the slightest shadow of a doubt the biggest purveyor of entertainment content to Western children today, and their properties are also among the best known brands in the world. While a child in rural China will probably not know who Steve Jobs is, he or she will almost certainly have at least seen the Disney-characters, and may in fact be fluent in the Disney mythology. Disney Publishing worldwide reaches an average of 100 million readers monthly, publishes more than 250 magazines and sells some 120 million children's books each year, with additional millions seeing the TV-shows, the DVDs, the computer games, the websites and so on.

In the Disney universe, Scrooge McDuck stands as one of the oldest and best-known figures. He is Donald Duck's uncle, incredibly wealthy ('The Richest Duck in the World™'), and obsessed with money. He is definitely a quadzillionaire, and his total wealth has at one point been valued at five multiplujillion, nine impossibidillion, seven fantasticatrillion dollars and sixteen cents. A born entrepreneur [in Kirzner's (1985) sense], he will do almost anything to get richer, and becomes physically ill when forced to part with even the slightest sum. His desire to hoard cash (and swim in it) has been the object of awe for generations of children, and his money bin overlooking Duckburg has in all likelihood been coveted by hundreds of thousands of children at some point in their life – I myself had an unhealthy childhood fascination with Scrooge's treasure. Interestingly, while McDuck obviously is the most well-known entrepreneur and capitalist in the world, there is little to nothing written about him from a management point of view (see, however, Dorfman and Mattelart, 1971/2003). Assuming that childhood impressions affect how we learn things in adult life, as I believe one can, this omission seems strange indeed. As Scrooge is one of the first examples of a clearly identified businessman most children come in contact with, one can assume that this meeting will color how children (and in extension adults) will view such things as entrepreneurs and capitalists. In fact, as the figure of Scrooge is so clearly iconic, we might even say that he establishes an archetype in our culture, that of the businessman as greedy, obsessive and single-minded.

However, the subtext of Scrooge's adventures establishes something much more complex. While it is true that the figure in itself is painted as eccentric and even slightly ludicrous (his attachment to the Number One Dime – the first coin he ever made – could, if analyzed by Slavoj Žižek, probably be fodder for an entire book), it also establishes that business is an adventure, and that cunning and thrift is a good way to become a success. Whilst the strive for evermore money might be presented as somewhat odd, the results of Scrooge's passions tend to be fantastic: mystical treasures, cultural experiences and various kinds of hi-jinx. The simple case of sourcing raw materials for a kind of chocolate may in the world of Scrooge very well involve discovering a long-lost tribe and culture, negotiating a complex business deal – interestingly enough, there seems to be an almost endless line of tribes who have massive amounts of a raw material like oil or metals and who want to trade these for soda-bottle caps (Veiled critique of capitalism or the fevered dream of Adam Smith? Let the children judge.) – and often enough a happy end for all. This final point is the most important one. Scrooge's adventures do not always result in the best possible outcome for himself, but instead tend to assure the greatest possible benefit for the greatest possible amount of people – utilitarianism defined and prettily presented.

In other words, even though Scrooge is presented as an eccentric, and as somewhat pathological, he is also shown as a necessary and natural phenomenon in the world. His desires, odd though they might be, lead to exciting adventures and often result in happiness for a surprising amount of people. In fact, it is not uncommon for the *denouement* of an adventure being that Scrooge acts completely against his nature, giving away things, saving Christmas (i.e. acting like his namesake Ebenezer Scrooge), and so on. Although a superficial reading of the character (and his ubiquity in global children's culture) might either emphasize the sheer mental imbalance of the character, thus making it a case of subtextual critique of capitalism, or look to the success of the selfsame and thereby seeing it as a cheap ideological trick played on children, the fact is that reading Scrooge may be a multilayered learning set. What children learn from reading Donald Duck is not a straightforward paean to the market economy, but rather that the economy is both many-faceted and comes with a complex moral order. Scrooge may seem like *homo œconomicus*, but is in fact driven by strong passions and is quite capable of acting 'against' his nature.

So, what does this show us? Much of what has been stated in the previous parts of this text could be discounted by simply stating that it is quite natural that popular culture mirrors the society it exists. There is nothing inherently interesting in the fact that popular culture contains depictions of the business world, nor that managers play certain roles therein. Even though I contend that one needs to pay attention to the patterns and iconic descriptions that children consume and that might have an impact on how they will view similar things later in life, the consumption of such popular depictions should probably be seen as a normal and even necessary aspect of culture. Obviously, we cannot generalize from a single case, not even from such a culturally pervasive one as Scrooge. Yet, what this case shows us is that not only do themes of organization, management and business exist in children's culture – it would be a stunning result indeed if they didn't – they can be understood as a form of 'sentimental education'. The few studies on the business organizations in this field have tended to emphasize the ideological taint in such representations (see Grey, 1998), or in the case of Ingersoll and Adams's (1992) work, inquire into how 'technical rationality' is learnt at an early age. Here, the underlying assumption tends to be that children are uncritical, that children's culture is a simplified version of adult culture, and that the themes that we can find are simply reduced varieties of greater narratives from the 'real' world – that is children's worlds are assumed to be unreal, undeveloped, and therefore fairly unimportant. I would contend that this only captures part of the whole of children and management. Instead of seeing Scrooge (or any other cultural representation) as a one-way communication/brainwashing, can we understand the sphere of childhood as having a management dimension all of its own?

I would, in a manner at least partly reminiscent of how Rhodes (2001) has analyzed *The Simpsons* as a carnivalesque challenge to more mainstream understandings of management and organization, claim that an understanding of Scrooge cannot be reduced to merely seeing him as a caricature of ravenous capitalism. Monty Burns, the evil capitalist in *The Simpsons* is both a menace and laughably decrepit, and this dual portrayal should not be flattened out. A reading of Rhodes would say that it is at the moment when Burns is made to look like a fool when he in fact becomes most dangerous, as it is at such moments when we are led to believe that he is unthreatening. Similarly, the important part in the chronicles of Scrooge might not be the ones where he is portrayed as greedy and profiteering, but rather the moments when he does good. For what is the nature of the foremost capitalist in the world? The social theorist Slavoj Žižek has in a series of books (see e.g. Žižek, 1991, 1992) suggested modes of reading popular culture that both takes their surface effects seriously, but also tries to inquire into what these effects are the symptom of. In the case of Scrooge, both the effects and their cause seem very simple at first. Scrooge is greedy (for capitalists are greedy), so he is cheap and tries to trick people. The lesson, then, would be that capitalists are not to be trusted (and misers). But a reading in the spirit of Žižek would turn this analysis around, and instead see what alternative story lies underneath. Here, Scrooge's greed could be understood as a symptom, and the adventures are ways in which he tries to feed his greed, knowing full well that he will never have hoarded enough money. However, the moment of catharsis does not come when Scrooge makes more money, but when he is acting 'against' his nature – such as when he donates toys to Duckburg's children or saves Christmas. This is the moment when he overcomes his symptom, and finds happiness by curing the underlying trauma that has resulted in his greed. In the scope of a comic book, such things are possible. What is insidious here is that children may well read this story with greater subtlety than adults are capable of (cf. Zipes, 1983). In this reading, Scrooge becomes a rather lovable character – capable of doing an enormous amount of good by being insanely rich, and always having the possibility of acting in a way that brings the greatest possible happiness to the greatest number of people. Children might thus come away learning that all the avarice and exploitation that adults see in Scrooge in fact are means to an end, as business will end up saving Christmas.

In other words, learning about business is no easy matter, and involves an engagement with children's culture that adults may have either never had or already forgotten. Further, this learning is not simply one of transmitting ideals, but makes demands on children, who may learn in ways very much different from what we initially assume. Still, this initial stop on our whistle-stop tour of children's culture is admittedly a very abstract one, where the child will be reading about things that may not feel particularly real. To flesh out this understanding, we need to consider the labor process.

Learning to work

One of my most cherished possessions is a set of toys for dress-up and make-believe play (cf. Parker, 2007). Such sets have been popular playthings for as long as commercial toys have existed, and can probably be traced back to the use of masks and outfits in tribal cultures. Iconic games like dressing up to play cowboys and Indians, or toy versions of a doctor's equipment and trademark white coat, have played a part in children's culture for a very long time. The set I bought is in one sense a continuation of this, but in another sense something much stranger. Its full name is the 'My First Business Day Playset' (cf. Rehn, 2004), and contains over 20 pieces of playtime goodness, including but not limited to an attaché case in blue plastic, a wallet with playmoney and credit cards, a PDA (with incoming email and a displayed pie-chart), a mobile phone, keys for the office (one of which *might* lead to the executive bathroom) and security ID tag (this last item fascinates me no end). On the box, a boy of four or five years is displayed wearing a crisp white shirt, a tie, talking into the playphone (held between ear and shoulder, trader-style) and taking notes on his PDA.

This could obviously be interpreted as the most dystopic toy ever created, where little Timmy or Tammy Trader are schooled and cowed into white-collar hell from preschool onward, where the business PDA and the ID tag's connection to a personal identity-destroying surveillance regime is naturalized through the medium of toys. Another reading of the same might emphasize the educational benefits of teaching children what a lot of people are doing all day, and thus make the world of the adult a little less threatening and incomprehensible. One could even in the spirit of Slavoj Žižek (1991) suggest a complete turn of the interpretive gaze and see this playset as something of a critical break. A Žižekian reading would suggest that our culture is creating these weird symptoms of the capitalist order not in order to make it more palatable to children, but as a way to handle the trauma that much of the adult world of management is rather childish and jejune. There would in such a reading be no 'serious' core to the toy, no need to read anything into it. The most radical possibility might in fact be that there is no agenda to the playset – it is just a small version of another set of toys, a surface standing in for another surface. By creating the playset through which even a four-year old can pretend to be a businessman, we can in part deal with the inanity of working life, and in a sense transfer our unconscious suspicion that it is all a game of dress-up. The child thus carries the trauma of the adult, not in order to train the child for what is to come, but rather to handle the adult's sense of fundamental irreality present in business life.

Such a reading would be close to the notion of queering and performativity that has been suggested by Martin Parker (2002). Here Parker has suggested that one could see and study management at least partly as a form of role-play, drawing on queer theorists like Judith Butler in arguing that just like we need to learn how to play at being 'woman', we need to learn how to put on the role of the manager – complete with suit and accouterments. For a person that feels there is too much uncertainty, upholding the boundaries partly becomes an evermore intense desire of finding the proper role and fitting costume. The playset does something similar, but whereas the role-play suggested by Parker seems to be driven by uncertainty and fear, the play of the child seems a lot less neurotic. One could even see that the anguish that Parker identifies is transferred to the child, who may be better equipped to carry it. Where management is part of the social construction of adulthood (Harding, 2003), there may – and I am here referring to the ways in which Žižek has called attention to the traumas that are created when a united subject such as, for example, an adult, professional manager is attempted – be a need for a dissolving of this construction, a breathing space for management.

Regardless of which kind of reading one prefers, such playsets – in which we could also include computer games consoles and mobile phones, not to mention board-games – present to the children that play with them a business life with a Janus-like face. On the one hand we can see a clear socializing aspect to them, a way to train children in the harsh reality of office life (see Parker, 2007), but at the same time these open up for the kinds of rebellion and subversion that play has always been good at (cf. Huizinga, 1955). When the accouterments of the grown-up world of management are brought into play, they also show how easy it is to ridicule, mock and pervert the iconic act of 'being a manager' (see also Harding, 2003). The child who, armed with the 'My First Business Day' playset, goes around the schoolyard firing friends and teachers is not only playing at being a manager, he or she might be engaging in the quintessential form of critique available to children, that of questioning through play. This should obviously not be confused with the adult forms of critique (Why are we always so quick to assume that children are not capable of having their own, separate cultural forms?), but might instead point to what management *is* to children.

A more extreme example of this is the 'My First McJob' playset. Its real name is different ('The McDonald's Drive-Thru Playset'), but I have taken to using the more apt name, as the set consists of a full, child-size outfit of a McDonald's employee, complete with a simple cashier's point and a headset with which to take orders. Created as a collaboration between McDonald's and a toy manufacturer, this fun little set of toys in effect makes it possible for the child to pre-train him- or herself for the exciting world of working for minimum wage in the fast-food industry. From the perspective of the corporation, this is obviously very close to the perfect product. Not only does McDonald's get paid for products that serve as advertisements for their products (we should also note that while advertising to children is curbed and discouraged in many countries, making toys with logos is perfectly legal), they further get the added bonus of children making themselves (slightly) more prepared to act as workers. Selling commodities, branding and the labor process, all wrapped up in shiny plastic – like something from a CEO's wet dream. But at the same time, this assumes that children are at best receptacles of managerial and corporate discourses, that children in their everyday life are unable to form their own opinions and their own understandings of that which they are subject to.

While it is quite obvious that children do react to advertising and that children's critical faculties are different (and quite probably less developed) than adults, the important thing to note is that while children's everyday lives are inundated with discourses and material artifacts that communicate managerial imagery and organizational frameworks, this does not mean that the transmission of the managerialist ethos is total and perfect. Drawing on the work of Fleming and Spicer (2003) one could postulate that children at least could use the described playsets in ways that would signify resistance and a cynical distance to the world of work, and at the very least we can assume that the way in which management templates are introduced into the world of children is changed to accommodate the lifeworld of the same, in a way that creates a much more hybrid cultural form than might be deduced from the material instantiations themselves.

In other words, the ways in which management is present in children's everyday life should be studied as a dynamic that is created through the interaction of two forces. On the one hand we have a very clear colonization of a sphere that we often implicitly assume exists 'beyond' management, where both the tools (as in playsets) and discourses (as seen in comics and other cultural forms) are introduced as normal and 'real'. Such forces arguably work to socialize and indoctrinate children into late capitalism (Ingersoll and Adams, 1992). But on the other side of this we have the very real and easily observed fact that child's play is a powerful transformative force, capable of turning things on their heads (cf. Bakhtin, 1939/1984; Huizinga, 1955; Rhodes, 2001). We simply cannot know the ways in which the accouterments of corporate life are appropriated by children, and may need to pay much more attention to how the lifeworld of the kids is constructed, and how in extension management is constructed therein. At the moment, there is very little research into anything like this, as we tend to assume that children's everyday life is merely a less developed version of adult's. This myopia has hindered our understanding of how one can take things such as the My First Business Day-playset and from this develop novel and creative interpretations of corporate life, and has in other words hindered our understanding of how we actually learn about work. Succinctly put, while we teach the children, the children teach us, or in the words of Wordsworth, 'The Child is father of the man'.

So far, we've worked from a position where children are either consuming culture or putting themselves into situations where they are in a subjected position. Clearly, much of economic life can be learnt through this, as much of the average wage-earners life can be described as a cycle of subjugation and consumption. However, for the purposes of this text, it is important that the juvenile agency that I've implied must be interrogated when discussing management in children's culture is brought more to fore. I will thus move onto discussing how children get to manage businesses.

Learning to manage

An obvious sphere within which to investigate this dynamics of children creating a 'management of their own' would be to look at computer games. Obviously, children are not the only ones playing such games, but they do represent an avid group of players, and with the proliferation of information technology, it is increasingly common that a child learns about the world at least partly through the mediation of digital entertainment (Wolfe and Perron, 2003; Poole, 2004). This becomes particularly pronounced when it comes to the sphere of management and learning to handle the complexities of a larger organization, and the case of business games serves as an excellent example of just how children are socialized in the arts of commerce.

In 1990, genius game developer Sid Meier together with Microprose published the game *Railroad Tycoon*. The game, which is played on a mostly green map with heavily stylized graphics, simulates the running and development of a railroad company during the boom time for such endeavors. Gameplay consists mainly of planning tracks between stations and cities, and managing an increasingly complex network of logistic exchanges, where matters such as train carrying capacity, their cargo, shifting prices, varying demand and similar problems of preference, coupled with the odd unforeseeable event, come into play. The game attempts to mimic the market economy, complete with a small stock market where you can buy and sell stock in both the company you're running and in competing companies. Many found the strategic gameplay boring, but it also won over a cadre of dedicated fans. The game spawned several sequels and expansion packs, and also became a template of sorts. In 1991 the same Sid Meier would come to release *Civilization*, considered by game aficionados to be one of the best games ever made, as well as slightly more addictive than heroin.

Railroad Tycoon was not the first business simulator, as there were primitive equivalents on the very first personal computers, and many games before it that contained business elements. In 1984, the first version of the now almost deified *Elite* was released, a game which built on space trading and a complex economic model. In fact, business games have always had a niche of their own in the world of computer gaming. *Railroad Tycoon* was however different in being both a pure business game (*Elite* had a wider framework of space exploration and combat) and a mainstream success. It also started the trend of specific business simulations, many of which borrowed the word 'Tycoon' for their titles. Thus the original later begat *Airport Tycoon, Lemonade Tycoon, Zoo Tycoon, Pizza Tycoon, Casino Tycoon, Coffee Tycoon, Transport Tycoon, Monopoly Tycoon, Mall Tycoon, Rollercoaster Tycoon, Moon Tycoon, Transport Tycoon, School Tycoon* and *Prison Tycoon*, to mention a few. As this list should make clear, several of these were geared toward children, and one – *Lemonade Tycoon* – even went so far as to map out the way one (supposedly) could turn the iconic child's enterprise (a lemonade stand) into a corporation. Together with *Civilization, Railroad Tycoon* can be said to have ushered in the 'management game', where the most important aspect is the ability to administer an increasingly large network of activities. Although the

Sim-games, which got their start with *SimCity* (originally released in 1989), have a similar form of gameplay and development-history, their structure is closer to that of a civics lesson, and they exhibit a more complex relation to business.

Some of the newer releases in this series include *Prison Tycoon* and *School Tycoon*. In the former, the challenge is to establish, run and develop a prison, for maximum efficiency (and profit). By collecting fees, staffing, buying buildings and additions to these, the player tries to create the best prison he or she can. At set intervals, after reaching certain goals, one is afforded the chance to improve the facility further, all the way to a super-max prison. During all this, one has to check that one has money for the pay-roll, that the prisoners do not riot, and look out for the occasional fire. In *School Tycoon*, this same format is replicated, but now the important thing is not to build secure blocks, but athletic venues and new school buildings, and manage a school in a way that optimizes academic ability, how the school does in sports, discipline and so on. On one level these are simple building games, where the setting could just as well be a mall or a factory, the context being mainly to lend flavor to the game. For instance, whereas the two events clearly are different, there is a structural similarity between an infestation of farm pests in *John Deere American Farmer* and a prison riot in *Prison Tycoon*, as both stand as major events onset by a planning failure (often built in as a necessary result in the game) that need to be managed. Seen in this light, all games are structured in more or less the same way, as a series of problems to be solved by the player. All management games would likewise be similar, based on a structure of developing an endeavor and balancing conflicting forces. However, the way in which the Tycoon games show how endeavors can be turned into profitable companies, and how 'management' consists of a series of small decisions, with the surrounding world portrayed as a continuous chaos and an abstract adversary, might give us some insight into how children perceive the economy. The Tycoon series also communicates that the world needs, nay *demands* management. With everything from soda-machines at schools to the building of a railroad being positioned within the context of 'managing', such games create a framework which make management seem like a natural and fun endeavor, as well as enabling children to 'play the corporation'. Looking at how children actually engage with games (see Sutton-Smith, 1997), we can see that they do not necessarily play 'according to the rules', but instead test and tweak the game, submit it to various kinds of stress (such as building impossible structures or trying to kill everyone through starvation), and so on. Playing at being a manager is thus not merely training in doing good and producing value, but also a form of hacking, where the role of management becomes something akin to leading a game or experimenting. The way in which children learn to manage might thus not be so much a process of learning the rules, but learning what can be done in a specific context – and experimenting with the rules. Again, the sphere that is created when popular cultural representations of management and corporate behavior meet the tinkering minds of children shows us several faces, making the field of 'children's management' a much more complex area of inquiry than we might immediately assume.

The great game

On 8 February 2006 DIC Entertainment publish a press release announcing that they have partnered with investment guru and iconized billionaire Warren Buffett to create a direct-to-DVD animated series entitled 'The Secret Millionaire's Club', scheduled for a first run of 13 episodes. The premise of the series is worth quoting at some length:

> An unscrupulous developer buying up properties in Omaha is foreclosing on the rundown local Youth Center. Its last four members are cleaning out the attic when they find a box of old sports memorabilia–including, among other rare and valuable items. They put everything up for bid on an online auction service–and make millions! After they pay off the mortgage on the center, the 'secret millionaires' ask local celebrity Warren Buffett for advice on how to invest the money.
>
> With Warren's help, the four kids meet secretly to decide what local companies and businesses to invest in. Each week, Warren guides them to discovering new aspects of his investment philosophy, by using the Socratic Method to help them put his rules into practice, and helps them learn sound financial management skills–like avoiding debt! At the same time, the kids become involved in adventures as they deal with dishonest owners, corrupt accountants, security guards, corporate raiders, crooked politicians, and, of course, the unscrupulous developer.

Commentary on the project tended to focus mostly on the amusing notion of turning the frumpy Warren Buffett into an animation hero (it should however be noted that there exists a cartoon biography of Buffett, and that this sold well in Japan, so the stretch isn't that great). More interesting here is the fact that the premise was presented without a hint of irony, and that the implicit assumption in it is that (a) children can relate to becoming millionaires, (b) children can be made interested in how to invest in companies, and (c) this makes good edutainment. When it comes to the first point, this is obviously not the first time wealthy children have been made cartoon heroes. Richie Rich, 'The Richest Kid in the World', had his own comic book from the 1950s (he debuted in a Little Dot-comic in 1953) and an animated series in the 1980s. And while Richie was a good guy, cartoons have always had nasty little rich boys and girls in them, foils put in to explicate the moral implications of wealth without responsibility. What is special about the secret millionaires, however, is that they are presented as empowered by wealth and also active in the management thereof.

The latter points, regarding the potential interest and educational value of the program, are slightly more difficult to disentangle. One reading of the premise would suggest that no actual children were consulted when developing this project. Rather, it seems like a heavy-handed attempt to position a product so that concerned parents will buy the DVDs, hoping to both impart economic acumen and entertain the kids. At the same time, the concept might be understood as a perverted kind of realism, a tip of the hat to the fact that corporate raiders and scurrilous accountants are far more likely threats in today's society than the mad scientists and militia leaders, and that financial skills may be a more potent weapon than collaborative efforts or friendship. We could thus (again) read this in a manner reminiscent of how Žižek (1991, 1992) tends to analyze popular culture, that is not merely as superficial trivialities, but as a staging of underlying traumas in the social unconscious. While the surface notion of a TV series where the animated avatar of a real investment Tycoon gives 'Socratic' lessons in fiscal responsibility and financial moves could be understood as a superficial attempt to naturalize the existing economic order, the unconscious subtext of it could be read as a critique of the same, in the same manner that Žižek shows how the omnipresence of conspiracy theories in Hollywood movies can be understood as attempts to handle a paranoid streak in the postmodern subject. The program is in effect showing kids that they live in a society where cash is king, where money is the most important thing of all, and where corruption and unethical dealings are rampant. This is further enhanced by the fact that the 'real' Buffett now appears as a cartoon character, emphasizing the virtuality and the fundamental irreality of today's money markets. In late capitalism, financial skill becomes a weapon, accountants wield power, and the 'big players' exist in an altogether different world, where breaking a major currency or doing a multibillion deal is 'normal'. The cartoon might in fact teach children much more than it tries to, assuming that children are not merely receptors of information and propaganda and can read between the lines. Where Bugs Bunny cartoons at best managed to make hunters look foolish (through the character of Elmer Fudd), the Secret Millionaire's Club plays out a whole host of dramas that can be transferred into how children look at the world around them. Suddenly, the accounting class isn't quite as innocent as previously imagined. Bank managers are no longer just old men, but potential villains. The business pages, where Buffett is prominently displayed, whisper 'Here be monsters...'

Yet again, children's culture can show us a much more complex picture than might at first be evident. My contention, thus, is that we need to pay the same attention to this assumedly simple form of culture than we usually do, and that in order to fully comprehend it we need to be as subtle (or subtler) in our readings as when analyzing other forms of popular culture. Just stating that children are subjected to forms of culture that try to naturalize and normalize an ideological state is not enough, as this completely disallows any form of children's agency, in the face of how children have always appropriated culture for their own usages. The great game of business can be played on many levels, including that of the children. But is it the same game? Or something much more hybrid, mutated, adapted?

Child's play and kid's management

What I have tried to show throughout this text is that there is a dialectic of sorts at play when we talk about children and management, and that any analysis of this field risks getting caught up in one of three traps: one, the fallacy of perfect transmission; two, the fallacy of ascribed resistance; three, the adult-centric fallacy.

I started this text by pointing out that children are subjected to management discourses and ideas at an early age, and that this is often ignored when talking about how we internalize management as a discursive field. Children's culture contains a wide range of imagery and cultural artifacts that communicate ideas about management, business and the economy, and I have tried to highlight some of them in this text. A proto-fallacy that comes before the three traps I outline above would be to ignore this, and assume that there is no such thing as a 'management for children'.

Most people will however agree to there being such a field if one points it out to them, but the interpretation of this will vary widely. A common reaction and part of the public discourse is that this is an atrocity, that children should not have their lifeworld sullied with such things and so on. At the root of this reaction is the fallacy of perfect transmission. We often implicitly assume that children are *tabula rasa*, and that the imagery of management will imprint itself upon them with an indoctrinating force that can only be defeated through adult action. My contention in this text has been that this is a simplified view, and that children can well be capable of reading and adapting in a more complex way than we often assume – and that this should be researched further.

This does however invite the second fallacy, namely that children are not affected or that they are capable of creating 'resistance' through play and appropriation of the imagery and discourses they are subjected to. Even though we know that play can function in such a way, it is important not to ascribe too much to such potential counter-agency. Children are affected, and just like adults their capacity to handle the onslaught of discursive regimes is limited, and some would say that it is far less developed than the similar faculties in adults. What we can state is that it is different, and that the ideological constructions that children form in the field between management as cultural colonization and play as resistance are a cultural field unto themselves.

This leads us to the third fallacy, namely the tendency to project our adult views and preoccupations onto the world of children, assuming our view of the world to be a template that can be transferred directly onto the kids. My main contention in this chapter is that children have cultural forms of their own, and while it is true that material culture and discourses from the adult world of management are fodder for these and form them, this does not mean that the understandings of children can be reduced to rudimentary forms of adult understandings. Instead, we should study the lifeworlds of children as spaces where novel and idiosyncratic understandings of, for example, management are formed, and study these as cultural forms unto themselves.

In other words, this text could be understood as outlining a research agenda for studying management in the everyday life of children, but with a focus on what children do to management, not the other way around. Now, will somebody please think of the children?

References

Bakhtin, M. (1939/1984) *Rabelais and His World*. Bloomington: Indiana University Press.

Dorfman, A. and Mattelart, A. (1971/2003) *How to Read Donald Duck: Imperialist Ideology in the Disney Comic*. Oakland, CA: AK Press.

Fleming, P. and Spicer, A. (2003) 'Working at a Cynical Distance: Implications for Power, Subjectivity and Resistance', *Organization* 10(1): 157–179.

Grey, C. (1998) 'Child's Play: Representations of Organization in Children's Literature', in J. Hassard and R. Holliday (eds) *Organization/Representation*. London: Sage, pp. 131–148.

Harding, N. (2003) *The Social Construction of Management*. London: Routledge.

Hancock, P. (2008) 'Cultures of Sleep: Organization and the Lure of Dormancy' *Culture and Organization,* 14(4): 411–424.

Hancock, P. and Tyler, M. (2004) '"MOT Your Life": Critical Management Studies and the Management of Everyday Life', *Human Relations* 57(5): 619–645.

Huizinga, J. (1955) *Homo Ludens: A Study of the Play Element in Culture*. Boston: Beacon Press.

Ingersoll, V. and Adams, G. (1992) 'The Child Is "Father to the Manager": Images of Organizations in U.S. Children's Literature', *Organization Studies* 13(4): 497–519.

Kirzner, I. (1985) *Discovery and the Capitalist Process*. Chicago: University of Chicago Press.

O'Dell, F. (1978) *Socialisation through Children's Literature: The Soviet Example*. Cambridge: Cambridge University Press.

O'Doherty, D. (2007) 'The Question of Theoretical Excess: Folly and Fall in Theorizing Organization', *Organization* 14(6): 837–867.

Parker, M. (2002) 'Queering Management and Organization', *Gender, Work and Organization* 9(2): 146–166.

Parker, M. (2007) 'The Little Book of Management Bollocks and the Culture of Organisation', in R. Westwood and C. Rhodes (eds) *Humour, Organization and Work*. London: Routledge, pp. 77–91.

Poole, S. (2004) *Trigger Happy: Videogames and the Entertainment Revolution*. New York: Arcade Publishing.

Rehn, A. (2004) *The Serious Unreal: Notes on Business and Frivolity*. Åbo: Dvalin Press.

Rhodes, C. (2001) 'D'Oh: The Simpsons, Popular Culture and the Organizational Carnival', *Journal of Management Inquiry* 10(4): 374–383.

Rhodes, C. (2002) 'Politics and Popular Culture: Organisational Carnival in the Springfield Nuclear Power Plant', in S. Clegg (ed.) *Management and Organization Paradoxes*. Amsterdam/Philadelphia: John Benjamins, pp. 119–138.

Sutton-Smith, B. (1997) *The Ambiguity of Play*. Cambridge, MA: Harvard University Press.

Wolf, M. and Perron, B. (eds) (2003) *The Video Game Theory Reader*. London: Routledge.

Zipes, J. (1983) *Fairy Tales and the Art of Subversion*. New York: Wildman Press.

Žižek, S. (1991) *Looking Awry*. Cambridge, MA: MIT Press.

Žižek, S. (1992) *Enjoy Your Symptom!* London: Routledge.

Chapter **10**

Managing conflict

The curious case of neuro-lingustic programming   *André Spicer and Mehdi Boussebaa*

Introduction

One of the great inevitabilities of people getting together is that conflict will inevitably rear its head. Whether it be a marriage, a business partnership, a neighbourhood committee, an international scientific project or a nation state, we can be almost certain that conflict will appear. The thought of conflict might conjure negative images in our minds – we may think of unpleasant arguments, children squabbling over a toy, or even a vicious and bitter war. It seems only natural to long for an end to these nasty scenes. The question of whether we will ever witness the end of conflict is one that has exercised some of the greatest thinkers. While some of these thinkers have shied away from conflict, modern political philosophy assumes that conflict is a natural product of human relations. As Hannah Arendt (1970) suggests, power (and we would add conflict) appears as soon as people get together to do something. In other words, conflict is an inevitable part of being human and living with other people whose interests and priorities might not always converge with our own.

Many modern philosophers have become comfortable with the idea that conflict is something from which we cannot escape. However, a range of more recent 'visionaries' have offered us a world without the *Sturm und Drang* of human conflict and upheaval, suggesting that conflict is something that can be disposed of through careful and considered management. Kindly garden designers, power-hungry city planners, well-meaning scientists, drug addled artists and crazed dictators have all put forward conflict-free zones. However, they have often been found to be severely lacking or very fragile. In a world which has moved 'beyond left and right', these utopians have begun to look decidedly last century. The utopians of today have given up on dropping acid or cleansing unwanted elements from society. Instead, they have donned Armani suits, gone to business schools and bought memberships to exclusive health clubs. That's right, they have become consultants.

Today, a whole class of consultants offers us cures for the various conflicts that plague our societies. For these miracle workers, any conflict is potentially solvable. Youths on miniature motor-cycles ransacking a local housing estate, irate customers storming a local IKEA to claim the last of the *Ramberg* bed-frames on sale, or a worked up anti-war protestor intent on closing down a forlorn military camp in some rain-swept field can all potentially be calmed with the 'powerful techniques' on offer. Some experts even claim to be able to manage deeply entrenched conflicts such as the tensions in Israel and Palestine, Kashmir, and Northern Ireland. For them, conflict is a disorder that, with their help, can be carefully managed out of existence.

In this chapter, we want to investigate claims that conflict can be managed. In order to explore this proposition, we begin by asking how conflict has typically been conceptualised in Western thought. We find that at least since Machiavelli, conflict has been thought about as a natural and inevitable result of human interaction. However, during the late nineteenth century, some began to argue that conflict could be disposed of if a society or group was effectively and rationally managed. As a result, the focus moved from attempts to take advantage of conflict to attempts to develop techniques for engineering conflict-free space. There has been a profusion of popular psychological techniques which people are entreated to use in their professional and everyday lives to manage conflicts and struggles. One well-known example is Emotional Intelligence training which seeks to alert its users to the emotional dynamics of conflictual situations. We investigate one equally popular technique that has recently proved particularly alluring in the management of conflict: neuro-linguistic programming (NLP). NLP has been offered as a powerful tool that business people can use to manage their relationships, the way they present themselves, the way they communicate and, of course, the way they engage with conflicts. It is increasingly seen as a must have by many an aspiring business person. However, its appeal goes far beyond the business world. NLP is used by public sector workers, people in non-profits, professionals and home-makers. In fact, NLP has become a technique that is increasingly used in people's everyday lives to deal with many of the problems and challenges that they confront. We argue that whilst NLP may provide some alluring techniques for feeling mastery, such techniques internalise conflict, making struggles something that we need to 'work through' within ourselves rather than 'work out' with others. The ultimate result is that people feel that conflict is something that must be done away with through an act of internal psychological will. Any residues of conflict are simply to be blamed on an imperfect use of the technique. This ultimately results in people who try 'working through' conflicts being trapped in a heightened state of anxiety.

Conceptualising conflict

A world without conflict is one where everyone knows his or her place. This is the kind of statement that would not be out of place at the Conservative Club of some village in middle England. It is an old chestnut that has been warmed on the coals of Tory fires for generations. The assumption underlying this statement is that there are a series of natural positions that people occupy in a society. Each of these positions is charged with certain roles, responsibilities, skills and behaviours. The crucial thing is that people should stick to the position they occupy. Seeking to do something that they are not charged with will inevitably lead to mistakes, incompetence and, of course, useless struggles. According to our conservative friend, the Butcher is good at providing meat to people, but he or she is not so good at ruling the village. Similarly, the local mayor might be good at ruling the village, but he or she would prove to be hopeless at tending an orchard. The message is clear – a place for everyone, and everyone in his or her place.

This image of a perfectly ordered and conflict-free Arcadia can be traced back at least to Plato's *Republic*. In this foundational work of political philosophy, Plato offers a rational and well-ordered scheme on which society should function. In the *Republic*, Socrates recommends 'working at that which he is naturally best suited' and 'to do one's own business and not to be a busybody' (1945: 433a5–433b). In other words, in a perfect society people would stick to their given position. Following from this supposition, the *Republic* also offers each individual a place and a domain of power as well as a strict hierarchy which specifies who should have power over whom. The office of the Ruler is given to philosopher kings who are charged with the skilful and wise creation of just rules and orders. The second office of the Soldier is given to those who seek to carry out and defend the rules and orders that are issued by the Rulers. The third, and perhaps the largest group, are Producers whose task it is to follow the rules and orders that are laid down by the Rulers and enforced by the Soldiers. The result is a utopian order that would avoid conflict if people remain in their pre-destined roles. It also produces the assumption that a society without conflict is one that is ruled over by a small group of carefully selected elites who know what is best for society.

Plato's plan for a conflict-free society proved to be very alluring. It sparked a long tradition of attempts to sketch out the coordinates and characteristics of a perfect society where conflict would be a thing of the past. These range from the careful systematisation of Plato's *Republic* that we find in Aristotle's *Politics* through to perfect Christian plans for worlds without conflict such as Augustine's *City of God*. The golden thread that runs through each of these works is that alluring assumption that careful planning on the part of particularly clever people could alleviate society of many of the petty struggles that take place.

This golden thread was abruptly cut during the Renaissance by one erstwhile political consultant and student of the dark arts of power called Niccolò Machiavelli. The work of Machiavelli (1515/1997, 1517/1983) has shocked and astounded readers for centuries. This is largely because it eschews attempts to develop a perfect scheme for the government of society that would banish conflict as a fantasy that masks the realities of power and ongoing struggle. Instead of a perfectly ordered world, divided in an elaborate scheme of different classes, Machiavelli presents a world where actors are 'ungrateful, fickle, false, cowardly, covetous, and as long as you succeed they are yours entirely; they will offer you their blood, property, life and children, as is said above, when the need is far distant; but when it approaches they turn against you' (Machiavelli, 1515/1997, Chapter 17). Social life involves the constant attempt by egocentric actors to advance their interests, often at the expense of others. The result is that politics is a space where mutually mistrusting actors are consistently locked in conflict to gain political advantage. This conflict is not bound or constrained by any external reference points. There is no grand plan of perfection. The only thing there is for Machiavelli is a brutal and constant calculation of power.

Images of a social world founded on conflict can be found in another foundational work of modern political philosophy: Thomas Hobbes's (1651/1985) theory of the modern state. Hobbes argues that people are largely equal in physical and mental abilities, but tend to overvalue their own ability vis-à-vis the ability of others. This gives rise to a situation where people will seek to use their abilities to obtain a resource they desire from another person. Because of the limited nature of these resources, actors begin to fear attack from others, they seek to pre-empt an attack on their own interests and life through consolidating their power. During this time there are no human institutions outside of mutual struggle, 'a state of nature' reigns whereby the only important dynamic is perpetual conflict. In this state of nature, people are condemned to lives that are 'nasty, brutish and short'. Hobbes points out that people desire an escape from this state of consistent war and voluntarily submit their power to a sovereign who will guarantee them order and life. What Hobbes reminds us is that the ground zero of politics is a situation of mutual, interlocked fierce conflict and struggle. Law and order is only something that comes after the fact to prevent its negative effects (Chapters 14–17). For Machiavelli and Hobbes, the plans and schemes of a leviathan are only interim solutions. The state of nature of perpetual conflict is what continues to trouble and plague any grand scheme.

The image of conflict as lying at the basis of society is taken further by Hegel's (1807/2005: IVa) famous discussion of the master and slave. According to Hegel, conflict is not just an inevitable plague that we must stoically cope with. Rather, it is actually a kind of productive force. In particular, he argues that through dialectical struggle with another, we come to be conscious of ourselves. Instead of this being a process of exploring ourselves and gradually revealing what is there, Hegel argues that we come to know who we are through a struggle with another person: 'Self consciousness exists in itself and for itself, in that, and by the fact that it exists for another self-consciousness; that is to say, it *is* only by being acknowledged or recognized' (Hegel, 1807/2005: 229). Here, he maintains that our own sense of who we are is to be found only through interaction with another person. For Hegel, the nature of this interaction with another person is struggle. He notes that two individuals enter into a 'life-and-death struggle' to 'bring their certainty of themselves, the certainty of being for themselves, to the level of objective truth'. This life-and-death struggle is exemplified by the antagonism between the powerful Lord and the dependent Bondsman. The Lord feels that they are independent of the Bondsman because they have control over them and can tell them what to do. In contrast, the Bondsman experiences himself or herself as dependent upon the Master because they are often simply an extension of the Master's wishes. Hegel shows us that both these figures, at least initially, are dependent on the other for their sense of who they are. The Master would not be a Master without the Bondsman to recognise them as such and do their biddings. Similarly, the Bondsman would not have an identity without the recognition and fear experienced in the face of their Master. Hegel goes even further by noting that the Bondsman has a relationship independent of their relationship with the Master, namely the relationship with the object of their work. It is through this struggle with the object of work that the Bondsman develops a sense of recognition and self-consciousness that is independent of the Master. The central point we can take from Hegel's argument about the relationship between the Master and the Bondsman is that each of these figures only exists to the extent that they stand in relation to one another.

Hegel shows us how through the conflict and struggle between two actors (whether they are individuals or social collectives) each group gains their sense of identity and existence. This suggests that actors do not just arrive on the scene and then engage in struggle. Rather, they develop a sense of themselves as actors through the very process of struggle. This theme has been picked up in many subsequent studies of specific conflicts. For instance, Marx and Engels (1848) argued that societies are defined by the class struggles they revolve around, and that the conflict between the capitalists and the workers produces the internal dynamics and explosive creativity of capitalism. Some feminists claim that the dominant conflict which characterises patriarchical societies is the struggle between men and women. More recently, Honneth (1995) has argued that many justice movements are underpinned by a dialectical struggle for recognition of a certain social group. What these very diverse studies share is the common assumption that social life is underpinned by conflict and struggle. Moreover, these conflicts and struggles are the wellspring and font of many social processes ranging from class to group formation to gender to identity. Following this Hegelian line of thought, struggle and conflict is not something that we might seek to banish. Rather, it is what brings the social world to life.

Despite these insistencies on the importance and vitality of struggle in modern political thought, the last 200 years has seen repeated attempts to revive the dream of vanquishing conflict. This has often involved attempts to invoke the notion that conflict could be dealt a fatal blow by ensuring the proper ordering of society. The crucial difference that we find between modern foes of conflict and their classical counterparts is the question of who was going to expunge society of conflict and just how they were going to achieve this difficult feat. Classical thinkers assume that an elite who is given their position due to noble blood would do away with conflict. Modern thinkers assume a new elite who find themselves in the position of philosopher kings due to their unique talent. Instead of drawing on a stock of 'noble lies', carefully argued rhetorical feats, or interpreting the words of God, this new elite was to seek to reorder society through the systematic application of rationality. Through this mixture of an elite selected on the basis of their talent and a set of rational techniques, it was hoped that modern societies would be able to tame and triumph over the great scourge of conflict that had beset all hitherto existing societies.

Following the traumas of the French Revolution, a range of rationalisers appeared who set their sights on applying systematic reason to social relations. One of the most well-known of these was Saint-Simon who sought to replace the general upheavals experienced during the French Revolution with a rationally ordered society. For him, this involved uprooting conflict and replacing it with organisation. He argued that the revolution had meant that 'all the existing relations between the members of a nation become precarious, and anarchy, the greatest of all scourges, rages unchecked, until the misery in which it plunges the nation … stimulates a desire for the restoration of order even among the most ignorant of its members' (cited in Wolin, 2004: 337). Saint-Simon saw his task as uprooting this conflict and retaining order through the systematic application of reason. This involved envisaging a time when the world of politics and conflict would be governed by a set of rational and specifiable rules. For instance, Saint-Simon suggested that 'in the old system society is governed essentially by men; in the new it will no longer be governed except by principles' (cited in Wolin, 2004: 322). In order to achieve this vision of a perfectly rational society, it would be necessary to draw out the rational laws on which politics operate through rational and sustained investigations. The aim would be the rational administration of conflict through the systematic application of rules. Because these rules would be rationally derived, they would be treated as impersonal. Rulers should not posit or invent rules. Rather, they should try to rationally and impersonally administer these laws. The unplanned, surprising and even miraculous character of conflict would slowly diminish as it was brought within the realm of rational planning and administration. The central way this could be achieved, Saint-Simon argued, was through the rational organisation of societies.

The injunctions of Saint-Simon invite a whole series of social technologies that have the explicit aim of rationally managing conflict out of society. For instance, the spirit of Saint-Simon can be found in the schemes of nineteenth-century industrialists who sought to develop model towns where the systematic application of reason would expunge class conflict that had previously characterised cities. Similarly, industrial engineers like F. W. Taylor hoped to root conflict out of the production process through the rational organisation of production that would allow an increase in the efficiency of each individual worker. Likewise, large-scale social scientific endeavours such as the Hawthorne studies sought to render the 'irrational' social drivers of workplace conflict visible to rational scientific analysis and managerial manipulation. The tools and techniques of social sciences were also applied to the many conflicts that beset broader society. Whether it was racial tensions in a neighbourhood, conflict between a parent and a child, or even an endemic war, social science promised to deliver a set of rational rules which, if followed, could do away with conflict.

The curious case of NLP

The quest to do away with conflict was driven by stoic technocrats and welfare experts during the last half of the nineteenth century and first half of the twentieth century. It was something which required strict rule following to ensure a disciplined social body that fitted into the timetables and administrative schemes developed by technocrats (Foucault, 1979). However, what is striking is that these attempts to engineer conflict out of social relations did not only involve the external enforcement of laws and legislation; they also entailed a requirement from those targeted by the disciplinary technology to begin to 'govern themselves' (Dean, 1999). This involved a continued process of self-monitoring, self-assessment and self-questioning on the part of individuals, as a way of bringing them into line with the demands of a 'governmental technology'. Perhaps one of the most striking ways by which people have been enticed into schemes of self-governing behaviour is through the plethora of therapeutic technologies (Burchell et al., 1991).

One of the most popular of these therapeutic techniques is NLP. NLP has become something of a self-development phenomenon over the past two decades. There is now a plethora of NLP books promising to help us grow 'more fully human' (Andreas and Andreas, 1989), build 'better relationships' (e.g. Prior and O'Connor, 2000) and even become 'thin' (McKenna, 2005). Not only is there a veritable library proposing to make us better human beings, NLP 'gurus' conduct a range of seminars designed to put theory into practice. The most famous of these reunions is Anthony Robbins' 4-day *Unleash the Power Within* seminar, the climax of which involves participants being encouraged to walk barefoot over hot coals. A growing number of companies (e.g. *International Teaching Seminars*; *NLP Comprehensive*) now offer a range of action-oriented NLP workshops from which participants can also get certified as 'NLP Practitioners', 'Master NLP Practitioners' and even 'NLP Trainers'.

But what exactly is NLP? No single definition seems to exist but it generally refers to a methodology designed to help people achieve *excellence* in what they do. The story of this 'new technology of achievement' (Andreas and Faulkner, 1996) began in the 1970s at the University of California when Richard Bandler, a maths undergraduate, teamed up with Dr John Grinder, an assistant professor in linguistics, to conduct research into 'human excellence'. They sought to understand what made the difference between people who were merely competent at any given skill and people who excelled at the same skill. To do so, they studied how a number of exceptional professionals – hypnotherapist Milton Erickson, Gestalt therapist Fritz Perls and family therapist Virginia Satir – achieved their excellent results with the patients they treated. The outcome of that research was two books, *The Structure of Magic* (Bandler and Grinder, 1975) and *The Structure of Magic II* (Grinder and Bandler, 1976), detailing the linguistic and behavioural patterns of the therapists. This structure was then adapted for general communication and effective personal change (Bandler and Grinder, 1979). The authors essentially claim to have uncovered ways to identify and codify the specific skills by which excellent people achieve their goals or as Virginia Satir put it, 'the ingredients of the *what* that goes into making the *how* [of excellence] possible' (1975: viii, original emphasis).

How exactly does this work? The basic premise of NLP is that people are influenced by internal 'maps' which they construct and organise according to their five senses: auditory, gustatory, kinaesthetic, olfactory and visual. NLP claims that the way this information is stored can be identified by paying attention to how individuals use their five senses. In this sense, NLP is 'the study of the structure of subjective experience' (Dilts et al., 1980). By studying such a structure in exceptional people, one can essentially 'model' it and adopt it as one's own. Thus, one can, in principle, become excellent at anything. For instance, business school academics inspired by the success of Henry Mintzberg, by modelling him, should in theory be able to reproduce his excellence. Similarly, revolutionaries aspiring to the heights of Che Guevara or footballers aiming for the glory of Zinedine Zidane simply need to model their heroes. The message is clear: 'excellence' can be analysed, codified and reproduced. In short, excellence can be managed.

NLP's interest in excellence and focus on action-oriented techniques has made the discipline increasingly appealing to the managerial world (e.g. Adler, 1996; Molden, 2000; Knight, 2002), where companies are seeking to achieve excellence not only in terms of client service but also vis-à-vis the selfhood of their employees. NLP promises corporate citizens the ability to achieve excellence at a wide array of skills: communication, creativity, goal-setting, leadership, learning, negotiation, presenting, problem-solving, selling, team-building, to name just a few. CEOs, directors, managers and their employees are increasingly being seduced by NLP, seeing in this technology a unique opportunity to achieve corporate success and fulfil their dream of winning the rat race.

One of the promises that NLP makes to potential users is the ability to successfully manage the various conflicts that beset their everyday lives. In a rather grand statement, one of the three therapists whom the founders of NLP 'modelled' suggested that the technique might be part of

> the beginning of the end of people relating to each other through force, dictatorship, obedience and stereotypes ... It is a question of whether the old attitudes will die and new ones be born or that civilisation dies out. I am working on the side of keeping civilisation going with new values about human beings. I hope that now you are, too. (Satir, 1972: 303–304)

So how exactly do practitioners of NLP hope that these grand promises of a world without conflict can be delivered?

Some of the early work on NLP directly broached the issue of 'conflict resolution'. In *Reframing*, Bandler and colleagues (1982) contend that conflict is not the result of divergent interests, long histories of hostility or structural antagonisms. Rather, it is the result of a lack of 'rapport' between participants as well as the lack of a common 'outcome frame'. If only two assailants were able to develop a sense of rapport and agree on a common outcome frame, then conflict would dissolve. In order to do this, various techniques of conflict resolution have appeared. At the core of these techniques is an attempt to alter how people think and talk about a situation. This often involves a process of getting conflicting parties to move from a 'solution frame' (this is what I would like to see happen) towards an 'outcome frame' (this is what I would like to achieve). By doing this, advocates of NLP argue that it is possible to identify what each group actually wants and what is disposable. Underlying this approach is a faith that if only each actor understood what the other really wanted, then they would be able to come to the realisation that both parties have similar interests after all, and could quickly come to a mutually agreed upon solution.

This kind of unitarist assumption is common to many forms of conflict resolution. What NLP adds, however, is a curious idealist twist: it argues that what needs to change is not just what actors' various demands are – these are secondary to how the participants involved in a conflict think about them – but their mental models, which block them from truly bonding with each other. If only they were able to switch their 'blame frame' into an agreed upon 'outcome frame', then it would be possible to overcome conflict. The central assumption is that conflict can be minimised by creating a common language between participants and getting them to minimise the difference between how they think. In other words, conflict is viewed as being simply the product of unhelpful patterns of speech and thought.

NLP usually involves some fairly unitarist assumptions about the nature of conflict. Here is an example from a brief paper offered by one practitioner of NLP:

(1) Meet people in their own model of the world – and respect their world view, (2) The meaning of any communication is represented in the response you get, (3) In any situation, a person makes the best choice with the resources available to them at the time, (4) In any interaction, the person with the greatest behaviour flexibility has the greatest influence over the outcome, (5) There is a focus on causes rather than solutions. So how questions are probably more useful than why questions, (6) Always add choices – never take them away, (7) The resources an individual needs to affect a change are already within them, (8) *Every* behaviour is appropriate in *some* context. (Davies, 2005: 1)

What is interesting about these statements is that they reflect many of the widespread liberal assumptions on which therapeutic techniques of governmentality are based. For instance, the core assumption appears to be that what is key is individuals' solipsistic 'models' of the world they have constructed neurologically. This suggests that the world is not something that exists outside of us, or between us, or even in our interaction. Rather, the world is simply our unique mental precepts of it. Conflict can be simply put down to a lack of understanding, acceptance and engagement with the unique worlds individuals solipsistically dwell within.

To create changes in different participants' representations of the world, NLP practitioners offer a plethora of tools and techniques. Some of these are process models that promise to guide parties through the dire straits of conflict. For instance, Bandler and colleagues (1982: 162) offer an exercise for constructing 'agreement frames'. This involves the following steps:

1. Ask A and B what, specifically, they want, and then restate it to their satisfaction as a pace.
2. Ask both A and B what their specific outcome will do for them (their meta-outcome) and restate it.
3. Find a common outcome such that when you state it, both A and B agree it is what they want.

The assumption here is that, through a process of framing and reframing what each party says it wants, it is possible to craft some kind of agreement. On other occasions, NLP simply provides a set of questions that the facilitator can ask in their attempts to massage the thinking of the groups they are working with. For instance, they might seek to draw out hidden assumptions that lie in talk. Gareth C. Davies gives us a well-trodden example of this kind of intervention:

Statement – He makes me angry when he does that Challenge (draw attention to the flaw in the cause/effect relationship) – It is interesting that he has that level of control over the emotions your produce. (Davies, 2005: 2)

Once again, the assumption underlying this kind of therapeutic intervention is that it is possible to overcome what appear to be insurmountable hurdles by changing how an individual talks and thinks about particular social interactions. There are many other potential models and processes of conflict resolution that draw on NLP. Indeed, there is a veritable industry around different models and methods. It is not our intention to dwell on them any further here; all we have hoped to do is briefly sketch out some of the broad assumptions underlying such interventions.

The end of conflict?

How far, in practice, can NLP deliver on its promises? Despite its popularity, NLP remains controversial. Some question its scientific validity (e.g. Sharpley, 1987; Drenth, 1999; Devilly, 2005) whilst others criticise it for not being subject to any regulatory standards and professional ethical codes (e.g. Schütz, 2007). Having recently attended an NLP workshop, one journalist (from the *Financial Times*) concluded that NLP was little more than a mix of mumbo jumbo, pop psychology and pseudo-science (Sanghera, 2005). But what is most troubling about NLP are the basic presuppositions on which it rests. NLP maintains that subjective experience has a structure and that by changing that structure, one can literally change one's world. In other words, NLP offers us a kind of individualism that begins from our internal world. There is no world in which we exist. The world is only a mental representation that may be altered and changed through skilled manipulation.

By beginning with one's mental models, NLP effectively involves a turning away from the world. To eradicate conflict, one needs only to dive into one's interiority and tune one's subjectivity in accordance with that goal. Conflict is no longer thought to be something that has anything to do with unequal resources, systematic patterns of discrimination and disrespect, or fundamental antagonisms in social life. Rather, it is something that is the result of a misalignment between mental frameworks and how we communicate. The result is that conflict is effectively internalised; it becomes about one's interior world rather than the world between us. Conflict is thought of as something that is a deviation from a world of perfect inner calm and communion between our individual mental models.

At one level, this turn away from the world implies that we can simply ignore some of the more deeply rooted and ingrained conflicts that exist within societies. For instance, struggles around resources are seen to be a product of faulty mental models on the part of both parties. This effectively overlooks the ongoing and deeply embedded historical distribution of value and rewards in societies (Bourdieu, 1984). Similarly, the distribution of status attributed to women in societies is thought to be the result of particular modes of thinking. This leads us to ignore utterly how institutions that distribute status such as schools, universities and professional bodies often operate with a degree of masculine bias (Bourdieu, 2001). Conflict around the laws is seen as something produced by a fundamental mismatch between mental models of the governed and the governing. This effectively ignores how collective conflict is often highly conditioned by cultures of collective conflict that go back hundreds of years (Tilly, 1977). It also pays no attention to how collective patterns of contestation are shaped by the opportunities which the state and other social structures give to groups to engage in conflict (Tarrow, 1994). We could go on and point out the many other aspects of collective social life that are effectively ignored or simply side stepped by NLP. But all these criticisms point in a single direction: if NLP does indeed hope to manage conflict out of existence, then it cannot simply do so by focusing on internal mental structures. This is because many of the dynamics of conflict and struggle are not located within our head. Rather they involve ongoing and collective social processes that are far greater, far more concrete and perhaps far more intriguing than our own mind.

To only focus on managing the inner world, NLP does not just fall short in explanatory power by ruling out nearly any external 'social' variable. It also makes a far more fundamental and perhaps more dangerous move: it continues to promote a culture of narcissism and inwardness that seems to have plagued many of the minor therapeutic approaches to self-management that have appeared since the 1960s (Lasch, 1984). What is particularly concerning about this movement is that it represents not just a change in technique but also a change in worldview. It represents a moment when one's attention and efforts shift from an engagement with the Other (in whatever form this Other might take), to a focus on the self. The core assumption is that the greatest hope we can have is to try to alter and change oneself. Changing the world is thought to be a hopeless task. Even if it were possible to achieve these changes in the world, they would be seen as somewhat ethically distasteful due to the fact such a project may involve asking people to do things which they do not immediately want to do. Indeed, some postmodernists would go as far as to call such interventions 'totalitarian' because they harbour a kind of utopian desire and a plan for society (Žižek, 2002).

The problems with this 'turn inwards' are many. At the most obvious level, they foster a relatively safe situation of inaction whereby any attempts to actually engage in meaningful social change projects are immediately dismissed as being hopelessly doomed to failure, utopian and even possibly a road to totalitarianism. The result is that plans for social change and broader demands are abandoned. In their place, what is offered is the endless therapeutic road of 'healing oneself'. This means that energy that could have been channelled into changing the way we interact and organise is suddenly channelled into how we relate to ourselves. A certain cynical distance towards the world is established whereby we seek to change what we think about the world, but do not seriously even hope that we change the world itself (Sloterdijk, 1984). But what is perhaps most dangerous about this movement is that it represents an abandonment of the terrain on which politics and conflict can actually take place – the space between us (Arendt, 1958). The result is a world where collective action becomes individual action and politics becomes therapy. Managing conflict simply becomes managing oneself.

In addition to promoting a turn inwards, NLP presupposes that the techniques for managing and mediating conflict are liberally available to everyone. Additionally, NLP assumes that people have all the resources they need inside themselves: memories, sensations, thoughts can all be mobilised to construct new mental maps designed to achieve personal goals. It is no wonder that NLP has become so popular in our culture. Subjectivity is seen as something that can be 'managed', improved and 'reprogrammed' in order to actualise the potential of individuals, to allow them to achieve higher levels of 'performance'. Those in positions of authority and responsibility can effectively give up on the task of managing conflicts and governing. This is something which each individual is made responsible to do themselves. In the ideal world of NLP, each individual would become a kind of conflict manager who continually monitors and assesses their interactions with others and seeks to create rapport and eradicate conflict. The blame for conflict would no longer lie externally to a subject. Rather, it would become something that they should negotiate and deal with.

The problem with this extreme form of subjectivism is that it further contributes to the responsibilisation of the individual and the 'ideology of "Just do it!"' (Salecl, 2004: 50). In so doing, it tricks individuals into believing that, by altering one's 'mental models', anything is possible. Thus, individuals fall prey to the idea that the eradication of conflict is a question of subjectivity management and individual choice. This pushes a lot of work such as dealing with, negotiation and seeking to resolve conflicts back onto the individual. In practice, this means a kind of intensification of the identity-work that employees already endure in the workplace (Sveningsson and Alvesson, 2003). It also typically gives rise to an experience of anxiety whereby individual workers are consistently asked to engage in this self-work themselves (Salecl, 2004). Individuals are forced to always ask themselves whether they have made the right decision, how they could have done something differently, and whether their failure to build rapport created conflicts.

The turn inwards leads to an internalisation of tensions between what Higgins (1987, 1989) calls discrepancies between different 'self-domains'. Borrowing Higgins's terminology, one is torn apart by one's 'actual self' – one's representation of what one really is here and now; one's 'ideal self' – one's representation of what one wishes to become; and one's 'ought self' – one's representation of what one thinks significant others expect of oneself. Such discrepancies heighten emotional vulnerabilities, leading to anxiety, disillusion and stress. Thus, rather than making us 'excellent', NLP has the potential to exacerbate our feeling of a *lack* of excellence. This means that any manifestation of conflict, whether it be in a relationship, a business transaction or inter-faith relationships is no longer something that is a natural and inevitable part of social relations. Rather, it is due to individuals' patterns of thinking. Moreover, conflict is something that may be managed by individuals manipulating their psychic life.

Conclusion

In this chapter, we have argued that in the last century we have witnessed repeated attempts to expunge conflict from the social world. This has often come in terms of attempts to develop formal administrative systems that will manage conflict out of existence. The first set of attempts to create such systems largely focused on changing the external relationships between people. However, this attempt to manage conflict shifted to the internal psychological terrain in the latter part of the twentieth century. The central intuition this is based on is that creating psychic harmony through the tools and techniques of psychology can give rise to social harmony. This leads us to assume that external conflict is the product of a lack of internal control.

To expunge nasty conflicts from our everyday lives, psychologists have offered a profusion of popular tools that promise psychic calm and relational harmony. NLP is only one of the most recent examples of such tools. We have argued that it is particularly appealing because it assures users that by managing their internal psychological world they can manage their external social world. Getting rid of conflict becomes a matter of changing how we talk to others. We have suggested that this approach is very appealing because it provides simple tools and steps that allow people to feel like they can manage the conflicts that beset their lives simply through the civil and skilled manipulation of words. For the acolyte of NLP a world without conflict is only a few words away.

While NLP may offer some comforting and perhaps even useful techniques, it rests on some dangerous assumptions. In particular, it assumes that conflict is an internal psychological issue. For NLP, managing our neurological life is managing our social life. We argued that this assumption disregards the fact that there is a whole range of external factors that affect how competent one might be in managing one's internal life (Illouz, 2007). Moreover, the kinds of conflict one is confronted with are also systematically organised by external social structural processes. The result is that the middle-class users of NLP may find themselves faced with far less insurmountable conflicts than an illegal immigrant who has fled a war zone and landed in a conflict-ridden public housing estate. Finally, and perhaps most worryingly, NLP represents yet another example of the great 'turn inwards' where we seek consolation for our struggles by turning away from our fellow humans and engaging with our more manageable psychic world.

References

Adler, H. (1996) *NLP for Managers: How to Achieve Excellence at Work*. London: Piatkus Books.

Andreas, C. and Andreas, S. (1989) *The Heart of the Mind*. Moab, UT: Real People Press.

Andreas, S. and Faulkner, C. (1996) *NLP: The New Technology of Achievement*. London: Nicholas Brealey Publishing Ltd.

Arendt, H. (1958) *The Human Condition*. Chicago: University of Chicago Press.

Arendt, H. (1970) *On Violence*. San Diago: Harcourt Brace.

Bandler, R. and Grinder, J. (1975) *The Structure of Magic I: A Book About Language and Therapy*. Palo Alto, California: Science and Behaviour Books.

Bandler, R. and Grinder, J. (1979). *Frogs into Princes: Neuro Linguistic Programming*. Moab, UT: Real People Press.

Bandler, R., Grinder, J., Andreas, S. and Andreas, C. (1982) *Reframing: Neuro-Linguistic Programming and the Transformation of Meaning*. Maob, Utah: Real People Press.

Bourdieu, P. (1984) *Distinctions: A Social Critique of the Judgement of Taste*. Cambridge, MA: Harvard University Press.

Bourdieu, P. (2001) *Masculine Domination*. Palo Alto, CA: Stanford University Press.

Burchell, G., Gordon, C. and Miller, P. (eds) (1991) *The Foucault Effect: Studies in Governmentality*. London: Harvester Wheatsheaf.

Davies, G. C. (2005) *NLP in Workplace Conflict Mediation*. Total Conflict Management. www.tcmsolutions.co.uk.

Dean, M. (1999) *Governmentality: Power and Rule in Modern Society*. London: Sage.

Devilly, G. J. (2005) 'Power therapies and possible threats to the science of psychology and psychiatry', *Australian and New Zealand Journal of Psychiatry*, Vol. 39(6), pp. 437–445.

Dilts, R., Grinder, J., Bandler, R. and DeLozier, J. (1980) *Neuro-Linguistic Programming: Volume 1, the Study of the Structure of Subjective Experience*. California: Meta Publications.

Drenth, P. (1999) 'Prometheus chained: Social and ethical constraints on psychology', *European psychologist*, Vol. 4.4, pp. 233–239.

Foucault, M. (1979) *Discipline and Punish*. London: Penguin.

Grinder, J. and Bandler, R. (1976) *The Structure of Magic II: A Book about Communication and Change*. Palo Alto, California: Science and Behavior Books.

Hegel, G. W. F. (1807/2005) *The Phenomenology of Mind.* Oxford: Oxford University Press.

Higgins, E. T. (1987) 'Self-discrepancy: A theory relating self and affect', *Psychological Review,* Vol. 94, pp. 319–340.

Higgins, E. T. (1989) 'Continuities and discontinuities in self-regulatory and self-evaluative processes: A developmental theory relating self and affect', *Journal of Personality,* Vol. 57, pp. 407–444.

Hobbes, T. (1651/1985) *Leviathan.* London: Penguin.

Honneth, A. (1995) *The Struggle for Recognition.* Cambridge: Polity.

Illouz, E. (2007) *Cold Intimacies: The Making of Emotional Capitalism.* Cambridge: Polity.

International Teaching Seminars, http://www.itsnlp.com. Accessed on 13 April 2007.

Knight, S. (2002) *NLP at Work: The Difference that Makes a Difference in Business.* London: Nicholas Brealey Publishing.

Lasch, C. (1984) *The Culture of Narcissism.* New York: Norton.

Machiavelli, N. (1517/1983) *Discourses on Livy.* London: Penguin.

Machiavelli, N. (1515/1997) *The Prince.* London: Penguin.

Marx, K. and Engels, F. (1848) *The Manifesto of the Communist Party.* London: Penguin.

McKenna, P. (2005) *I Can Make You Thin.* London: Bantam Press.

Molden, D. (2000) *NLP Business Masterclass.* London: FT/Prentice Hall.

NLP Comprehensive, http://www.nlpco.com. Accessed on 13 April 2007.

Plato (1945) *The Republic of Plato.* Oxford: Oxford University Press.

Prior, R. and O'Connor, J. (2000) *NLP & Relationships.* London: Thorsons.

Salecl, R. (2004) *On Anxiety.* London: Routledge.

Sanghera, S. (2005) 'Look into my eyes and tell me I'm learning not to be a loser', *Financial Times,* 26 August.

Satir, V. (1972) *Peoplemaking.* Palo Alto, California: Science and Behaviour Books.

Satir, V. (1975) 'Foreword', in Bandler, R. and Grinder, J. (eds) *The Structure of Magic I: A Book about Language and Therapy.* Palo Alto, California: Science and Behaviour Books.

Schütz, P. (2007) 'A consumer guide through the multiplicity of NLP certification training', http://www.nlpzentrum.at/institutsvgl-english.htm, accessed on August 2007.

Sharpley, C. F. (1987) 'Research findings on neuro-linguistic programming: Non supportive data or an unstable theory', *Journal of Counseling Psychology,* 34(1), pp. 103–107.

Sloterdijk, P. (1984) *The Critique of Cynical Reason.* Minneapolis, MN: University of Minnesota Press.

Sveningsson, S. and Alvesson, M. (2003). 'Managing managerial identity: Organizational fragmentation, discourse and identity struggle', *Human Relations,* 56(10), pp. 1163–1193.

Tarrow, S. (1994) *The Power in Movement.* Cambridge: Cambridge University Press.

Tilly, C. (1977) *From Mobilization to Revolution.* Reading, MA: Addison-Wesley.

Wolin, S. (2004). *Politics and Vision,* 2nd ed. Princeton, NJ: Princeton University Press.

Žižek, S. (2002) *Did Somebody Say Totalitarianism?* London: Verso.

Chapter **11**

'When I'm sixty five'

The shaping and shapers of retirement identity and experience   *Stephen Fineman*

Introduction

In July 2007, the vast Olympia Exhibition Centre in London opened its doors to The Retirement Show, billed to exhibitors as '*the best opportunity to interact with the UK's fastest growing and most asset-rich population ... the pot of assets and cash held by people over 50 is valued at over £175 billion*'. The retirement 'products' offered to the 'affluent visitors' concerned health, mobility, finance, holidays, property, hobbies, as well as 'last orders' – coffins, wills and other accoutrements of death and dying. This last, sombre, note was, however, well offset by the upbeat style of the show, augmented by celebrity presentations, tango lessons, games and gardening tips. The message was clear: retirement was a time for planning, fun, opportunity and, above all, consumption.

My purpose in this chapter is to examine how those 'retired' from the normal structures of work and employment are met by eager identity definers – specialist service and product providers. In their different ways, these agents capitalise on the material and/or existential fears of retirees to transform them, at a price, into a 'positive lifestyle project'. They reflect a twenty-first-century zeitgeist that defines retirees as a special brand of consumers who are expected to look to the marketplace for a new sense of being, security and purpose. For those who have the wherewithal to purchase the products and services of the likes of The Retirement Show, there is a cornucopia of exciting pastimes and projects to help them on their way. For the less prosperous, identity reconstruction presents a starker challenge. I will show how these processes and practices are cross-cut by dominant societal discourses on the management of self and others, on ageism and youthfulness.

Constructing retirement

In the late 1980s a shift emerged in discourses about retirement. Rather than a period to be spent in 'God's waiting room' – in decline, dependent and awaiting death – images of 'positive retirement' appeared in the media and academic literature (Featherstone, Hepworth and Wernick, 2004). The positive retiree could leave the workforce to enjoy a 'lifestyle' (suggesting life can be 'styled') of carefree pleasure and fun where age, per se, was little or no barrier. While the clock could not be stopped, it could certainly be stalled or obscured for a while. The deal, however, was that the lifestyle benefits were not an automatic provision or entitlement; the individual bore the responsibility, costs and risks of their choices (Salisbury, 1997).

With increases in longevity and a bulge of baby-boomers entering their senior years (in 2007 there were, for the first time in the UK, more pensioners than babies (Self and Zealey, 2007)), neither the state nor employer has been willing to meet the costs of retirement. Pre-retirement 'goals', 'planning' and 'investments' were, therefore, seen as essential features of the end-of-work experience. The self is a 'development project' enacted through rationalistic discourses and market resources, mirroring the very language and practices that epitomise the 'well managed' industrial organisation and the much vaunted 'pursuit of excellence' (Peters and Austin, 1985). The UK Government's 2007 advice to retirees encapsulates this self-help/self-management rhetoric (see Figure 11.1). Common to the popular retirement-marketing literature, the narrative is enlivened with a photograph of a smiling, healthy looking, heterosexual, couple:

Guide to planning for retirement

Figure 11.1   UK Government Advice on Retirement Planning

Planning for your retirement is important. You may look forward to your retirement as a time when you can have the freedom to do what you want, or as the time you will be rewarded for working all your life. The changes involved in retiring can be rewarding and positive or stressful, confusing and frustrating. It's up to you how you adapt.[1]

Retirement is individualised. It is presented as a time of opportunity; a transition to a new, golden, period of life – but only if you choose to make it so and organise/plan; 'it's up to you'. The call to individual agency and adaptation is blurred, however, by the social and emotional realties of the switch. The absence of welfare or pension entitlements and 'the death of the social' (Rose, 1996) isolates retirees who have failed, or been unable, to make provision for themselves; women, especially, are likely to be particularly disadvantaged (Age Concern, 2007; Roberts, 2007). In aggressive self-help, self-management, cultures, such as the USA, it can leave victims feeling guilt-ridden for their circumstances – they have 'brought it upon themselves' (Kemp and Denton, 2003).

Fears of 'known' and 'unknown' varieties can conspire to make retirement an unpredictable, often bumpy, ride (Atchley, 1976; Fineman, 2003). Vickerstaff and Cox's (2005: 85) study of UK public- and private-sector retirees and near-retirees reveals most of them to be unprepared and fearful for what lay ahead:

> Well it's the unknown really. I said before, for 41 years I don't know anything else. (Male manager, Transport)

> It's a very big step to go from working full-time to stepping over into what looks like the abyss of retiring and it's a psychological thing that you've got to come to terms with. One minute you've got the security of a wage coming in, which is a good wage. ... The next you're just a dog's body. (Male manager retired, Transport)

Such reactions echo Blaikie's observation that many of us are not especially interested in later life 'until we get there; and when we do we find ourselves disoriented by the crossing to a new land' (1999: 2; see also Hayden, Boaz and Taylor, 1999).

In sum, without the social capital, psychological resilience and actual purchasing power, many can only window gaze at retirement's positive offerings, while those who are able to enter the retirement market may or may not find solace; without firm boundaries and a context to anchor their new meanings, the choices on offer can appear bewildering. As psychoanalytic writers have noted, choices can be disorienting when uncoupled from the occupational and social structures that typically contain them (Fromm, 1942; Jahoda, 1982).

Youth, ageism and gerontophobia

Any discussion about retirement is pervaded by a meta discourse – the cult of youth. The veneration of the community, tribal or family elder as fount and transmitter of wisdom has all but vanished in post-industrial societies. In its place, youthfulness is celebrated. As Fischer puts it of the USA, 'The people of early America exalted old age; their descendants have made a cult of youth' (Fischer, 1977: 4). A cult of youth is symbiotically attached to ageism – discrimination against older members of society.

Ageism is expressed in the discriminatory provision of social care, of education, of medical treatment, of welfare benefits and of jobs (Morgan and Kunkel, 2001). All reflect a decline in the perceived economic value of the old in capitalist societies. No longer part of mainstream society they become a social burden; passengers rather than crew (Phillipson and Biggs, 1998). Retirement typically marks the passage from the productive worker to an unproductive 'elderly person', or, more euphemistically, 'senior citizen'. But as consumers, the well-off can offset their status losses and ageist attributions – for a time. The stigmas of older age are more pressing for the elderly poor, many of whom are relegated to shadowlands of subsistence-level state benefits.

Ageism blurs into gerontophobia – a fear of aging and the aged. A gerontophobic society manifests what Menzies-Lythe (1988) has termed social defenses against anxiety – social and organisational practices that neutralise or deflect threats to self-integrity or self-image. Typical anxieties include existential fears about the inevitability of death and the bodily decline and decrepitude that precede it. Popular culture responds defensively to such anxieties in two contrasting ways: by presenting retirement and older age as a rather nice time of life, or by distancing it through humour. The former can be found in greeting cards for the retired which offer clichéd portrayals of the golfing/fishing/bowling retired, the feet-up-in-front-of-the-television sort and (more wryly) the new sexual pleasures that are in store. Humour can be seen in mocking or satirising the 'afflictions' of the retired and the older person. Americanreetings.com, for instance, sells an 'over the hill' range of birthday cards containing strap lines such as 'old and neutered', 'fifty ain't pretty', and an animation of 'senior survivors' racing each other on their wheel chairs. Magazines aimed at the over 60s, such as *The Oldie*, offer their readers a light-hearted jaunt through their 'predicament' – a mix of mild grumpiness and humorous quips. Through humorous discourse, old age is made to appear more bearable, safer for public consumption, while, simultaneously, easier to marginalise and distance.

The stereotypical image of the curmudgeonly, confused, old person has been exploited in prime-time, comedy, television programmes, such as the BBC's telling-titled *One Foot in the Grave*. Humorous caricatures of the elderly allow us to confront decline (our own, others') safely, at a distance. Other distancing practices can be found in 'overaccommodation' by younger people – the tendency to speak to old people simply (they are cognitively impaired), loudly (they are deaf) and over-politely (they are intolerant) (Nelson, 2005). All such practices help protect those wanting to dissociate themselves from the actual or socially constructed debilities of aging (Woodward, 1991; Palmore, 1999).

Positive retirement and age work – the antidote?

Advice on positive retirement can be seen as something of an antidote to gerontophobia: constructing the old as still young – at heart, if not in body. As a powerful discourse, shaped by marketers and governmental agencies, positive retirement offers the elderly an honorary membership of 'normal' society with renewed access to its pleasures, especially consumption and exceptional goal-attainment of some sort. This is well illustrated in 'lifestyle' magazines for the retired.

Senior Journal, for example, illustrates its regular section on health and fitness with accounts of sporting achievements of 'ordinary' 65-year-olds, 'senior stars' who have sailed round the world, completed marathon horseback rides or survived the rigours of cross-country cycling.[2] *Active Adult, Retired* and *Senior One Source* magazines take a similar line, but use actual celebrities as role models – 'At 75, William Shatner is flying high'; 'Petula Clark – sixty years a star and still shining'. Unsurprisingly perhaps, ex-doyens of industry readily slip into managerialist/careerist language in constructing their retirement: 'Lee Iacocca – don't say retired! Never underestimate the importance of a project or in setting a goal'.[3] *Saga Magazine* reports on 74-year-old management 'guru', Charles Handy, an enthusiast for 'reinventing' himself with a 'portfolio career' to smooth the 'bonus years' of his life.[4] The implied seduction is, 'if they can do it, so can you'. But of course, 'they' typically command material resources out of reach of most of the retired proletariat.

Television has also responded to (or capitalised on) popular gerontophobia in a more corporeal sense – through 'makeover' programmes where *managed* bodies take centre stage. In the UK, *Trinny and Susannah* transform, before the camera, the aged and 'dowdily dressed' into new, youthful, versions of themselves, while *10 Years Younger* confronts participants, in clinical detail, with their decaying bodies and proceeds to reverse them through cosmetic surgery and corrective dentistry. The compliant subjects often appear dazzled by their 'instant' new looks, stirred by effusive praise from the presenters. We learn nothing, however, about what happens after the studio lights are extinguished or how they live with their re-sculpted forms.

In these settings the body managers, orchestrated by media celebrities, work in distinct ways to transform a low-capital body (old, wrinkly and irregular) to one that, putatively, has high social capital and worth (smooth, youthful and cool). Managing the body, even by drastic interventions, offers promise of a 'fitter' old age for a gerontophobic society – enhanced social acceptability and employability. In short, a sound 'investment'. Indeed, the *investment* potential, along with its managerialist expectations, is blatant in many presentations of cosmetic surgery for the older person – female and male. Ricci, a TV 'money' journalist, puts it as follows:[5]

> An increasing number of men admit to feeling threatened by age at work, and believe appearing more youthful, with younger-looking skin and a full head of (not-greying) hair will give them better job prospects. Indeed, the Harley Medical Group reports a boom in 'silver surgery'. The proportion of its cosmetic surgery patients over 50 has risen from 5% to 21% in the past five years. *With a lot of thought, research and realistic expectations of what surgery will achieve, going under the knife for the right reasons can prove to be a worthwhile lifetime investment.* [Italics added]

Ricci further notes Phillip Hodgson's opinion that 'it's sad but true that young, attractive people will always be more successful in every aspect of life, and that includes getting the higher-paid jobs and staying in them for longer'.

In these ways, a systemic prejudice in society is addressed symptomatically through a regime of body improvement, where capital is extracted from the aesthetics of youthful appearance – a shift from a tradition of brawn as capital, or more recently, knowledge. The structures and values that discriminate are left untouched and the door is open to the services of body managers. There are distinct echoes here of industry's 'stress fit' programmes where employers facilitate, and sometimes prescribe, exercise and related practices to help combat the physical and psychological rigours of, in effect, over-demanding or oppressive work (Newton, Handy and Fineman, 1995).

An extreme manifestation of body-improvement processes can be found among pop stars, fashion models and media celebrities, icons of glamour/youth societies. The physical effects of aging are a persistent hazard to a marketable social image, threatening to spoil a professional identity and public persona (Goffman, 1963). A remedy, that we can term *age work*, is a melange of body enhancement, aesthetic labour, anti-aging potions, positive thinking and constructive denial (Witz, Warhurst and Nickson, 2003; Hancock and Tyler, 2008). In her late 60s, actress Joan Collins explains her version of age work:

I mean, retire, what is that? Retirement – when you retire, very shortly thereafter you die. I don't want to do that, not yet. It's just something that I like, and I also don't buy into the ageism theory. I don't buy into you're on the slag heap when you're 40 or 50 or 60 or 70 or whatever. I think health is another exceedingly important thing. And I think of that again as I've written in several of my beauty books, a lot of health comes from the proper eating habits.[6]

'Life extensionists' have approached age work meticulously, with managerial precision, working compulsively and orderly on the edge of scientific possibility. Appleyard explains:

Since the seventies, wealthy boomers have tended to be fussy about their health, exercising, dieting and taking supplements. But those who know about the possibility of life extension have gone much further. I have encountered self-prescribing doctors using drugs to keep their blood pressure and cholesterol levels at phenomenally low levels, scientists taking 250 supplements a day and exercising furiously and, most extreme of all, calorie restrictionists living on two-thirds of the food intake one thought necessary. Not much of a life you may say, but, on the other hand, if it works out as planned then one day they will be able to abandon all the punishing regimes and live as they did in the sixties. (Appleyard, 2007: 9–10)

We might endorse Blaikie's (1999) suspicion of these efforts. Disguising the physical manifestations of aging, he argues, simply shifts the stigma burden to 'deep' old age, when no amount of bodily correction, or euphemism, can make a difference:

Deep old age suffers from yet greater distancing, stigmatisation, and denial. The 'positive' ageing discourse effectively eclipses consideration of illness and decline, yet final decay and death take on heightened hideousness since these will happen, regardless of whatever cultural, economic, or body capital one might possess. (Blaikie, 1999: 75)

One reading, and indeed aspiration, of the positive aging discourse is that it contributes to the inclusivity of older members of society. Yet perversely, if it does, it is not by valuing or celebrating older age in its own terms, but in terms of what it cannot really be: young. It buttresses the hegemony of gerontophobia, where older age becomes progressively more stigmatised, to be danced around in common, facing saving, interaction rituals of the sort, '*surely you're not that old; you certainly don't look it!*' (see Goffman, 1967). Age work and its 'positive' companions create a cryogenic bubble in which one can claim *not* to be 'like' one's chronological age and that there is an ageless self that belies the aging body reflected in the mirror (Kauffman, 1986; Featherstone and Hepworth, 1991). The trick is to bring the body into line with the youthful self through a range of technologies and interventions. Management – its rhetoric and procedures – is axiomatic to the realisation of such a 'project'. The 'well managed' body/self involves aims, targets and objectives for improvement. It involves support, surveillance and feedback from experts or advisors. It involves systematic or bureaucratic regimes and rules to track one's performance. It involves attention to the latest fashions – blends of scientific and quasi-scientific knowledge that promise different, quicker or cheaper routes to the corporeal 'excellence' or change that one seeks. Planning and plans – at the very core of rational management processes – are embedded in the lexicon of such practices, such as Giampapa, Pero and Zimmerman's (2004) '*5-Step Plan to achieve an anti-aging solution – which will actually repair your DNA!*'. Their recipe includes nutritional supplements, skin 'makeovers' and exercise, all carefully planned and prioritised through your 'personal aging equation' and by you 'taking charge'.

Marketing the Grey

The positive narrative is, as suggested, a business opportunity for marketers, significant agents in the power/knowledge regimes that shape the identities and lifestyles of the retired and elderly. Their taxonomies bring the market firmly to the forefront of aging and retirement as a consumerist experience. Negative stereotypes of the elderly population give way to more nuanced ones (Woodward, 1991; Palmore, 1999). For example, Moschis, Euehun and Mathur counsel marketers to 'properly stereotype mature Americans' who are ' … better-off financially … with the main focus on enjoying life rather than trying to "make it in life"' (1997: 289), while Williams, Ylanne and Wadleigh (2007: 19) identify 'new ground for images of older people by providing role models for ageing well – active, healthy, attractive, romantic and sexy'.

'Segmented profiles' facilitate marketers' 'product-specific strategies' (Coleman, Hladikova and Savelyeva, 2006). The profiles range widely in form and quirkiness. Moschis, Euehun and Mathur (1997), for example, identify 'healthy indulgers' (they like travel, home care services and town houses), 'frail reclusers' (need overdraft protection, exercise equipment and home health care) and 'ailing outgoers' (require investment products, health club membership and special clothing).

Other taxonomies give a colourful, if not bewildering, array of identifiers – such as 'woopies' (well-off older persons), 'glams' (grey, leisured and moneyed) and 'grumpies' (growing number of mature professionals) (Blaikie, 1999). The JWT Mature Marketing Group divides the 'mature market' into 35 'lifestyles', to include 'strapped seniors', 'the gold "n" gray', 'wired wanders', the 'urban upper crust', and 'credit commandos'. Together, these labels provide marketers with a deconstructed 'old' population to target with different products and services and, de facto, for the elderly to construct their identities.

The financial services and pensions industry plays a significant role in this process, especially attuned to the retiree, or potential retiree, who is 'unprepared'. Its Web sites tend to trade on fear and insecurity:

> Are your finances ready for retirement? Many people in the UK overestimate the value of their retirement savings and how long they will last – particularly as we are all living longer. (Fidelity International)[7]

HSBC sounds a similar note of worry:

> According to the Social Security Administration, Social Security will only provide approximately 40% of the income you'll need for a comfortable retirement and company pension plans are no longer the dependable source of income they were once considered.[8]

Others mix fear with the enticement of a positive-retirement dream. CNNmoney. com, for example, gives financial advice to retiring 'boomers', warning them that 'the "R" moment looms closer than ever', but 'if you get serious now, you can still catch the magic bus.' The 'bus' transports one to new lifestyles, such as 'a house on a beach' or 'opening an inn', and enables one to 'be the 30-year old you still think you are' and meet the costs of 'the many procedures out there that can – sort of – reverse time'.[9] All these measures aim to profit from the uncertainties and fantasies of older members of society. The old and retired may be moving, or have moved, from employment, but as long as they can be defined as consumers – be it for financial security, or of an active, leisured lifestyle – they merit marketing attention.

Managing the Grey

In shaping the elderly as significant consumers, grey marketing sets the ideological frames and sub-frames for managing the grey. The harnessing of powerful marketing rhetoric can succeed best when it manipulates or colonises the aspirations and behaviour of its target population. The grey consumer, while not a passive agent, is, in Foucauldian form, a part-product of the knowledge and persuasive structures to which they are exposed. Managerialism, thus, is embedded in the way marketing 'assists' in defining what the elderly and retired 'should' be planning for, should be investing in, should be worried about, should be wanting and should be dreaming about. We see this most intensely, and tangibly, in the retirement village, a microcosm of grey-management mechanisms and ideals.

Sun City Center – Florida's Best Retirement Community for Active Seniors
Sun City Center, America's premier retirement community, where you will love the sunshine and year round activities offered. Explore our community and you will arrive at one conclusion: What a great place to live!

No need for two cars here. Residents use golf carts to travel throughout the community on public streets. Drive to the golf course, go shopping, visit friends. You can maintain an active, independent lifestyle without the added expense of a second car. Meet great people and enjoy the many recreational activities available to residents.[10]

Richmond Retirement Village – Don't Put off Getting the Most out of Life ....
We take great pleasure in providing villagers with the best possible care and assistance, this gives villagers all the time they need to relax and get to enjoy their retirement as much as possible.

Whether you live in an Independent Apartment, Luxury Close Care Serviced Apartment or a Residential Care Room, you will experience a new zest for life in a Richmond Retirement Village. With stunning retirement homes for sale across the country, you can keep your independence and be part of a real community. A community brimming with excitement, activity, events, clubs and as much entertainment as you want. No two days are ever the same in a Richmond Retirement Village.[11]

Sun City Center's advertisements parade a montage of smiling, elderly, people, doing various things: on exercise machines; swimming; playing cards, snooker or golf; and eating fine meals together. Managed activities and busyness, in its many forms, appears an imperative for successful, happy, aging in the village; individual identity is affirmed through a 'busy ethic' (Ekerdt, 1986). Indeed, there is something of a postmodern irony when a particular stratum of society seeks independence and individuality by joining others who purportedly share the same agenda (Blaikie, 1999).

Village residents are literally buying into an age-segregated community where 'doing things' is facilitated – a serious playground for the elderly. Richmond Retirement Villages are based in the UK and are less expansive in their public relations than their US cousin – more restrained, rather more 'British' – but still strong on a zestful, positive, lifestyle. Many villages are careful to target clientele who are 'active' by stressing that they are 'not care homes', but places to *live*, happily and *safely*, tapping into latent fears about crimes committed against the elderly (Lucas, 2004). There is some evidence that residents are pleased to endorse the safety message. Graham and Tuffin (2004a: 187), for example, report the views of those living in an Australian retirement village, iron-gated and located within 2m-high brick walls. They regarded the wider community a threat, but, in the words of one, 'You never have to think about that here'. Retirement villages wed the identity of the retired to a specific physical place and geographical location. As 'communities of identity' (Gilleard and Higgs, 2005) it falls to residents to work at creating a community spirit that meets their own desires – but desires already well-circumscribed by the extant facilities and the commercial aims of the village's owners and professional managers.

The village phenomenon originated in the USA, post World War II, but is relatively recent in the UK – which has less vacant land for the development of such communities. In their early years the phenomenon drew sharp criticism from social critics – describing it variously as 'socially unnatural' and 'golden ghettos' (Hunt et al. 1983: 1). As gated, luxury, warehouses for the elderly, they were seen to separate residents from the wider community and a 'normal' life course – so fostering greater stigmatisation and societal fragmentation (see Grant, 2006). This view remains; but there is now a competing one, fuelled by the considerable growth of the elderly population and its business potential: that any image of the *active* aged will challenge negative views of aging (Croucher, 2006). This is especially pertinent to the rapid growth of such communities in the USA, some of which resemble mini suburbs or towns.

Those who have made the sometimes tough choice of uprooting from their traditional home and moving to a retirement village have a vested interest in justifying their decision to report positively on their village experiences. Nevertheless, what we know of life on the inside indicates much that is experienced as nurturing, supportive and socially dynamic for this self-selected group (Grant, 2006). But there is also an impression that those who are socially reticent, or become so, are less comfortable, and less welcome, in a setting where committee membership, participation in managing activities, and community leadership is celebrated (Graham and Tuffin, 2004b). It is a place for joiners and active followers – who are more likely to be middle class, white and ethnocentric (McHugh and Larson-Keaghy, 2005).

How, then, do such communities, that strive for homogeneity, manage inevitable differences? Retirement villages are not static communities, frozen in the cheery image of their promotional literature. As they age and mature; as people leave, die and others join; we would expect (like other complex organisations) a variegated, politically complex, social organization (Folts and Muir, 2002). There is a dearth of research on this question, but there are some intriguing hints. Streib and Metch (2002), for example, challenge the perception that retirement communities offer an idyllic, conflict-free lifestyle for the retired. Conflict, while not exactly rife, is reflected in many structural divisions, such as between new and long-term residents; between neighbours within the community; and between residents and the management, owner or developer. An ethnography of a ten-year-old Florida retirement village, Eldorado, by Kestin and Hoonaard (2002), adds substance to these observations, exposing details of social boundaries and cliques. The researchers found that certain groups – 'snowbirds', newcomers and the widowed – lived on the margins of the community. Snowbirds spent just half the year in the community, escaping the inclement weather of their hometown. They were criticised by year-round residents for their lack of commitment to the community, for breaking the continuity of card games and for being ignorant of the management issues facing the community. Newcomers spoke of their difference from the 'older generation' of the community, especially (and ironically, given the 'activity' spin of village promotion) their lack of activeness. They also found that the longer-term residents did not readily befriend them. Finally, there was widowhood. In the early days, some 9 per cent of Eldorado residents were widows; ten years later, this had climbed to nearly 30 per cent. Death bites greedily and partially (more frail males) in a community that is already in its senior years. Kestin and Hoonaard (2002: 60) apply Goffman's notion of stained identity to characterise the sentiments of the widows. They saw themselves as second-class citizens compared to married couples, and were shocked to be dropped by their married friends. Their rules of survival were reactive and defensive:

> They wait for couples to call and invite them out; they make sure they pay their own way; they defer to their couple friends in decisions regarding where to go out for dinner or what movie to see. In addition, they must not turn down invitations or they risk not receiving any other ones.

Married couples, in contrast, were convinced that the widowed 'like to keep to themselves', so reinforcing the separation. The glossy image of bonhomie among the elderly, joined in common purpose, was further punctured by the discomfort expressed by non-Jews in a community where Jewish residents were in the numerical majority.

The positive spin on retirement communities is orchestrated by a number of stakeholders, particularly governments, co-joined with real estate and tourism developers and managers. Together they present a seductive vision of 'choice', a Shangri-La for the elderly. But the studies of life inside suggest a more intricate, less idealised, picture. Perhaps the ultimate irony for the ageism debate is the indication that retirement communities can begin to reproduce, within their solid walls, a version of the very ageism to which residents 'outside' are exposed.

Being busy in the slow lane

Positive retirement embraces, without question, busyness – being busy, keeping occupied and doing stuff. Busyness is expressed in the many formally, micro-managed, activities for retirement village residents. For example, Rocky Creek Retirement Village in Tampa, Florida, proudly boasts that it 'has so many activities it is hard to choose!'[12] Figure 11.2 reproduces their veritable supermarket of offerings, leaving no day without scheduled games, exercises, events or entertainment. These events are constructed and managed by paid, full-time, organisers, and by the residents themselves.

Activities overview

- Horseshoe pits
- Puzzles
- Walking club

- Swimming pool
- Billiards

- Shuffleboard
- Books and magazines

Weekly overview

- Sing-a-longs
- Triva
- Arts and crafts
- Bowling
- Greenhouse
  (gardening)

- Current events
- Bunco
- Ceramics
- Arm-chair traveling
- Bridge

- Painting
- Stretcher size
- Uchre
- Water aerobics
- Bingo

Monthly overview

- Dinner theater
- Kitchen band

- Pet therapy
- Guest speakers

- Dinner outings

Annual overview

- Canadian's Farewell
  Dance
- Easter Dinner/Bonnet
  Parade
- Grandparent's Day
  Picnic
- Halloween Party and
  Dance
- Resident Christmas Play
  and dinner

- New Year's Eve Dinner
  and Dance
- Valentine's Day Dance

- St Pat's Day Talent
  Show
- Memorial Day Picnic

- Veteran's Day Picnic

- 4th of July Picnic

- Labour Day Picnic

- Volunteer Banquet

- Thanksgiving Dinner

- Resident Bizzare

Periodic overview

- Golf outings
- Plays and shows

- Tournaments
- Mini vacations

- Museum tours

Figure 11.2 Activities at Rocky Creek Retirement Village, Florida

Managed activity and consumerist ideologies converge; a logic that derives, in part, from gerontologists' long-held belief that activity can be used to index 'adjustment' to old age. For example, Cavan et al.'s (1949) 'adult activity inventory' defines healthy adjustment in terms of participation in a wide range of leisure, religious and friendship activities. Other writers speak of 'high investment activities', and 'serious leisure' as indicators of successful aging (Katz, 2000). Classifications of these sorts are laden with both moral and power dimensions: who defines what is a good and right activity for the elderly, and how the elderly, in turn, come to define and evaluate themselves by such categories. Indeed, Katz draws attention to the way that activity has become professionally and managerially appropriated as a disciplinary and market discourse, such that the 'inactive', or activity resistant, risk being stigmatised or pathologised.

Conspicuously absent from the professional discourse on activity is a critical examination of the class and gendered assumptions that gerontologists themselves hold. Activity checklists are typically anchored in middle-class conventions and morality with no mention, for example, of sex, drinking or gambling (Katz, 2000). There is little evidence of the cultural and sub-cultural meanings of activity that the elderly themselves value, or on what basis actual 'pastimes' common among the elderly, such as watching television, taking a nap, reading or simply sitting around musing, are marginalised or discounted.

What we learn from such discussions is the force of managed 'activity' as an ethic, commodity and socially constructed source of meaning during retirement. At its most potent, it could be seen to colonise the identity of the elderly and retired, such that a life without much 'organized' activity is experienced as incomplete; something to feel uncomfortable, or guilty, about. It invites age work and emotional labour – giving the *impression* to others that one is, indeed, happily, active, contrary to initial appearances. For those who feel oppressed by exhortations to be active, by being micro-managed or mismanaged by their peers or recreation leaders, a degree of resistance could be expected. Dorothy, a resident of a Florida retirement village, describes her feelings about the recreational director's tightly packed event programme:

> You have no idea – exercise – it's just like you were back at school, as if you're such imbeciles you couldn't think of a thing to do yourself. When people say, 'Oh, you should take line dancing', I say, 'Oh, I'm not old enough'. Inside this body, that may look like it's aging to you, is still a fourteen year old screaming to get out. (Katz, 2000: 146)

There is a hint here of what Gabriel (1995) has termed the 'unmanaged organization', a space where micro-management fails and a self-authored identity is expressed. It also suggests tensions between the market-friendly, customer-focussed, image of retirement villages and the overt and covert control that such enterprises require to keep the activity-ball rolling (see also Simpson and Cheney, 2007).

In conclusion

Managerial and marketing languages and practices now permeate the construction of the retired and retirement. Neo-liberal social policies, and a withdrawal of state support, have created a huge retirement industry aimed at capturing the surplus financial capital of the retired, both fuelling and assuaging their fears and, accordingly, shaping their identities. The corporate world, sensing an expanding market, has turned its well-oiled marketing and management tools to making retirement seem an enticing consumer experience and comfortable security net.

Many such practices trade on a cultural obsessiveness with youth and activity, symptoms of societal unease about the actualities of aging and its bodily and psychological deteriorations. Some of these 'afflictions' are camouflaged by enticing, 'rejuvenating', products and procedures, others are re-framed as positive in the glitz of retirement activities and retirement villages. The latter can provide solace for many of their residents, many willingly (it seems) captured by a community of managed activity; others, though, finding themselves at odds with the pressure to 'do', and uncomfortable with the unfolding social divisions of the community. Notwithstanding their growing popularity, we could regard these village developments as more a symptom of societal failure and social-policy mismanagement. Ghettoed retirement communities can bleed wider society of a mix of talent, wisdom, and side-by-side comprehension, across the generations. A challenge, surely, lies in helping to create in situ, mutually supportive, mixed local communities, not facilitating their further break-up – for a privileged few.

Who we are and who we can be in our retirement and old age are, in part, a product of the discourses that inhabit our identities – and the choices that we can then make. The positive offensive contains existential, ideological and moral baggage that needs unpacking, especially in its notions of activeness and management. At one level, as Moody (1988) has noted, activity per se can be a substitute for emptiness of meaning, just as workaholism can anaesthetise a dull or troubled life for those in employment. As the state has retreated, marketing and management, in its various persuasive guises, has stepped into the vacuum to promote 'activity' lifejackets for the aged and retired. An activity ethic, however, distances participants from reflectivity about how, alone or with others, they could differently shape their selves and identities in retirement. And it effectively postpones the likely crisis when the infirmities of old age prevent activity – at least of the sort pedalled by marketers of a youthful or ageless retirement.

A further consideration, alluded to at various points in this chapter, is the eliteness of current conceptions of activity aimed, as they are, at the fit-for-purpose retiree. The individual is constructed as a vibrant consumer of retirements' products with a desire to 'keep young, look young, and feel young'. They are seen as ready for a customised, keenly managed, lifestyle of activity and leisure. Yet such upbeat messages would appear foreign, if not bizarre, to the mass of old and retired who do not enjoy an affluent, baby-boomer, lifestyle and struggle with poor health, financial difficulties or loneliness. For them, the positive retirement discourse and its management/self-management messages carries with it exclusion and stigma.

Finally, positive constructions of aging, much like the recent celebration of the 'positively deviant' in management and organisational theory (Fineman, 2006), are remarkably unreflective in their presentation. They are rarely, if ever, qualified by the commercial 'aging' industry, or by mainstream gerontologists; their critique resting in hands of a small band of critical sociologists. This attests, in part, to the counter-culturalism of questioning anything in human affairs that has a 'self evident', positive label, attached to it, and partly to the unfashionability of conducting research among the old and retired – especially within the broader fields of management and organisational studies. This should change – because everyday life is, evermore so, a life beyond 65 years of age.

Notes

1. http://www.direct.gov.uk/en/Over50s/RetirementAndPensions/PlanningForRetirement/DG_10027113
2. http://www.seniorjournal.com/SenStars.html
3. http://www.activeadultmag.com/; http://www.retiredmagazines.co.uk/index.php; http://www.senironesource.com/LeeIacocca.html
4. http://www.saga.co.uk/magazine/lifechanges/planretirment/ReinventingRetiremment.asp
5. http://www.channel4.com/money/feature.jsp?pageParam=5andid=489
6. Interview with Joan Collins, CNN Larry King Live, 11 November 2002 – 21:00, http://transcripts.cnn.com/TRANSCRIPTS/0211/11/lkl.00.html
7. http://www.fidelity.co.uk/direct/planning/plan/retirement/index.html
8. http://www.us.hsbc.com/1/2/3/personal/other-services/retirement
9. http://money.cnn.com/magazine/moneybag/babyboomer/
10. http://www.suncitycenter.org/
11. http://www.richmond-villages.com/lifestyle.php
12. http://www.rockycreekretirementvillage.com/activities.html

References

Age Concern. 2007. *Counting the Cost of Caring: A Women and Pensions Survey.* London: Age Concern.

Appleyard, B. 2007. *How to Live Forever or Die Trying.* London: Simon and Schuster.

Atchley, R. C. 1976. *The Sociology of Retirement.* New York: Wiley.

Blaikie, A. 1999. *Ageing and Popular Culture.* Cambridge: Cambridge University Press.

Cavan, R. S., Burgess, E. W., Havighurst, R. J. and Goldhamer, H. 1949. *Personal Adjustment in Old Age.* Chicago, IL: Science Research Associates.

Coleman, L. J., Hladikova, M. and Savelyeva, M. 2006. The baby boomer market. *Journal of Targeting, Measurement and Analysis for Marketing,* 14(3): 191–209.

Croucher, K. 2006. *Making the Case for Retirement Villages.* York: Joseph Rowntree Foundation.

Ekerdt, D. J. 1986. The busy ethic: Moral continuity between work and retirement. *Gerontologist,* 26: 329–244.

Featherstone, M. and Hepworth, M. 1991. The mask of ageing and the postmodern life course. In M. Featherstone, M. Hepworth and B. S. Turner (Eds), *The Body: Social Processes and Cultural Theory.* Newbury Park, CA: Sage.

Featherstone, M., Hepworth, M. and Wernick, A. 2005. Images of aging: Cultural representations of later life. In M. L. Johnson, P. G. Coleman and T. B. L. Kirkwood (Eds), *The Cambridge Handbook of Age and Ageing.* Cambridge: Cambridge University Press.

Fineman, S. 2003. *Understanding Emotion at Work.* London: Sage.

Fineman, S. 2006. On being positive: Concerns and counterpoints. *Academy of Management Review,* 31(2): 270–291.

Fischer, D. H. 1977. *Growing Old in America.* New York: Oxford University Press.

Folts, W. E. and Muir, K. B. 2002. Housing for older adults: New lessons form the past. *Research on Aging*, 24(1): 10–28.

Fromm, E. 1942. *The Fear of Freedom*. London: Allen and Unwin.

Gabriel, Y. 1995. The unmanaged organization: Stories, fantasies and subjectivity. *Organization Studies*, 16(3): 477–501.

Giampapa, V., Pero, R. and Zimmerman, M. 2004. *The Anti-Aging Solution: 5 Simple Steps to Looking and Feeling Young*. Hokboken, NJ: Wiley.

Gilleard, C. and Higgs, P. 2005. *Contexts of Ageing: Class, Cohort and Community*. Polity Press: Cambridge.

Goffman, E. 1963. *Stigma: Notes on the Management of Spoiled Identity*. New Jersey: Prentice Hall.

Goffman, E. 1967. *Interaction Ritual*. New Jersey: Anchor Books.

Graham, V. and Tuffin, K. 2004a. Retirement villages: Companionship, privacy and security. *Australian Journal of Ageing*, 23(4): 184–188.

Graham, V. and Tuffin, K. 2004b. Retirement villages: Companionship, privacy and security. *Australasian Journal on Ageing*, 24(4): 184–188.

Grant, B. C. 2006. Retirement villages: An alternative form of housing on a ageing landscape. *Social Policy Journal of New Zealand* (27): 100–105.

Hancock, P. and Tyler, M. 2008. It's all too beautiful: Emotion and organization in the aesthetic economy. In S. Fineman (Ed.), *The Emotional Organization: Passions and Power*. Oxford: Blackwell.

Hayden, C., Boaz, C. and Taylor, F. 1999. *Attitudes and Aspiration of Older People: A Qualitative Study. Department for Social Security Report 102*. London: HMSO.

Hunt, M. E., Feldt, A. G., Marans, R. W., Pastalan, L. A. and Vakalo, K. L. 1983. Retirement communities: An American original. *Journal of Housing for the Elderly*, 1(3/4): 1–277.

Jahoda, M. 1982. *Employment and Unemployment*. Cambridge: Cambridge University Press.

Katz, S. 2000. Busy bodies: Activity, aging, and the management of everyday life. *Journal of Aging Studies*, 14(2): 135–152.

Kauffman, S. 1986. *The Ageless Self: Sources of Meaning in Late Life*. Madison, WI: University of Wisconsin Press.

Kemp, C. L. and Denton, M. 2003. The allocation of responsibility for later life: Canadian reflections on the roles of individuals, governments, employers and families. *Ageing and Society*, 23(23): 737–760.

Kestin, D. and Hoonaard, V. D. 2002. Life of the margins of a Florida retirement community: The experience of snowbirds, newcomers and widowed persons. *Research on Aging*, 24(1): 50–66.

Lucas, S. 2004. The images used to 'sell' and represent retirement communities. *The Professional Geographer*, 56(4): 449–459.

McHugh, K. E. and Larson-Keaghy, E. M. 2005. The white walls: The dialectic of retirement communities. *Journal of Aging Studies*, 19: 241–256.

Menzies-Lythe, I. 1988. *Containing Anxiety in Institutions: Selected Essays*. London: Free Association Books.

Moody, H. R. 1988. *Abundance of Life: Human Development Policies for an Aging Society*. New York: Columbia University Press.

Morgan, L. A. and Kunkel, S. 2001. *Aging: Second Edition*. Thousand Oaks, California: Pine Forge Press.

Moschis, G. P., Euehun, L. and Mathur, A. 1997. Targeting the mature market: Oppportunities and challenges. *Journal of Consumer Marketing*, 14(4): 282–293.

Nelson, T. D. 2005. Ageism: Prejudice against our feared future self. *Journal of Social Issues*, 61(2): 207–221.

Newton, T., Handy, J. and Fineman, S. 1995. '*Managing' Stress: Emotion and Power at Work*. London: Sage.

Palmore, E. B. 1999. *Ageism: Negative and Positive*, (2nd ed). New York: Springer.

Peters, T. and Austin, N. 1985. *A Passion for Excellence*. New York: Random House.

Phillipson, C. and Biggs, S. 1998. Modernity and identity: Themes and perspectives in the study of older adults. *Journal of Aging and Identity*, 3(1): 11–23.

Roberts, Y. 2007. Ageism is still the real enemy of better care. *Community Care* (1663): 16.

Rose, N. 1996. The death of the social? Re-figuring the territory of government. *Economy and Society*, 25(3): 327–356.

Salisbury, D. L. 1997. Retirement planning and personal responsibility: The changing shape of the three-legged stool. *Generations*, 21(2): 23–26.

Self, A. and Zealey, L. (Eds) 2007. *Social Trends No. 37*, Office for National Statistics. Houndmills: Palgrave Macmillan.

Simpson, M. and Cheney, G. 2007. Marketization, participation, and communication within New Zealand retirement villages: A critical-rhetorical and discursive analysis. *Discourse and Communication*, 1(2): 191–222.

Streib, G. F. and Metch, L. R. 2002. Conflict in retirement communities: Applying an analytical framework. *Research on Aging*, 24(1): 67–89.

Vickerstaff, S. and Cox, J. 2005. Retirement and risk: The individualisation of retirement experiences? *The Sociological Review*, 53(1): 77–95.

Williams, A., Ylanne, V. and Wadleigh, P. M. 2007. Selling the 'elixir of life': Images of the elderly in an Olivio advertising campaign. *Journal of Aging Studies*, 21: 1–21.

Witz, A., Warhurst, C. and Nickson, D. 2003. The labour of aesthetics and the aesthetics of labour. *Organization*, 10(1): 33–54.

Woodward, K. 1991. *Aging and Its Discontents: Freud and Other Fictions*. Bloomington: Indiana University Press.

Epilogue

Epilogue

Chapter 12

Bringing everyday life back into the workplace

Just be yourself! *Peter Fleming and Andrew Sturdy*

> Have the confidence to let people be themselves. Tolerating different approaches and expressions of individuality can make life much more complicated and disruptive for leaders ... Yet, compliance and conformity are less likely to help leaders come up with ground breaking ideas than conflict and challenge ... letting them [employees] express their views and their individuality freely are key determinants of building an authentic and meaningful environment. The upcoming X and Y Generations certainly expect it.
>
> *(Bains et al., 2007: 251)*

Introduction

While the other chapters in this volume address how managerialism has colonized various aspects of everyday life '*outside*' the work organization, this chapter explores a reverse (yet related) process. In particular, we argue that recent approaches to managing employees seek to appropriate and re-construct ostensibly non-colonized aspects of everyday life within the workplace. With the rise of market rationalism combined with a recognition of the managerial limitations of homogeneous corporate cultures, greater attention is given to diversity. Here, the private, individual and authentic identities, feelings and lifestyles of employees are seemingly celebrated and thereby utilized as an emergent and yet insidious form of identity management and construction. For example, firms seek to encourage the experience of 'fun' at work by promoting a party atmosphere whereby diverse sexualities and consumer lifestyles are reconstructed and the experience of concomitant routine work downplayed. We suggest that this reconstruction is possible, in part, because everyday life is now constructed to such an extent that what it means to be diverse or authentic is already largely compatible with the productive demands of late capitalism, or comes to be so.

There is a long history in modernity of more or less conscious efforts to shape the feelings, values and orientations of individuals in advance of, and preparation for, a life of paid employment. Respect for authority, a sense of time discipline and work ethic and the suppression of extreme and 'negative' emotions continue to play a part in our socialization and increasingly, those in industrializing regions of the world (e.g. Thompson, 1967). Although employer preferences are diverse and subject to change, these early forms of the 'management' of everyday life can be seen to help provide employers with an already disciplined labour force. Of course, the persistence of conflict and tension in the employment relationship and elsewhere suggests that such efforts have had, at best, partial success (Abercrombie et al., 1990). Nevertheless, in all but the tightest labour markets, employers' recruitment practices select those who seem to have been suitably formed (Thompson and Callaghan, 2002). This is the base line for normative control which then continues to reinforce and transform values through various means.

Despite the preparation and filtering of labour prior to entering the world of work, distinctions remained between what was required and expected within and beyond work, even in the various forms of paternalistic regimes (Abercrombie and Hill, 1976). Bureaucratic, political (e.g. liberal) and/or occupational (gendered) discourses assigned norms to separate domains (Ferguson, 1984). Although by no means wholly independent, work and everyday life were then considered largely separate realms for all except, perhaps, the elites (Kanter, 1977). In particular, bureaucratic concerns to bracket off reason and effect helped ensure some existential and normative boundaries (Albrow, 1997). However, this was to change. Echoing elements of both paternalism and human relations, organizational control regimes emerged which placed greater emphasis on the normative characteristics of the ideal employee (Ray, 1986). Here, the new 'corporate culture management' went a step further in defining, screening and then seeking systematically to cultivate and reinforce values.

But this did not mark the end of the work–non-work divide. Firstly, the prescribed norms were organization, as well as, work specific (e.g. the 'HP Way') such that other aspects of employees' lives continued to be out of bounds (Kunda, 1992). Secondly, although intrusive, culture initiatives allowed for employee compliance where a cynical distance from the prescribed values helped protect a sense of a 'real' self, including that rooted in aspects of everyday life. In short, the emotionless 'Organization Man' of the 1950s (Whyte, 1956) was replaced by the 'company-specific' person and values of the 1980s and 1990s, but the realms of work and everyday life remained, clearly, if not completely, distinct.

Much of the above overview is well documented elsewhere and in a way which is more sensitive to historical and situational context (see Guillén, 1994). Our concern is with what we see as a parallel development to that discussed in all the other chapters in this volume. In particular, we are concerned with one aspect of a wider development whereby traditional conceptions of organizational boundaries are breaking down. Here, some of the realms of everyday life which had been deemed as either irrelevant/obstructive to employers and/ or as comprising a protected existential space for employees have become the object of management. This might be termed 'the management of everyday life *at work*' and we seek to show how this can be linked to a recognition of some of the dysfunctions of corporate culture management and the emergence of an individualistic discourse of market rationality.

Market rationality can be seen as a paradoxical combination of a laissez-faire economics, normative concerns with generic values of entrepreneurship and innovation as well as our particular focus, the celebration, appropriation and construction of various features of everyday life. As intimated in the prescriptive quote at the beginning of the chapter, recruits should be 'existentially empowered' in that they should not share the organization's values, and should even oppose them. They should also break another traditional work/non-work boundary by 'having fun' at work and express more of their 'true' selves. Diversity and incongruence with (traditional) organizational norms are key. This resonates both with earlier human relations interventions in terms of engaging with employees' informal involvement in work and with contemporary political and social discourses of equal opportunities and multiple identities, in relation to sexuality and lifestyle for example. In short, employees are to be encouraged and even legislated to 'be themselves'. It is almost as if market society at large has imbued employees with enough of a 'value orientation' that today's firms need no longer expend resources on the selection and constitution of engineered selfhoods.

In order to make this argument, the chapter is organized as follows. Firstly, we explore some of the literature on corporate culture management and identity before turning to the apparent rise in market rationalism. Secondly, we examine recent developments in the management of identity, including the celebration of diversity and 'fun' at work. Thirdly, we introduce case study research and present data on the application of such a management approach in an American-owned call centre in Australia. We conclude with a discussion of the broader implications for the organization and experience of work and control in contemporary (individualist) societies.

From corporate culture management to market rationalism

The massive popularity of culture management in the 1980/1990s prompted the development of concepts that clarified the intersection of power and selfhood in organizations (e.g. Willmott, 1993). According to Kunda (1992), for example, the wave of management ideas grouped around the 'culture gurus' like Peters and Waterman (1982) fundamentally changed the experience of work. Control mechanisms were based upon commitment and extreme organizational identification as much as on bureaucratic systems. In this sense, then, *employees become part of the company*, but coercion was also evident – 'you either buy into their norms or you get out' (Peters and Waterman, 1982: 77).

Kunda's (1992) analysis highlighted the resulting tension among employees between absorbing the designed membership role as their own and maintaining a private reserve that was 'truly' theirs and beyond the corporate collective. Employees adopted a number of tactics to cope with this, including depersonalization or distancing of self. As a result, 'the emotions experienced as part of the organizational self are presented as distinct from other aspects of emotional life and at some remove from one's "authentic" sense of self' (1992: 183). One consequence of this was burnout, but there are limits to what the company wants to know about this side of its culture – 'Keep that kind of shit to yourself' (Kunda, 1992: 203). Thus, while bureaucratic traditions were partially eroded, clear limits remained on what was allowed in to work (Ashforth and Humphrey, 1993).

Such forms of degradation formed part of a growing critique of corporate culture management. Some pointed to its totalitarian and coercive nature – workers must pretend to be someone they are not, someone different to everyday life (Hochschild, 1983; Willmott, 1993; Parker, 2000). Others suggested that it had only limited efficacy in generating shared values (e.g. Van Maanen, 1991). At the same time, emphasis on strong organizational loyalty was exposed as counterproductive in the case of organizational mergers, downsizing and competing value targets such as customer service (Cartwright and Cooper, 1996; Sturdy et al., 2001). More significantly, recent critiques have focussed on normative control more generally. Here, as we shall see, imposed value conformity and homogeneity is seen as organizational *groupthink*. This is seen as having adverse effects on innovation, initiative, learning and creativity in rapidly changing product markets (Brown and Starkey, 2000) and increasingly, short-term financial and stock markets (Sennett, 1998).

While culture management has certainly not lost its appeal *in toto* (Adler, 2001), Kunda and Ailon-Souday argue that such developments mark a new paradigm of managerialism which re-scripts the organization as a contract-based marketplace – 'market rationalists seem to have little patience for culture, no matter how strong' (2005: 203). Rather, control is assuming laissez-faire characteristics. Employees are expected to receive little more than remuneration and the opportunity to develop their skills portfolios for the open market. The focus is 'on causing workers to behave like an organization rather than to inspire them to feel for the organization ... ' (ibid: 207). This does not simply represent a move from normative control, but from bureaucracy as well. Indeed, it is congruent with the post-bureaucratic form that celebrates organizational 'thinness' and flexibility and challenges the traditional boundary between work and home (also see Webb, 2004).

In emphasizing an apparent shift from normative control, Kunda and Ailon-Souday (2005) underplay the normative basis of market rationalism such as individualism, entrepreneurial risk taking and self-reliance, even these are not organizationally specific. Nevertheless, the changes seem to allow for a certain degree of 'freedom' in relation to values, identities and lifestyles in the workplace. Indeed, for more optimistic commentators, they create an unprecedented free space or what might be seen as existential empowerment. As we will now outline, popular business pundits recommend an anti-organization workforce who are free to manage not only their own tasks, but their identities (even to the point of disloyalty).

Just be yourself ... or else: Recent developments in identity management

For Kunda and Ailon-Souday (2005) then, management are no longer so interested in shaping the identities of workers. Fear of job loss, ostensible task autonomy and self-interested careerism are enough to control the labour process. By contrast, we suggest that a new, emergent form of identity management, beyond that which calls for entrepreneurial and self-reliant selves, is becoming prevalent. In this section, we describe a growing wave of popular management rhetoric and associated practices that encourage difference, diversity, idiosyncrasy and the expression of authentic feelings in the work environment. This invitation to 'be your self' sits comfortably with the idea that markets cater to individual variation, tastes and differences. Here, consumption, lifestyle factors, sexuality and humour, for example, are not externalized in favour of a collective normative alignment nor barred from the organization in the bureaucratic tradition, but 'celebrated' as a useful organizational resource (see also Janssens and Zanoni, 2005).

The celebration of difference and the defiance of management

Much of the guru literature in the last ten years speaks of the redundancy or decline of the corporate culture management. For example, following long humanist and essentialist traditions, Peters (2003) argues that workers are *naturally* inclined to be innovative, curious, risk-taking, imaginative and exciting. But he is not simply calling for renewed emphasis on job discretion or 'enrichment', but for a challenge to outdated management ideologies that desire conformity and deference. In direct contrast to his own earlier human relations-informed demand for organizations to provide employees with meaning and values (Peters and Waterman, 1982), a laissez-faire approach to norms is the new imperative (Peters, 1992). Indeed, some managerialist writers now recognize that the problem is as much employee cynicism or depersonalization as it is conformity to prescribed corporate norms.

Many individuals have adopted inauthentic and self-protective strategies that ultimately destroy meaning for both parties. However, the po-faced corporate uniform and caricatured observance of protocol that once stood for professionalism is not a feature of Meaning Inc. companies. They work to create belonging cultures that allow people to be authentically themselves, and reap substantial rewards in the process. (Bains et al., 2007: 258)

In the same vein as Fierman (1995) and Semler (1993), Peters (1994) encourages a 'joyous anarchy' in which zanies, nutters, mavericks and freaks are hired and celebrated. Because the market is based upon differentiation and variation, organizations should follow suit. Indeed, 'chaos is with us ... but the way to deal with it is to pursue variation, not to manage it' (Peters, 1994: 51). Underlying this 'be yourself' ideology is the notion that employees are free agents. In Semler's *Maverick!*, which describes his own firm's practices, workers are told: 'now control is passé and a badge of incompetence. Now, you are free' (1993: xiii). The freedom to be yourself also extends to expressing dissent and recalcitrance towards management (Peters, 1994: 47). In its most extreme form, even traitors are celebrated (Peters, 1992: 588). All the tropes of the free market are here.

The celebration of difference is not simply concerned with the rejection of corporate conformity and hierarchical deference in favour of the 'freedoms' of the market. It also absorbs liberalist motifs in relation to minority groups such as gay and ethnic minority people and others who have long been disenfranchised or rendered invisible in corporate settings. Difference along these dimensions should be openly encouraged and used by the firm. Indeed, some workplaces have seemingly approached diversity legislation as an opportunity for increased effectiveness (Janssens and Zanoni, 2005). Raeburn's (2004) study of US organizations that embrace sexual diversity, for example, indicates that they generally benefited from more motivated and dynamic work environments.

Having 'Fun'

Bringing sexuality into the workplace in such an explicit, formal fashion is a clear illustration of the management of what was long considered a domain of everyday life (as well as of the informal organization). This breaking down of bureaucratically informed boundaries is recognized in guru accounts and more generally, particularly in relation to the idea of expressing an intrinsic desire to be playful and curious rather than suppressing it in the name of sober productiveness and a 'bottom-line mentality' (Deal and Key, 1998: 6). Indeed, Deal and Key see a key constraint to having fun at work as the 'tendency to partition life and work ... only to recover our humanity once we return home' (1998: 16). Similarly, Semler (2004) advocates a 'seven day weekend' in order to enhance the individual pleasure of work. Here, the plurality of strange and colourful identities and tastes found in the marketplace and home are invited into work. Indeed, some have suggested that it can make work more existentially meaningful than the traditional home. For example, in *Happy Mondays* (2001), Reeves argues that organizations now provide purpose, fun, creativity, friendship networks and love (see also Hochschild, 1997).

The attention given to playfulness can be linked to a desire to foster innovation in work tasks as well as appeal to anti-bureaucratic preferences for informality from key workers such as in the hi-tech industries and firms like Google. However, it can also be seen as an effort to compensate for the rigours of economic relations such as downsizing and highly routine and stressful work tasks such as in call centres. If workers are able simply to express themselves freely or, as Deal and Kennedy (1999: 234) suggest, if the 'Fun Quotient' is high in a firm, then employees will be more committed to their tasks and everyone will benefit. Such practices are quite widespread among the 'best companies to work for' at least. For example, Kwik Fit, a car servicing chain in the UK, has a full time 'Minister of Fun' managerial position (*Sunday Times*, 2004, 2005). Similarly, Bains et al. (2007: 253) describe how at Virgin, in 'place of robotic announcements and mechanical service are jokes, frivolity and a sense that you are part of a party rather than a drill'. Such practices are not only seen as appealing to the (late) modern preferences of what Bains et al. call 'X and Y Generations', but seek to tap the energy, innocence and openness associated with younger people. For Peters (1994: 204), for example, the ethos of the unruly youngster is often drawn upon – 'go for youth'.

The prescriptions and descriptions of various commentators of managing employee identity in seemingly new ways highlight a number of themes. In particular, distinctions are made between both bureaucratic traditions of formality, work-everyday life boundaries and emotion suppression as well as between more recent concerns with conformity to designed corporate cultures. Rather, difference and individuality are celebrated as well as the expression of playful and youthful emotions and, to a lesser extent, sexuality. In each case, bringing in 'everyday life' is quite explicit. To these developments, we might have added others which also fit with a more widespread extension of the reach of identity management in the workplace. For example, a number of studies have pointed to the more systematic and widespread use of employees' accents, bodies and dress styles which have accompanied the growth of the service sector in many western economies – aesthetic labour (see Sturdy et al., 2001). Similarly, the management of fun is closely linked to what others have observed as attempts to deploy and appropriate humour in workplaces for productive ends (Collinson, 2002). Likewise, reference has already been made to the idea of friendship within work contexts and others have pointed to ways in which this can be transformed into a commodity, in the form of social capital for example (Grey and Sturdy, 2007). Indeed, this has parallels with human relations, although here the target of control was informality and mutual support produced largely within, rather than beyond, the workplace.

The apparent extension of the management of everyday life in work is presented by its advocates as not only organisationally effective, but as something of value more generally, as morally and politically good in enhancing personal and emotional freedoms and celebrating, rather than suppressing, diversity. While recognizing that some advances in equality of opportunity may have resulted from such developments, our position is a more critical one. In particular, we are sceptical about whether this development is simply a kind of liberation or 'existential empowerment'. Rather, it may better or also be seen as 'existential exposure' – a process through which the organization seeks to manage, appropriate and therefore help construct, the complete person – a potentially insidious form of 'neo-normative' control (see also Fleming and Sturdy, 2007). Why might this be the case? Firstly, we shall argue that there are clear limits to the extent of diversity an organization will tolerate. Secondly, in much the same way as contemporary marketing practices utilize consumer diversity as a resource in product development, existential 'empowerment' actually appropriates values and identities, even the 'inner preserves' which lay behind the cynicism associated with corporate culture management. Thirdly, it can be seen as self-disciplinary in pushing individuals back upon themselves in accounting for their worth while other forms of control are obscured. However and finally, such approaches provoke forms of resistance, however bizarre the notion of resisting being yourself may seem. We now develop this argument through the use of a case study which demonstrates some, but not all, of the developments discussed above.

The case of sunray

An 8-month study was conducted at Sunray Customer Service (a pseudonym), an American-owned call centre with around 1000 employees based in an Australian city. Sunray deals with outsourced communication functions and puts much emphasis on customer service skills. The company was founded by James Carr (another pseudonym) in the 1990s and he remains the cultural 'figurehead'. Sunray was selected for this research project because of its broader reputation as a 'high commitment' organization and 'best place to work'. This was of particular interest given the often draconian and Tayloristic methods used in call centres to organize and motivate workers (Frenkel et al., 1999).

The initial objective of the research project was therefore to understand how Sunray manages the culture and how employees respond to this. To this end, a sample of three Human Resource Managers and 30 employees was selected and interviewed at various intervals over the 8 months. The initial selection process was random. However, one interviewee introduced the researcher to his 'cohort' consisting of three other workers, which then became a keen focus in the project. Given the qualitative nature of the project, this sample was not therefore purely representative.

Following Spradley (1979), a high degree of flexibility was retained in the interview schedule in order to allow the conversation to flow in unpredictable directions. It was derived from speculative assumptions regarding possible interpretations of the culture, and later modified to target some of the concerns discussed in this paper. Employees were interviewed both on-site and outside the firm (in homes, cafes, etc.). Although 45 interviews were conducted overall, data from a selected group will be primarily used in this chapter. The average age of the telephone agents interviewed was 23. This is significant for the research findings, as will be discussed shortly.

Identity management at sunray

> Forget lone rangers – at Sunray we have free-rangers! It's hard to have fun when you're confined to a workstation like a battery hen, so we encourage you to enjoy the freedom and latitude you need in order to fulfil your obligations to Sunray. (training manual)

Sunray initially appears as a classic example of culture management. For example, a key role is attributed to the founder and CEO who has inspired a veritable mythology that incorporates the firm's humble beginnings. Similarly, a core and persistent theme and explicit vision here is 'the 3Fs: Focus, Fun, Fulfilment.' Janis, who oversees the culture program at Sunray, explains its significance:

> Without the culture the place would be drab, and in most workplaces people can't wait to leave. But at Sunray they love to work and really get into it. You know, just the other day I heard someone say 'I can't believe they pay me to have fun!' and that is exactly what happens.

The explicit management rationale behind this is mainly to detract from, and compensate for, the hard and mundane work required of agents who receive calls from customers in 8-hour shifts, with two 15-minute rest periods and a half-hour lunch break. In addition, there is some, albeit tokenistic, emphasis on creativity and innovation such as the use of vocabulary – 'do it creatively … personalize calls'. And again, Janis argues, 'effectively our people are their own bosses who make their own decisions … what this means is that team members don't have to ask to make changes. We tell them, Just do it'. But creativity is seen as resulting primarily from the emphasis on personal fulfilment. Indeed, the approach is, in part, explicitly inspired by Peters' idea of 'WOW'.

> Cubicle slaves … hack off your ties … flip off your heels … the work can be cool! The work can be beautiful. The work can be fun! Bash your cubicle walls! Rip up your Dilbert cartoons! The white collar revolution is on! Subvert the hierarchy! Make every project WOW! Be distinct or extinct! (excerpt from Tom Peters' 'Brand You' in training manual)

For example, the 3Fs slogan is not only a normative prescription ('you ought to be like this'), but also a description of the employees. According to Janis they are 'dedicated', 'diverse', 'fun', 'sexy', 'adventurous', 'professional' and 'playful'. The opportunity to express their unique individuality is especially considered a source of enjoyment for workers. This lies beyond traditional task autonomy and operates more as a form of 'existential empowerment'. Janis, for example, reports how:

> Everyone is different and we make sure that people can express themselves and will be accepted for who they are…. It all comes down to our environment – the culture, the freedom to enjoy being themselves and to enjoy being at work.

Likewise, the CEO is keen to promote life style, sexual and ethnic diversity.

> We've tried to create a workplace in which people of either sex, gay people and people from other places can come and really enjoy the time they spend with each other ... (Sunray: Magazine interview)

But the approach is not limited to one of 'diversity management' in the sense of utilizing particular groups represented by (constructed as) various socio-demographic characteristics. As the training manual suggests: 'You are encouraged to know yourself.... Our people are different ... Our culture is different'. Indeed, management practices are directed at reinforcing 'self-expression' more broadly. A selection of these and the employees' response are summarised below.

1. *The Expressive, Playful, Inner Child*

At Sunray, the recruitment strategy was to select people who had recently completed high school. Aside from cost considerations, the employment of young people is typically associated with the relative ease with which an organizational culture can be inculcated. However, the rationale given at Sunray reversed this logic in that 'young people find (the) ... culture very, very attractive because they can be themselves and know how to have fun' (Janis). In other words, young people were seen as more likely to be expressive and playful, including with identities, rather than impressionable. For example, in an observed induction session, workers stood and sung the Muppet's *The Rainbow Connection*. On another occasion, they were required to bring to work an item that 'best explains who you are – explain why.' One agent responded by bringing a surf board into the office.

Exhortations to behave in this manner included a range of activities which were more or less explicitly linked to those associated with the school room. For example, colourful, cardboard cut outs of animals such as Sesame Street characters were provided to decorate the workspace – the area dealing with an African-based airline project was decorated with cardboard jungle trees and photographs of cheetahs. Likewise, workers were asked to take home a rainbow-coloured pamphlet with a fill-in-the-blanks word puzzle reading, 'What are the 3Fs?' while other training and motivational games included mini-golf and quizzes. Similarly, annual 'awaydays' were seen as somewhere between a 'kind of school musical' and a 'party'. While most of the interviewees could see the rationale in this aspect of the management programme and found it fun, some were cynical. Jane, who answers calls for an insurance company, complained:

> Working at Sunray is like working for 'Playschool' [a children's television programme]. It's so much like an American kindergarten ... a plastic, fake kindergarten. The murals on the wall, the telling off if I'm late and the patronising tone in which I'm spoken to all give it a very childish flavour.

2. *Partying and Drinking*

While such practices might be seen as simply infantilising employees more than existentially empowering them, practices also incorporated the expression of explicitly adult identities under the theme of partying. In particular, employees were openly encouraged to drink alcohol. Job advertisements were headed with the phrase 'do you know how to party?' and management often said that Sunray life is similar to a 'party' because of the energy and 'good times' that distinguished the firm from other call centres. One training session, held in a nearby park, was analogous to an actual party with beer drinking and the open expression of sexuality and flirting. Likewise, the Christmas parties were described as 'really just big booze ups like any other. Although you get lots of gay boys prancing around in their Speedos and being very flamboyant' (Jules). Most employees interviewed appeared to experience such activities in a positive manner. John, a 24-year-old agent, described them as empowering and fulfilling:

> It's like this: when you leave work you don't feel drained – the fun allows you to focus not only on your work but yourself as well – you come out feeling fantastic and you like coming to work.

3. Sexuality at Sunray

The expression of sexuality and flirting among employees was not confined to parties nor simply a reflection of workplace life or, even, the demographics of the employees. Rather, according to some informants and confirmed by observations, it was openly condoned at Sunray. As one team leader said 'we like to think of our selves as fun, sexy and dedicated.' As already intimated and in keeping with the notion of 'being yourself', the sexual dimension of the Sunray culture did not conform to the heterosexist norm, but also had a strong gay focus. Rather than hiding their homosexual identities at work, Sunray was perceived by some workers as 'very gay' (see also Clair et al., 2005). For example, one agent, Joanne, said that ' ... they don't have to hide the fact that they are gay'. Likewise, others claimed that 'they (gays) like it 'cause they can be themselves' and that 'Sunray definitely promote it [open homosexuality] ... well, not promote it but, say, you are what you are and you are allowed to be that way'.

4. Dress Code as Identity

Part of the openly sexual and flirtatious culture at Sunray was its expression through clothing, encouraged through what some might see as a liberal dress code. For example, Joanne, a representative for a health insurance firm, referred to this, saying, 'you can wear what you want – people are allowed to wear low-cut tops and short skirts.' This practice cut across others such as the organized parties and events. On one of these, a 'fashion day' held by one team, 'many of the gay guys dressed in drag, in tiny mini skirts ... ' (Leanne). Similarly, in relation to the school theme, teams had dress-up days where employees came dressed as a superhero or in keeping with a particular theme such as 'The Tropics' (floral shirts and sun hats). In addition, the firm would hold occasional 'Pyjama Days'. Once again, most employees seemed to enjoy these team-building exercises, but some found it 'rather childish'. While these events were clearly in a similar spirit to 'dressing up', one element was to express yourself through otherwise private clothing worn outside the workplace, in everyday life.

Clothing and the seemingly relaxed and 'casual' dress code at Sunray also allowed for the expression of employees' identities as consumers, being centred on the latest fashion labels and promoted with the intention of creating a party-like atmosphere in the organization – the ritual of everyday consumption and shopping is a strong theme of the culture of fun. According to one employee, 'the idea is to get away from the boring office look and make things fun and happy like we are going out for the night'. This extended to 'fun' physical appearances among workers such as bright orange hair, visible tattoos and facial piercing; the comparison to 'parties', 'raves' and 'clubbing' is justified in this sense. Many of the employees interviewed relished this part of the 3Fs philosophy because they felt 'free to be who we are', as one agent put it. This use of clothing can be seen as a distinct form of aesthetic labour, not in the sense of attributes used directly in work tasks, such as accents or appearances to consumers, but indirectly, like smiling on the phone (Sturdy, 1998). But not all staff welcomed the approach. This exchange was recorded in a focus group interview:

Mark: People supposedly look at Sunray and see this hip, young, cool crowd.

Jackie: They don't, they see a bunch of pretentious fashion victims.

5. *Individual Attention – Health and Happiness in the Sunray Family*

In recognition of the physical strains of the work, staff are provided with various means of support such as a project coach who people can speak to when stressed. However, such practices are presented within the overall ethos of fun and attention to individual well-being needs. For example, a masseur attends to aching necks and backs and on mind/body days 'we can go to the park and do yoga'. Employees are also encouraged to give team members a hug and bring in gifts. One team leader reported that some employees go so far as to 'bring in their home made jams and give them to their team mates'. The home-work divide is also challenged in relation to more formal psychological support in that, in contrast to Kunda's (1992) *Tech* staff reported earlier, employees are encouraged to bring their problems into work, as Sarah, a team leader, explains.

We have a situation here where an agent can feel comfortable enough to say the reason why they've been coming late is because they have a serious problem at home.... We try to deal with them in a very caring way – and ask them how to fix the problem so they can be really great at what they do.

This departure from bureaucratic separations is felt to be valuable, with the results seemingly very similar to the aspirations of human relations and normative control more generally as Rob, an agent, admits.

I've had some personal problems and because of the way things are here I've had so much support I've overcome these. And I see it as my family, I don't see it as Sunray the company I work for – I come in and do more than I would normally do because of that.

As a result, Rob said he is 'fulfilled as a person, they allow me to grow and have fun. I could not see myself working anywhere else'.

The politics of everyday life at sunray

In many respects, the approach to managing Sunray employees matches the prescriptions of recent gurus of 'fun' and the publicized practices of 'leading' employers discussed earlier (see Figure 12.1 below). There is a strong emphasis on the expression of what hitherto might have been seen as the private, individual, authentic or freely chosen identities, feelings and lifestyles of everyday life and on the acceptance, and even celebration, of differences, of 'who they are'. The resulting freedom to be existentially expressive, combined with partially manufactured routines of fun, is seen to have a positive motivational impact and moral value. In addition, although there is little sign of Peters' hoped for subversion or 'white-collar revolution' and the work itself is highly constrained, the task-based innovation and creativity associated with such 'fun' regimes remains a management goal.

We have suggested, however, that such an apparently liberal approach to managing employees represents a form of identity management or control which appropriates and trades on the identities hitherto assigned to everyday life. Firstly, through both recruitment processes and the celebration of difference, Sunray reinforces broader societal constructions of identity in particular ways. Identity is produced as being multifarious, in keeping with late-modern constructions of society. Furthermore and echoing the work of Janssens and Zanoni (2005), diversity for both individuals and employees generally is constructed as a particular variant of sexuality, ethnicity, consumerism and playfulness rather than say occupational skills, familial roles, politics and community.

Secondly and most transparently, control is evident in the limits implicitly and explicitly imposed which contradict the rhetoric of a laissez-faire approach, revealing instrumentality and the manufacture of fun. For example, the numerous games and songs were largely prescribed and contained in time and space. Likewise, emotional

Fun management prescriptions	Sunray
Celebration of difference/variety	Yes
Openly antagonistic values	No
Child-like energy	Yes
Fun through individuality	Yes
Acceptance of 'non-work' problems (friendship)	Yes
Emphasis on connecting identity freedom to work creativity	Limited
Unruly youngsters	Yes

Figure 12.1 Sunray and 'Fun' Management Practices

negativity, including that associated with problems at home, was largely proscribed or segregated into a counselling space. In other words, emotional labour prevailed and even extended to non-customer, non-work task contexts. There was no room for the non-fun, non-'different' person in the organized events. Similarly, Sunray was strictly non-union and explicit resistance was suppressed. There was no place either, then, for a militant self or 'fun as sabotage'! Indeed, following the practice of bringing in homemade food for colleagues, one employee made hash cookies and was (unsurprisingly perhaps) dismissed for his efforts. In relation to visual aspects of identity, however, there was greater tolerance although this is clearly linked to the nature of the work with its lack of face-to-face customer contact. Indeed, more generally the instrumentality of the approach was clear.

But this is not the whole story. The regime was not just a managerial indulgence to compensate for hardship or even stimulate motivation. The third way in which it can be seen as problematic was in the appropriation (and partial construction) of identities and other unrewarded characteristics for productive ends. This is particularly evident in the recruitment and production of 'youthfulness', sexuality and enthusiasm. By allowing people to 'be themselves' in ways that facilitate the customer service function (e.g. positive sentiments, flexibility, discretion, creativity, etc.), the 3Fs philosophy enlists the once private or, at least, everyday dimensions of the individual as a corporate resource. This type of control appears to utilize authenticity, difference, diversity and lifestyle rather than bland conformity. The data suggest that Sunray does this by symbolically dissolving the private/public boundary. The motifs of fun, partying and sex, usually associated with the sphere of everyday life, are discursively integrated into Sunray's team exercises, social events and daily work interactions.

Moreover, where employees in a regime of culture management may have had 'private' reserves of identity through which to distance themselves from work roles and from which cynicism might emerge, at Sunray, these very qualities were brought out into the open. Indeed and fourthly, such a colonization of identities served as a form of self-disciplinary control in that individuals became accountable for their performance at an existential level. Because workers' everyday selves and identities were encouraged, more was visible to the managerial gaze in which certain attitudes were highlighted as problematic. Rather than say, motivational problems or insufficient correspondence with the company values, here, any failure is more personal. This was noted in the counselling dynamic of the 3Fs programme. Team members were policed on their own personal mental state: 'I will first recognize a difference in their attitude ... and I will say "What has happened? Is it the job or something at home? What can I do to help you with that?"' Contrary to Peters' exhortations about promoting dissent then, Sunray unsurprisingly favoured only a certain type of authentic identity, as the hash-cookie example above indicates.

The management of everyday life at work also has important implications for the ways in which employees engage in resistance. Under conventional corporate culture control regimes, employees often feigned identification and, to an extent, hid or protected other 'real' identities through role distancing and cynicism.

But when the control function operates by encouraging workers' to express these identities, what form, if any, does resistance take? Firstly, the cynicism and scepticism associated with corporate culture programmes continued – 'it seems to me that the individualism is forced here – to be yourself as the company wants you to be is not to be yourself at all'. Similarly, Jackie mentioned above also said 'I am empowered only in their terms, not mine … am I empowered to choose when to have my lunch break? No.' In addition, rather than simply pointing to the programme's contradictions, some employees sought to undermine it. In particular, the sentiment of diverse individualism was countered with a discourse that emphasizes solidarity, uniformity and collective subordination. Jane did this when she argued that the attention on 'being yourself' detracted from the proletarianized status of the work process:

> Well, to 'succeed' at Sunray you are basically gay, have to be really 'alternative' and Sunray likes people who have different coloured hair and who are into [*in a sarcastic tone*] 'being themselves'. Now I'm not too sure which one we fit into, but basically we are all plebs. Just plebs.

This directly challenges the identity management aspects of market rationalism and privileging of diversity by reminding fellow workers that the ultimate structural position of telephone agents was one of uniform subordination. Thus, while conventional corporate culture management provoked an assertion or protection of employee individuality, the new regimes prompted a, perhaps, late-modern form of class-consciousness whereby collectivity is emphasized, but not that which is defined by management.

Concluding remarks

We have argued in this chapter that the colonization of everyday life by management has involved an under-studied converse process in which the motifs of everyday life have been appropriated *inside* the organization. We have linked this observation to debates around the evolution of control and identity management in contemporary firms. In particular, the call to simply 'be yourself' at Sunray represents a kind of identity-focussed control that complements the market rationalism recently identified by a number of authors (e.g. Kunda and Ailon-Souday, 2005). Rather than indicate the absence of normative control, market rationalism influences the identities of employees in a much more profound manner. Previously, employees could maintain a preserve of private selfhood that separated them from the company, whereas it is this very preserve that is increasingly targeted by managers. The Sunray case is illustrative of this trend. While it certainly does not go so far as to advocate anarchy and rampant disobedience a la Peters (2003), it does appear to translate market rationalism into a distinct form of identity management.

This type of control draws significantly on selective aspects of the so-called whole person, which has generally been barred from the workplace in previous eras. Consumption, lifestyle factors, sexuality and humour are neither externalized in favour of a collective normative alignment nor barred from the organization in the bureaucratic tradition, but 'celebrated' as a useful organizational resource. The chapter has identified the controlling nature of the call to 'be yourself'. In the context of late capitalism this liberalist injunction is circumscribed by the production process in definite ways – everyday life has its uses, especially in relation to identity management in an age where cynicism, dissent and plurality are the norm. Recently, Thrift (2005: 46) has also argued that the liberalist call for open-ended identity has an obvious foundation in the new circuits of capitalism demanding flexibility, innovation and creativity. But while this may give the appearance of subjective multiplicity and difference *vis-à-vis* the staid 'organizational man' of yesteryear, the opposite may actually be the case:

> For all the commitment to an open-ended view of subjecthood, in practice the concept of the person … (is) a narrow one which involves super-exploitation of both managers (who are expected to commit their whole being to the organisations) and workers (who are now expected to commit their embodied knowledge). In other words, the net effect may well be to reduce the different conceptions and deportments of the person … and, worse, to transfer these reduced conceptions and comportments to other spheres of life.

In this sense, the chapter raises some profound questions about what freedom might mean in the emerging world of work. Until now, our message has been rather bleak. It almost appears that the values of work and non-work have been incorporated into a single logic of corporate domination from which there is little escape. Indeed, as Kunda and Ailon-Souday (2005), Sennett (1998) and others point out, the so-called freedoms championed by the ideology of market rationality also come complete with profound 'unfreedoms' associated with insecurity, uncertainty and disenfranchisement. Similarly, authenticity and self-expression, along the bastion of progressive workplace politics, are now appropriated to further regulate the identities of workers. Freedom to 'be yourself' is synonymous with organizational control since the 'practice of everyday life' (once celebrated by de Certeau [1984] as a site of resistance) is at least partially enlisted as a positive axiom of production. However, perhaps the new freedoms of the emergent workplace will have little to do with 'authenticity' and individualism, but swing back to a concern with solidarity and collective responsibility. This was certainly noted at Sunray. Some workers actually resisted 'being themselves' (as defined by the organization at least) by pointing instead to the uniform and standardised work task rather than the diverse identities around the task ('we are just plebs'). This highlights how the focus on identity appears to be impoverished if it does not correspond with task, job and role autonomy/creativity. Following Adler (2001), if both task and identity empowerment are achieved in a collective fashion that eschews the pathologies of market rationalism, then a different kind of workplace may appear.

References

Abercrombie, N. and Hill, S. (1976). 'Paternalism and Patronage', *British Journal of Sociology*, 27, 4, 413–429.

Abercrombie, N., Hill, S. and Turner, B. S. (eds) (1990). *Dominant Ideologies*. London: Routledge.

Adler, P. (2001). 'Market, Hierarchy, and Trust: The Knowledge Economy and the Future of Capitalism', *Organization Science*, 2, 12, 215–234.

Albrow, M. (1997). *Do Organizations Have Feelings?* London: Routledge.

Ashforth, B. E. and Humphrey, R. (1993). 'Emotional Labor in Service Roles: The Influence of Identity', *Academy of Management Review*, 18, 1, 88–115.

Bains, G. et al. (2007). *Meaning Inc: The Blue Print for Business Success in the 21st Century*. London: Profile Books.

Brown, A. D. and Starkey, K. (2000). 'Organizational Identity and Learning: A Psychodynamic Perspective', *Academy of Management Review*, 25, 1, 102–120.

Cartwright, S. and Cooper, C. L. (1996). *Managing Mergers, Acquisitions and Strategic Alliances*, 2nd edition. Oxford: Butterworth-Heinemann.

Collinson, D. (2002). 'Managing Humour', *Journal of Management Studies*, 39, 3, 269–288.

Clair, J. A., Beatty, J. E. and MacLean, T. (2005). 'Out of Sight But Not Out of Mind: Managing Invisible Social Identities in the Workplace', *Academy of Management Review*, 30, 1, 78–95.

Deal, T. and Kennedy, A. (1999). *The New Corporate Cultures*. London: Orion Business.

Deal, T. and Key, M. (1998). *Celebration at Work: Play, Purpose and Profit at Work*. New York: Berrett-Koehler.

De Certeau, M. (1984). *The Practice of Everyday Life*. Tran. S. Rendall. Berkeley: University of California Press.

Ferguson, K. (1984). *The Feminist Case Against Bureaucracy*. Philadelphia: Temple University Press.

Fierman, J. (1995). 'Winning Ideas from Maverick Managers', *Fortune*, 6 February, 40–46.

Fleming, P. and Sturdy, A. (2007). 'Just be Yourself, or Else: Towards Neo-Normative Control in Organizations?' Working Paper, Judge Business School. University of Cambridge.

Frenkel, S., Korczynski, M., Shire, K. and Tam, M. (1999). *On the Front Line – Organization of Work in the Information Economy*. New York: Cornell University Press.

Grey, C. and Sturdy, A. J. (2007). 'Friendship and Organizational Analysis: Towards a Research Agenda', *Journal of Management Inquiry*, 16, 2, 157–172.

Guillén, M. (1994). *Work, Authority and Organization in a Comparative Perspective*. Chicago: University of Chicago Press.

Hochschild, A. R. (1983). *The Managed Heart: Commercialization of Human Feeling*. Berkeley: University of California Press.

Hochschild, A. (1997). *The Time Bind: When Work Becomes Home and Home Becomes Work*. New York: Metropolitan Books.

Janssens, M. and Zanoni, P. (2005). 'Many Diversities for Many Services: Theorizing Diversity (management) in Service Companies', *Human Relations*, 58, 3, 311–340.

Kanter, R. M. (1977). *Men and Women of the Corporation*. New York: Basic Books.

Kunda, G. (1992). *Engineering Culture: Control and Commitment in a High-Tech Corporation*. Philadelphia: Temple University Press.

Kunda, G. and Ailon-Souday, G. (2005). 'Managers, Markets and Ideologies – Design and Devotion Revisited', in S. Ackroyd et al. (eds) *Oxford Handbook of Work and Organization*. Oxford: Oxford University Press.

Parker, M. (2000). *Organizational Culture and Identity*. London: Sage.

Peters, T. and Waterman, R. H. (1982). *In Search of Excellence*. New York: Harper and Row.

Peters, T. (1992). *Liberation Management: Necessary Disorganization for the Nanosecond Nineties*. London: Pan.

Peters, T. (1994). *The Tom Peters Seminar: Crazy Times Call for Crazy Organizations*. London: Macmillan.

Peters, T. (2003). *Re-Imagine! Business Excellence in a Disruptive Age*. London: Dorling Kindersley.

Ray, C. A. (1986). 'Corporate Culture: The Last Frontier of Control?' *Journal of Management Studies*, 23, 3, 287–297.

Raeburn, N. C. (2004). *Changing Corporate America from Inside Out: Lesbian and Gay Workplace Rights*. Minneapolis: University of Minnesota Press.

Reeves, R. (2001). *Happy Mondays: Putting Pleasure Back into Work*. London: Pearson Education.

Semler, R. (1993). *Maverick! The Success Behind the World's Most Unusual Workplace*. London: Arrow.

Semler, R. (2004). *The Seven-Day Weekend: Changing the Way Work Works*. USA: Penguin.

Sennett, R. (1998). *The Corrosion of Character: The Personal Consequences of Work in the New Capitalism*. London: W.W. Norton.

Spradley, J. (1979). *The Ethnographic Interview*. New York: Rinehart and Winston.

Sturdy, A. J. (1998). 'Customer Care in a Consumer Society', *Organization*, 5, 1, 27–53.

Sturdy, A. J., Grugulis, I. and Willmott, H. (eds) (2001). *Customer Service – Empowerment and Entrapment*. Basingstoke: Palgrave Macmillan.

Thompson, E. P. (1967). 'Time, Work Discipline and Industrial Capitalism', *Past and Present*, 38, 56–97.

Thompson, P. and Callaghan, G. (2002). 'We Recruit Attitude: The Selection and Shaping of Call Centre Labour', *Journal of Management Studies*, 39, 2, 233–254.

Thrift, N. (2005). *Knowing Capitalism*. London: Sage.

Van Maanen, J. (1991). 'The Smile Factory: Work at Disney Land', in P. Frost, L. Moore, M. Lewis, C. Lumberg and J. Martin (eds) *Reframing Organizational Culture*. Newbury Park, CA: Sage.

Webb, J. (2004). 'Organizations, Self-Identities and the New Economy', *Sociology*, 38, 4, 719–738.

Whyte, W. H. (1956). *The Organizational Man*. New York: Doubleday.

Willmott, H. (1993). 'Strength Is Ignorance; Slavery Is Freedom: Managing Culture in Modern Organization', *Journal of Management Studies*, 30, 4, 515–552.

Author index

Subject index